Mobility and Cultural Authority in Contemporary China

Mobility and Cultural Authority in Contemporary China

Pál Nyíri

UNIVERSITY OF WASHINGTON PRESS • SEATTLE AND LONDON

Publication of Mobility and Cultural Authority in Contemporary China
*was supported by a generous grant from the Chiang Ching-kuo Foundation
for International Scholarly Exchange. Additional support was provided
by the Donald R. Ellegood International Publications Endowment.*

University of Washington Press
P.O. Box 50096, Seattle, WA 98145 U.S.A.
www.washington.edu/uwpress

Library of Congress Cataloging-in-Publication Data
can be found at the back of this book.

To Julia Nyiri,

to the memory of Vladimir Gribov, and to Putao

Contents

Mobility and Cultural Authority in Contemporary China

Introduction

This book is concerned with the mechanisms by which the mainland Chinese state, the People's Republic of China (PRC), asserts cultural authority over an increasingly mobile population, and the ways individuals cope with that authority in the face of conflicting pressures regarding their movement.

In his influential article "Mobile Sociology," John Urry, drawing on Zygmunt Bauman's (1987) metaphor, suggests that we might be witnessing a return from the "gardening state," which "presumes exceptional concern with pattern, regularity and ordering, with what is growing and with what should be weeded out," to the "gamekeeper state," which is concerned with "ensuring that there was sufficient stock for hunting in a particular site but not with the detailed cultivation of each animal." He notes that East European societies under state socialism were "gardening" societies (Urry 2000:186). Put less benevolently, state socialism, despite important exceptions such as Tito's Yugoslavia, was associated with strict controls on population movement. Yet, since 1978 when the PRC embarked on the modernization drive that has become the supreme state ideology and social mantra, Chinese citizens have been challenged to travel. As Liu (1997) pointed out, a spatial hierarchy arose, in which "success" as a modern Chinese subject was linked to mobility. At the pinnacle of that hierarchy was international migration to the United States, the country that symbolized global modernity. Entrepreneurs, students, and workers who went abroad legally or illegally all assumed their places in the hierarchy. But a far larger number of them have moved within China, where a similar hierarchy arose.

While migration is almost the only form of human movement that attracts the attention of sociologists and political scientists concerned with the directions societies take, other forms of spatial mobility are privileged in the humanities in discourses of modern subjectivity. Tourism and travel in particular are persistent (and different) metaphors of (post) modernity (see MacCannell 1976 and Clifford 1992 for two influential and very different treatments of the subject), albeit exclusively of its Western form(s). In China, until the late nineties, the positive value of mobility lay in its strong association with capital accumulation. Since then, however, a culture of (mainly domestic) leisure travel, once reviled but now promoted by the state, has rapidly emerged as an attribute of modern urban lifestyle.

As people begin to move, they slip from the grip of Maoist systems of administrative control that are based on work units and household registration. In 1997, Laura Nader wrote that "when the use of *social* control becomes less culturally acceptable, especially for the middle class, the use of *cultural* control becomes more central for the mechanics of power." She had Western liberal democracies in mind, but her observation is pertinent to today's China. The party-state is eager to create capitalism, consumption, and a middle class without relinquishing control; in other words, it tries to become a "gamekeeper state" without ceasing to be a "gardening state." It is making great efforts to maintain cultural control over the processes through which the invention of the modern Chinese subject take place: for example, education, the media, advertising, the arts, and public spaces.[1] Every visitor to China witnesses one visible effort at cultural control: the innumerable slogans and posters exhorting citizens to study Jiang Zemin's "Threerepresents Importantthought"[2] or Hu

Jintao's "Eight Honourables and Eight Shamefuls," not to spit, and to be filial and patriotic. Instead of disappearing along with the Marxist ideology, these slogans have multiplied, adapted to the times, and been harnessed by a variety of government bodies as well as private advertisers. When Lee Kum Kee Oyster Sauce, popular from San Francisco to Penang but hardly known in Peking, puts up advertising billboards on Hong Kong's Chater Road with the caption "Love the Fatherland, love Hong Kong," and Bosideng Down Wear advertises itself on airplane seats as "World Brand, Pride of the Nation," it becomes clear that public displays of official language, far from being ignored relics, as they were in the last decades of the Soviet Union, are influencing everyday life in new ways.

Much of my previous work has been concerned with the construction and contestations of the image of the "new migrant" in Chinese public discourse, the media (Nyíri 2005ab), and new Chinese organizations overseas (Nyíri 1999, 2001, 2002b), as well as its effects on transnational migratory, economic (Nyíri 1999; Pieke et al. 2004), and religious networks (Nyíri 2003), gender strategies (Nyíri 2002a), and the education of one-and-a-half- and second-generation migrant children (Nyíri and Feischmidt 2006). The new migrant, I found, was a symbolic figure of a globally modern and yet authentically national, even racial, way of being Chinese. The image is of someone who is successful in the global capitalist economy and rises to a position of economic and political power in the country that epitomizes modernity and power, the United States. Yet he or she is able to do so precisely because of certain innate Chinese moral qualities, which include loyalty to the homeland and a natural, selfless interest in its development manifested in investment or donations. The narratives of success attached to the image of the new migrant have had profound effects on how Chinese migrants relate to China and their countries of residence, stake claims, and develop migratory strategies. They have enfranchised migrant elites and helped migrants justify some business or social practices that might otherwise be seen as deviant.

More recently, I have been interested in tourism in China. In *Scenic Spots* (Nyíri 2006a), I argue that state and market promoters frame tourism in China as the consumption of a defined set of bounded and classified "scenic spots" with clear narratives, which enables the maintenance of hegemonic cultural authority over them. To a large degree, the hegemonic representation of scenic spots and tourism by the state-market matrix defines the reading of the sites by mainstream tourists and their behavior as tourists. I argue that although alternative constructs of tourism that challenge this canon are emerging, the Chinese construction of the tourist site is useful for understanding the mechanisms by which the Chinese state has successfully resisted challenges to its authority to represent and interpret Chinese culture.

In the last few years, the countries that have served as spaces of accumulation for Chinese migrants have also witnessed the rise of leisure travel from China. To be sure, the migrants' and the tourists' encounters with foreign places overlap. Chinese tourists are important for Chinese migrant economies; local Chinese arrange their visits and accompany tourist groups. Through these frequent encounters, locals and visitors direct one another's gaze and shape one another's commentary on what they see. But leisure travel is not the purposeful kind of mobility that fits into the triumphalistic vision of linear progress expressed in the new migrant discourse.

As more Chinese begin to travel abroad with the primary purpose of leisure, new questions arise. How will they deal with the far less canonized meanings of sites they encounter outside China? How are alternative sources of authority established over the interpretation of such sites? How do mobile individuals cope with the conflict between the image of the borderless "globally modern Chinese" and the often humiliating experiences in which the mobility of PRC passport holders is frustrated by an immobilizing global migration regime? These questions are particularly important because of the central role of cross-border mobility in discourses of what it means to be Chinese in the modern world. So far, these discourses have interpreted mobility primarily as migration, driven by the purpose of capital accumulation, but they are likely to widen as the purpose of movement expands to include a consumption-oriented framework of travel as leisure.

Yet at home, the Chinese state also seeks to immobilize threatening and illegal migrants, those who used to be called the "blind flow" (*mangliu*) of rural-urban migration. Despite repeated liberalizations, the *hukou* (household registration) system remains in place, making China (along with Russia) one of the few remaining countries whose populations are not legally free to live where they wish. As Sun (2002) pointed out, there is an intimate link between representations of domestic and international migration and the formation of modern Chinese subjectivity. As the contradiction between the immobilizing imperatives of the global migration regime and the mobilizing imperatives of Chinese modernity becomes more apparent internationally, its representations will affect domestic migrants' own experiences of frustrated mobility. Both internationally and domestically, this contradiction produces a tension in which mobile Chinese subjects must live.

This book combines empirical material and conceptual frameworks from research on migration and tourism in order to explore how cultural authority is transmitted to mobile Chinese and what kind of challenges it encounters. First, I suggest that mobility, in its various forms, plays an important role in the dominant discourse of modernization in today's China, in part because it is seen as aiding economic growth, in part because it is viewed as an attribute of modern (Western) societies, and in part because it is linked to the goal of modernizing the countryside and "civilizing" its population. Of particular interest is the trope of the enterprising Chinese migrant who helps modernize poorer developing countries and stagnating Western economies and in the process becomes more modern himself, which exists simultaneously and contiguously with the idea of the domestic civilizing project that particularly targets remote areas and ethnic minorities.

My second argument is that the Chinese state is making great efforts to contain the subversive potential of mobility, and so far has been remarkably successful. This is due in part to the effective use of "hard" administrative instruments such as distinct household registration statuses and the involvement of state officials as owners and regulators in every tourism project. More important, however, are the "soft" means of transmitting and maintaining hegemonic representations of Chinese geography, history, and culture through a multiplicity of media, the design and use of public space, and very active politics of transnational mobilization of and economic exchange with migrant organizations. All of this is characterized by the mixture of state guidance and market mechanisms that is so typical of today's PRC, and results in a remarkably uniform understanding of what it means to be a good member of the Chinese nation. This hegemony of representations is, of course, challenged by a growing array of opinions, both inside China and from abroad, and increasingly by means of the Internet.

The first half of the book outlines how major forms of human mobility—internal and international flows of workers (manual and highly skilled), merchants, students, and tourists—evolved in post-1978 China, what efforts the state has undertaken to manage them, and how their public evaluation has changed. I draw on published scholarship on domestic migration and my previous research on international migration and domestic and, to a lesser extent, international tourism. The emerging phenomenon of immigration to China (both expatriate managers and low-skilled migrants from neighboring countries) gets only brief treatment because of the paucity of information on the subject. The second half of the book draws together the discussion of migration and tourism to analyze the state's ambivalent attitude toward mobility as an instrument of modernization and "civilization," but also as a potential threat that must be supervised and controlled.

The tension between encouraging and facilitating human movement on the one hand and limiting and controlling it on the other is by no means unique to China. Indeed, it is a feature of today's wave of neoliberal globalization (perhaps even, as Tim Cresswell argued in *On the Move* [2006], of modernity more generally). Many Western and non-Western states and cities have joined the global competition to attract the rich, the educated, and even the culturally diverse: being homogeneous is increasingly seen as an obstacle to economic growth. Yet, since these same states and cities are increasingly reluctant to underwrite the economic, social, and political costs associated with migration, getting through borders is increasingly difficult for the poor and the unpopular.

Thus, the Chinese experience has implications for the study of migration and its politics elsewhere. But China's case is distinctive for the speed with which its citizens have joined the global trend and the fact that it is still very much a "gardening state," engaged in an explicit pedagogical effort to both valorize and control mobility. In this respect, comparisons with other evolving systems of mobility, primarily Russia—another state with a newly mobile population and policies to limit internal migration—are instructive, as they show important similarities and significant differences with China.

Through this investigation of human mobility, my ultimate purpose is to trace the fine structure of the channels through which cultural authority is transmitted, contested, and possibly subverted, and the changes in the formation of the modern, global Chinese subject that this process may engender. I show how the formation of "Chinese-subjects-in-the-world" proceeds under the conflicting pressures of a discursive regime that calls on them to identify with the triumphant national imperative to pursue modernity/mobility; mundane barriers of mobility that frustrate that triumphalism; and competing individual and institutional narratives of modernity and pleasure. Through this analysis, I reposition China, and those who encounter it, in the concurrent and competitive processes of globalization.

The idea of this book was born in discussions with members of a working group on cultural mobility—Stephen Greenblatt, Rossitza Guentcheva, Heike Paul, and Ines Županov—during a stay at the Wissenschaftskolleg zu Berlin.[3] Parts of it were written during a Humboldt Research Fellowship at the Free University of Berlin. Grants by the Economic and Social Research Council (UK) and Macquarie University in Australia supported some of the research. I thank Putao and Sanshenggui for their assistance in gathering Chinese-language materials and Cheng Xi for letting me consult materials at the library of the Institute for Overseas Chinese History of the All-China Overseas Chinese Federation in Peking and generously providing me with copies of recent books. I am particularly indebted to Liang Yong for his invaluable help in gathering materials and setting up interviews. Finally, I thank Antonella Diana and the anonymous reviewers for the University of Washington Press for their thoughtful comments, and Lorri Hagman for the help and support she has given this book, as well as my earlier *Scenic Spots*.

1
Internal Migration in Reform China

I n controlling both internal and international migration, the Chinese
Communist Party copied the Soviet model. By the time the People's
Republic of China was established, that model, entailing extreme
restrictions on both foreign and domestic mobility, was well entrenched.
Ordinary citizens were only allowed to travel abroad as a political reward
in the form of strictly supervised group tourism. Emigration was regarded
as treachery from the very outset of Soviet power and, beginning in the
1930s, was allowed only on an ethnic basis, as "repatriation" for a limited
number of Jews, Germans, Greeks, Persians, and others. Even in these
cases, liberalizations were short-lived and were used as bargaining chips
in international politics.

Internally, the Soviet regime suppressed and controlled migration
through the household registration (*propiska*) system. In principle, the
system allowed for the planning of industrial and agricultural labor as

well as for the provision of goods and services. It also served to control the population and maintain surveillance of it. To reside other than where one was registered was illegal and deprived a person of access to work, education, and health care. To obtain *propiska* in a desirable location such as Moscow, one generally had to be admitted to an educational institution, be dispatched by the state to a highly skilled job, or marry somebody living there.[1] The lack of mobility among the rural population was sealed by not issuing peasants internal passports, which were necessary to move about the country. This immobility effectively meant a return to serfdom until the travel ban was lifted after Stalin's death. This suppression of individual and spontaneous migration was complemented by massive voluntary and involuntary migrations, including the use of deportation, banishment, and labor camps, organized by the Soviet government to suit political and economic aims (see, e.g., Polian 2001).

Most Eastern European state socialist regimes did not implement a similar system of total control over external and internal movement for any significant period of time, but China did, introducing the household registration system (known as the *hukou* system) in 1951, and fully implementing it by 1958 (Chan 1996:135–36). The following section provides an overview of the effects of the *hukou* system on migration control, relying mainly on Chinese sources published since 1978.[2]

The Hukou System

The new rules divided the population into agricultural (*nongye*) and nonagricultural, expelling peasants from cities (560,000 from Shanghai alone in 1958). Like rural *propiska* in the Soviet Union, the *hukou* was designed to keep the population in place by restricting access to food rations, education, health care, and old-age pensions (most of the benefits being reserved for urban residents). In addition to the *hukou*, the marriage and birth control system also functioned to keep the population in place. While food rationing was the most important instrument in keeping the population fixed before 1978, education, health care, and access to housing and employment became the main impediments during the reform period. Although no longer inaccessible without a *hukou*, they became—and remained—much more costly.[3]

Soon after the *hukou* system was implemented, explicit rules were set up requiring individuals to obtain clearance from the Public Security Bureau (PSB) before changing residences. In 1964, the "Draft rules of managing household registration transfer" approved by the State Council strictly limited the transfer of household registration from villages to cities and towns (Wang Haiguang 2003). In the name of prioritizing industrial construction and the proletariat, the provision of goods, education, and health care was far better in the cities than in the countryside, but this advantage could only be preserved if population growth in urban centers was kept under strict control.

Migration in China, as in the Soviet Union, was largely linked to state projects such as the industrialization of the Northeast, Inner Mongolia, and inland cities of the so-called three lines of defense against attack from Taiwan; the cultivation of fallows in central and northern China (involving 16 million temporary rural migrants during the Cultural Revolution decade of 1966–76 alone); and the removal of the surplus urban workforce, including the relocation of more than 17 million educated youths to the countryside during the Cultural Revolution (Lary 1999:35–42). Yet there were also large-scale spontaneous migrations; in addition to the estimated 30 million who migrated to the cities during the Great Leap (20 million of whom were forcibly returned), an estimated 4 million voluntarily migrated during the first two years of the Cultural Revolution when state control was relatively weak.[4] Nonetheless, the efficiency of the state's restrictions of nonplanned migration to cities is demonstrated by the fact that the percentage of urban population contracted from 18.4 percent in 1959 to 17.9 percent in 1978 (Zhang 2001:4). Ronald Skeldon and Graeme Hugo (1999:335) commented that "no other developing country has been able successfully to control its mobility to achieve state objectives in quite the same way."

In the 1960s and 1970s, changing from an agricultural to a nonagricultural registration was granted only for some state job assignments and labor requisitioning, and was denied for spouses and children in most cases (Chan 1996:137). In 1975, as the first educated youths began trickling back from the countryside, Article 90, guaranteeing freedom of movement, was removed from the new constitution of the PRC. According to the State Council's 1977 regulations on managing household registration transfer, rural-urban *hukou* changes granted to family members of urban residents were not to exceed 0.15 percent of the urban population annually (Wang Haiguang 2003).

Migration in the Reform Era

After the beginning of economic reforms in 1978, migration took off rapidly. Some of it, notably resettlement projects related to the construction of dams or the protection of grasslands, continued to be directly planned. Much of it was related to state projects, though less directly than before. For example, Special Economic Zones, such as Shenzhen, attracted millions of skilled and unskilled migrants to work in the newly allowed foreign- and joint-invested manufacturing enterprises such as the labor intensive textile/clothing industry. Issued in 1983, special "Regulations on the appropriate circulation of science and technology personnel"[5] facilitated the migration of skilled workers and investors, which was accompanied by a construction boom and, in turn, generated demand for construction workers, nannies, and workers in all manner of services, from hotels to prostitution. Rural areas, especially in South China, revived former traditions of entrepreneurial migration, sending out traders, hawkers, and repairmen, and forming compact colonies in major cities such as Zhejiang Village in Peking (see Li Zhang 2001). Meanwhile, increasing agricultural productivity because of the introduction of fertilizers and machinery created a surplus of rural labor inland, while rural industrialization and migration to cities (and in some areas to Hong Kong and abroad as well) created a demand for low-paid agricultural labor in some development pockets, mainly on the coast. The labor demand was filled by inland migrants, creating a two-tiered agricultural labor structure in many places. Finally, with the reopening of universities, students became another expanding flow of internal migrants.

The lines that had been drawn between town and country were now being redrawn, amidst continuous contention, between cities and rural townships, whose development was to be a buffer protecting large cities from the onslaught of migrants. The "surplus" agricultural population was encouraged to move to township enterprises (*xiangzhen qiye*) under a policy of "leave the land but not the countryside, enter the factories but not the cities" (*li tu bu li xiang, jin chang bu jin cheng*). This led to the first of a series of reforms that have continued gradually for over twenty years.

Beginning in 1984, peasants were allowed to obtain *hukou* in townships below the county town level (*jizhen*) if they had secured accommodation and employment or were engaged in entrepreneurship. This type of *hukou* excluded food rations and other urban benefits. (*Hukou* remained linked to food rationing until 1994.) Moreover, peasants transferring their *hukou* lost their allotted land plots.

A 1985 law introduced temporary residence permits (*zanzhuzheng*) to legalize the status of rural migrants in cities. Rural migrants were no longer necessarily poor, and town and city governments realized that selling permanent *hukou* was a good source of income. One of the first towns to do so, Laian, in Anhui, sold 773 permits at 5,000 yuan apiece in just six days (Wei Jun 2001:23). Tianjin was reportedly the first to introduce a city construction surcharge of 10,000 yuan, the equivalent of ten years' income for the average peasant.[6] Two years later, Shanghai set a construction fee at 10,000 to 40,000 yuan, depending on the district.[7] The State Council made repeated attempts to curb the sale of permanent *hukou*, but it continued in the guise of charging ever higher reception fees, education supplements, and so on.[8]

In the late 1990s, the government embarked on a prolonged series of sometimes contradictory attempts to reform the *hukou* system, with the long-term goal of phasing out rural-urban *hukou* barriers. In 1997, a policy granting permanent *hukou* to migrants who had had legal residence and a functioning business or employment for at least two years was piloted in 382 county towns, effectively extending upwards the policy introduced thirteen years earlier in smaller townships.[9] The two-year requirement was lifted in 2000 in a resolution that also prohibited discrimination against new *hukou* holders in employment, education, and housing (suggesting that such discrimination existed), and, importantly, allowed peasants who transferred their *hukou* to keep their land.[10] By this time, 540,000 people had obtained city *hukou* under the pilot scheme (Shi Yulong 2002). In 2001, the project was extended to all 20,000 or so towns at and below the county seat level,[11] while the State Planning Commission announced a plan to "gradually unify town and country in provinces and cities or economically developed regions that meet the conditions" in the next five years, abolishing *hukou* transfer quotas and the division of *hukou* into rural and urban (Yuan and You 2002:38). These measures were in line with the goals of the Tenth Five-Year Plan, issued in 2001:

> to reform the *hukou* regime in towns; to establish a mechanism for orderly urban-rural population flow; to abolish unfair limitations on the employment of rural labour force in towns; to guide an orderly flow of excess

rural labour between urban and rural areas and between regions. (*Renmin Ribao* 2001)

At the same time, a new government resolution published in 1998 permitted children to choose between the mother's and the father's *hukou*, old-age pensioners were allowed to obtain the *hukou* of their children who cared for them, and investors were allowed to obtain the *hukou* of the city they invested in.[12]

Implementation of the central directive on abolishing *hukou* transfer quotas varied widely. A number of more prosperous provinces, including Fujian, Guangdong, Jiangsu, Zhejiang, and Shandong, followed it and announced an end to the division of *hukou* into urban and rural (F. Wang 2004:120). But even within these provinces, cities of different sizes were allowed to define their own criteria for *hukou* applicants.[13] In small towns, rural migrants were often able to acquire *hukou* as long as they had a residence and a stable source of income, whereas larger cities usually stipulated a number of ways to acquire it, such as by joining close relatives with a local *hukou*; purchasing housing; investment; employment in the city; graduation from a university in the city; being born there; or having special skills. Some cities imposed age limits, wishing to attract young university graduates.

The larger and more prosperous the city, the more restrictive were the conditions for acquiring *hukou*. Some cash-strapped municipalities gambling on migration as a source of income experimented with more liberal rules (Liu Bowen 2004:11; Cheng Guanglong 2002). For instance, Shijiazhuang, the struggling capital of Hebei Province, allowed *hukou* acquisition for the families of all individuals employed in the city for at least two years who had purchased housing, started an enterprise, or graduated from university, as well as for residents' family members (Wang Wenlu 2003). By contrast, prosperous Canton declared that it would issue *hukou* only to those whose income tax exceeded 100,000 yuan (around US$13,000) for three years and limited benefiting family members to spouses who married "late" (in accordance with government policy) and had been married for at least six years (Yao Wen 2003; Ji and Xing 2004), as well as children under eighteen. Chengdu, capital of inland Sichuan, announced the abolition of *hukou* transfer quotas in 2003, but replaced them with regulations that require *hukou* applicants to belong to one of the following categories: outstanding (*youxiu*) graduates of higher education establishments; technical or management personnel with secondary vocational education; young or middle-age experts who have made an outstanding contribution to science or technology; and other urgently needed engineering, teaching, administrative, and management personnel (Zhang Xiaodong 2003). In 2001, Shenzhen, a city essentially built by post-1978 migrants, where the non-*hukou* population outnumbers the *hukou* population three to one, became the first city explicitly to allow a wide range of skilled professionals—such as accountants, doctors, real estate brokers, and anyone urgently needed by the city—to take up employment without *hukou* and still enjoy the same rights to social security and children's education (Cheng Guanglong 2002; Cui Dan 2002). The city government justified these reforms by the need to create "a better investment environment" (*Lingdao juece xinxi* 2003a).

Before 1978, migration from the more prosperous eastern regions to the less developed West, where ethnic minorities often formed the majority population, was part of the central policy of "supporting socialist construction in the borderlands." When the Great Western Development policy was announced in 1999, some provincial capitals in Western China, notably Urumqi, allowed everyone "with a stable legal income and abode" to obtain *hukou* for a fee of 3,000 to 8,000 yuan to promote economic growth (Xing Jiang 2001). Today, the provincial and local governments maintain more liberal *hukou* rules to create more attractive conditions for investments, even though in minority areas, especially Tibet and Xinjiang, Han Chinese immigration is a subject of controversy. In addition to managerial and technical personnel, economic growth in the West, particularly the growth of tourism, attracts both migrant construction workers and petty entrepreneurs from other parts of China. Tourism-oriented commerce in destinations is dominated by such migrants from the East. In Sipsongpanna, a popular 1990s tourist destination in Yunnan originally inhabited by the Tai ethnic group, there were 100,000 migrant workers and entrepreneurs in 1997, constituting about one-quarter of the population (Halskov Hansen 2005:68).

Shanghai, and especially Peking, remained inert to changes longer. For some years, these cities ran their own "immigration schemes" to attract what Chinese sources called investors and skilled migrants. In 1989, Shanghai officials (Shi and Ye 1989:41) described the city's *hukou* policy as "liberal on mid- and high-level special personnel; strict on ordinary personnel." As late as 2002, Shanghai still restricted the acquisition of permanent *hukou* to graduates of a small number of elite universities (*Huaxia Shibao* 2002). In 2004, however, the city adopted new rules allowing *hukou* to anyone with a business license or a work contract for over six months, or housing that had been purchased or rented on a contract for over six months (Wan Xingya 2004).

Peking continues to baulk at abolishing the *hukou* transfer quota, which officially remains around 15,000 per year (Tong 2004). The city government introduced a new green card system in 2003. Holders of green cards, or residence and work permits, were entitled to the same treatment as Peking *hukou* holders with regard to their children's education, purchasing housing and cars, employment, registering of businesses, and social insurance. But, out of a non-*hukou* population of 3 million, only 30,000 met the requirements for green cards (*Lingdao juece xinxi* 2003b) In the Zhongguancun district, designated a high-tech district by the Peking city government, only university graduates are officially allowed to settle.

Until 2003, Shanghai and Peking only granted *hukou* to children once they reached the age of five, and applicants had to bring proof of school enrollment and residence and certificates of registration from the local and provincial governments where the other parent's *hukou* was, even though the family no longer lived there (Liu Jing 1999:13). This process reportedly involved fees as high as 100,000 yuan, and the child was still excluded from most kindergartens in Peking (Wang Yutian 2003). In 2003, new regulations in Peking stipulated that all children born since August 1985 receive local *hukou*, but only if the father had it (*Guangdong Shiji* 2003).

The overall result of the reforms has been that the educated and "the rich have now achieved a *de facto* national mobility" (F. Wang 2004:122). Peking's 1997 "Regulations on outside labor and businesspeople in the capital" made this distinction clear by specifying that they do not extend to people hired to work in science and technology, arts and education, or finance and trade.[14] Only those who can afford to buy property are hired at a high level by important organizations or enterprises, run large businesses (employing at least 100 workers and paying no less than 800,000 yuan per year in tax [ibid.:120n25]),[15] or have good connections to local officials and thus can count on obtaining *hukou* in a major city. A number of state enterprises have the right to provide so-called group *hukou* (*jiti hukou*) to a certain number of employees from other cities. As a result, many individuals are nominally hired by such enterprises but in reality work in private firms that have nothing to do with the former. According to one author, such an arrangement cost between 10,000 and 30,000 yuan in Peking in 2004 (Tong 2004), but in order to obtain *hukou* for one's spouse and child as well, one had to be either "a multimillionaire investor" or the holder of a doctoral degree (F. Wang 2004:119).

At the same time, a Shenzhen newspaper observed: "For the vast majority of people, reforms or no reforms has not made much difference" (Tian 2003). This is true even outside large cities because in practice most nonelite rural migrants fail to meet the terms of stable legal income and residence, since they are generally interpreted to mean housing either owned or rented from a legal entity under official contract and employment under contract with social security contributions paid by the employer (Zhao Jin 2003; Jiang Yihua 2003). Yet, as we will see below, most employers prefer not to offer contracts or pay social security contributions to save costs; similarly, almost all migrants rent housing from private individuals without a contract (even though the Shanghai government has made attempts to corral them into hostels). This creates a vicious circle that keeps them out of *hukou* and in menial jobs. At the same time, the new regulations contain no provisions for the social welfare of those taking up the new unified *hukou*, meaning that a migrant has no recourse to social security payments if he loses his job. A further deterrent is that the regulations do not make it clear whether those taking up *hukou* in the city must give back their allotted land plots, which provide them with some sense of security in the absence of a welfare net.[16] As the head of the Propaganda Department of Jiangsu's Public Security Bureau admitted, the *hukou* reform "has only affected . . . a very small minority of peasants" (Zhao Jin 2003). Two years after Shijiazhuang implemented what was seen as a pioneer *hukou* reform, a survey showed that migrants with more education, higher income, and better employment were overrepresented among those who had acquired urban *hukou* (Tan Ke 2003:36).

For the majority of the outside population that remains without *hukou*, the regulations have remained largely unchanged since 1995. Although they vary somewhat from place to place, they generally include several elements. First, within a month of their arrival, migrants must register with the authorities. To do so, they must present a valid national identification card; the *hukou* booklet of the head of household if they are staying with a local resident; a copy of their lease if they are renting housing; and their family planning certificate if they are married women of reproductive age. (If they are staying within an employer's compound, the employer may apply for their registration.) If they have an Outside Employment Registration Card (*waichu renyuan jiuye dengjika*) issued by the local authorities where their permanent *hukou* is registered, they can then obtain a work permit (*wailai renyuan jiuyezheng*) and a temporary residence permit valid for a maximum of one year, which permits them to look for work or obtain a business license. For their part, employers must obtain permits to employ workers from outside the province, and the number of migrant employment permits issued is limited by a quota set by the local labor department.[17]

A range of socially and politically undesirable individuals is excluded from obtaining a temporary residence permit. In Peking, these people include "beggars and buskers; fortunetellers and other personnel engaged in feudal superstitious activities; unlicensed healers; manufacturers and vendors of counterfeit merchandise and vendors of documents and illegally made seals; and other individuals who harm social order and public safety."[18]

The Two-Tiered Society

Although the system of permits is supposed to limit migration and be adjusted in accordance with periodically revised guidelines—such as employers' plans for hiring outside labor—permits are often easy to obtain on the market. In addition, most migrants find work at open-air "slave markets" by employers who do not care about permits (Wang Minghao 2003). Arguably, therefore, the main function of the *hukou* system in China's major cities today—similar to the immigration systems of some Western countries—is not to keep unskilled migrants out but to keep them in a permanent position of legal and economic instability and vulnerability. The line—or as the liberal *Southern Weekend* newspaper referred to it, the "electric fence" (Li Changping 2003)—that nominally separated rural and urban *hukou* holders (and cities from rural townships after 1980) now effectively lies between official residents of the largest, most prosperous and desirable cities and all others, much as it did in Europe before the great homogenizing projects of the nineteenth century. Cities are no longer closed to outsiders; indeed, by the late 1990s, nonresidents outnumbered residents 9 to 1 in Dongguan in the Pearl River Delta (Li Ruojian 2001:57). Instead of closing their gates, cities divided their populations into two distinct halves endowed with different rights. Like in contemporary international migration or medieval European cities, they sustain a dual labor market, with the institutionally disenfranchised lower tier consisting of a flexible, disposable pool of temporary or illegal residents excluded from urban citizenship (Chan 1996). Indeed, as the permit system took shape in 1995, "Minister of Labour Li Boyong proposed to the National People's Congress that the authorities should set up a system for controlling the movement of internal migrants 'similar to international passport and visa requirements'" (Human Rights in China 2002a:35). Although recent moves rhetorically gesture toward the abolition of this system, real steps in this direction are likely to be slow.

Migrants without a permanent *hukou* tend to be employed, whether legally or illegally, in low-end jobs that locals do not take, or do not take for the same wages. Others are petty entrepreneurs, ranging from street cobblers to food vendors. Without a chance to be sponsored for permanent *hukou* by their employers, they are forced to remain in those occupations—though some are able to grow their businesses. Their access to housing is subject to official scrutiny and often to exclusion or higher rents than for local residents. As a result, a number of migrants find accommodation in illegally constructed housing. Although such housing does not resemble South American- or South Asian-style slums, there have been campaigns to demolish it (nearly 15,000 buildings in Shanghai in 1996 [Human Rights in China 2002a:28]), along with unlicensed businesses such as hairdressers' shops, food processing workshops, and ragpickers' depots (168 in the first half of 1998 in Shanghai alone [Wang, Sun, and Zhu 1998]).

Since the 1990s, as urban wages grew, the phenomenal growth of light industries (such as textile and electronics) has depended on the sustained existence of a dual labor market (Li Qiang 2000; cf. Piore 1970), in which rural migrants provide the lower segment, a dispensable and docile labor force without job security, training, or upward mobility. Wages, labor conditions, and the dependence on informal agreements or orders in this segment remain unaffected by the rising living standards of the urban/coastal population and the emerging body of minimum wage and labor standards regulations. Several studies from the mid-1990s to the mid-2000s concluded that migrant workers' incomes were between 50 and 70 percent of that of local workers (Li 2000:157; Lu 2002; H. X. Zhang 2006; Smart and Lin 2007; Luan's study [2000:90] showed a smaller differential).

In the following years, while urban wages grew, those of migrant workers remained practically the same; in 2004, they still averaged 780 yuan per month (under US$100) in the main urban centers (H. X. Zhang 2006). Moreover, Vice-Premier Zeng Peiyan said in late 2004 that employers owed migrant workers around 360 billion yuan in back wages (*China Rights Forum* 2004). Over 80 percent of workers punished or dismissed in the Canton and Wenzhou enterprises investigated by Luan (2000:51) were migrants. According to the same study, migrants who changed jobs often received lower wages at their new job than their previous one. And while migrants work in more dangerous jobs than locals—in one study, one-third of migrant workers suffered from work-related illnesses in the Pearl River Delta (Tan 2002; cited in Xiang 2005a:162)—fewer of them benefited from medical insurance, a pension scheme, or health care provided by the employer (Luan Jingdong 2000:78–88; Zhao Jin 2003; Guan and Jiang 2003; Xiang 2005a:169).[19] In a Peking survey, 93 percent of migrants had to cover all medical expenses themselves (Wen et al. 2003; cited in Xiang 2005a:164). Xiang (2005a) and H. X. Zhang (2006) point out that most migrants lack money for proper medical treatment and are therefore often refused admission by hospitals. Compounded by strict controls over migrants' fertility—even those women who would be entitled to apply for a birth permit cannot do so in practice because it would require liaising with the authorities at the place of their *hukou* registration—migrant workers' children have a high rate of infant mortality. Human Rights in China (2002a:76) maintains that in 2000 over three-quarters of all childbirth deaths in Canton were of migrant women.

As Xiang (2005a:169) points out, part of the reason for this precarious situation is that many migrants do not have formal contracts, and those who do tend to have short-term ones. In a study of car factories, Zhang Lu (2005) found that at Volkswagen's joint-venture factories 30 and 50 percent of workers were migrant workers on three-month and one-year contracts, respectively, with half the wages of permanent workers and no possibility to join the unions. The income gap is further widened by the fact that as temporary or "irregular" workers, migrants without a *hukou* are denied health care benefits and face payments of several thousand yuan per year or more for the primary education of their children in Peking, Shanghai, and Canton (Human Rights in China 2002b; Cui Chuanyi 2003:164; Guan and Jiang 2003:256). Even in the best case, this is five or six times the fee paid by local parents and can amount to two or three monthly wages of migrant workers (H. X. Zhang 2006).

Moreover, some schools do not accept migrant children at all, and others do not afford outside students (*wailaisheng*) the same treatment as locals (Sun 2000, cited in Jin Huanling 2005; Human Rights in China 2002b). According to one article, the principal of a government school in Yunlong, Ningbo Prefecture, declared that all migrant students with failing grades had to leave the school (Shen Ying 2004). Some students were expelled for various misdemeanors (such as stealing a watermelon), while others left voluntarily because they felt that teachers and local students had treated them badly. There was a mixture of reasons for refusing admission to migrant children. Schools are supposed to comply with student achievement targets, and they feel that migrant children come with less preparation and thus compromise their ability to meet these targets. On the other hand, local officials are unwilling to spend educational funding on migrant children, whom they see as parasites on local resources (ibid.).

This situation has resulted in a mushrooming of private migrant schools, where education is cheaper than at the state-run ones but chances of further education are low.[20] In 2005, 60 percent of migrant children in Shanghai were studying in such schools (Peng and Yao 2006:203), often in very poor conditions. In Peking, migrant schools were often located in "car-repair shops, public bath houses, coal storage facilities, or in the living space of migrant families" (Woronov 2004:296). Some cities, such as Canton, have licensed migrant schools and even provided them with assistance, but declared that children without *hukou* were *only* allowed to attend these schools. Other cities, including Peking and Shenzhen, periodically close migrant schools as part of cleanup campaigns targeting migrants (Human Rights in China 2002b:4, 17). Yet school fees in villages are also on the rise, resulting in more children dropping out of school altogether and migrating to cities on their own (Murphy 2002). According to Xie Jingyu (quoted in Human Rights in China 2002b:3), at least 1.8 out of 2.1 million migrant children in cities in the age group for which education is mandatory (from six to fourteen) were receiving no education in 1999.

Many Chinese and foreign authors have noted that the discrimination between local and migrant workers is reflected not only in differing wages but also in unequal working conditions. To begin with, because of the competition for urban jobs, they often have to pay the equivalent of one or two months' wages to be employed in the first place (Pun 2005a,b). In addition, some employers and local governments charge outside labor a monthly management fee, which, in the case of factories studied by Pun Ngai (ibid.), was as much as half their wage. In another factory, workers reportedly went unpaid for forty days and then were fired (Human Rights in China 2002a:88). Fires at migrant workers' dormitories have in some cases resulted in mass deaths because the workers were locked inside to prevent them from quitting their jobs.[21] In one factory studied by Pun, workers generally worked seven days a week, between seventy-two and seventy-seven hours, but earned relatively high wages (around one thousand yuan). Despite obvious discontent with these conditions, Li Qiang (2000:158) writes that rural migrant workers (*mingong, nongmingong*) fully expect to receive lower wages and be denied the benefits that urban workers (*zhigong*) enjoy. Maids, who are almost invariably migrant workers, frequently complain that their employers withhold their identity cards so they cannot run away or steal. This practice is illegal, but it is sometimes actively encouraged by local police (Bu Wei 2006).

Hukou discrimination is not limited to low-skilled workers. For example, in 2001, the popular *Peking Youth Daily* profiled a college graduate who landed a job with a Peking newspaper but, as a casual employee without a *hukou*, made a piece wage (eighty yuan, or about $10, per thousand characters) without the bonuses and social security afforded her permanent colleagues (Liu Juhua 2001). In addition, those without a Peking *hukou* may not own a motor vehicle, which is a significant obstacle for entrepreneurs.

In sum, the function of the *hukou* system has shifted from preventing population mobility to controlling access to economic resources, and finally to class and subject formation. It exercises this function by limiting the social rights, expectations, and status of most while granting exception to an elite minority who conform to the imaginary of modernization and success. A striking manifestation of the impact of *hukou* on social stratification is the rarity of intermarriage between urban and rural *hukou*, which, as Lu Yilong (2001) has shown, has effectively created two or more (big city, small town, and rural *hukou* holders) endogamous castes within Chinese society.[22]

Managing the Outside Population:
Toward Community Surveillance

The *hukou* reforms in the 1990s reflected a tacit acceptance of the need for migrant workers but erected institutional barriers to control the "blind flow" and to separate migrants from local society. As Zhang (1995:46) concluded, "the management of the outside population" (*wailai renkou*[23]) had to include a comprehensive system of "economic, administrative, [and] legal measures." This system reinforced the institutional and discursive division of polities into citizens and helots (see Luan 2000:34, 105).

Outside population management bodies within the police are vested with vague but sweeping authority to oversee all that concerns migrants: to control their employment and residence, to protect their interests, to deal with crime they perpetrate or suffer, and to repatriate them if they are unemployed.[24] They also determine the responsibility of employers and landlords in "managing" migrants. Moreover, employers, or village party committees, if migrants are employed in agriculture, are required to have personnel in charge of migrant affairs. In practice, local governments often sign agreements with major employers, delegating to them the task of supervising migrants (Luan 2000:107–9). As early as 1988, Shanghai set up municipal migrant management assistance teams consisting of 30,000 full-time and part-time members to "help *hukou* management organs enforce the management of outside population registration," chiefly by conducting checks (Shi and Ye 1989:42). In 1993, the city set up the Transient Population Management Coordination Committee, renamed the Shanghai Transient Outside Population Management Leading Group in 1998, with a vice mayor installed as chairman (Wang et al. 1998) and subgroups set up in every administrative subdivision of the city (Xu et al. 2000:2). Songjiang District created a network of "information officers," consisting of "core residents" and "enthusiastic landlords," who reported problems among the migrant population to the authorities (Xu Deming 2003:159). Similarly, the 1995 Rules of *Hukou* Management of Outside Personnel in Peking gave the Public Security Bureau the right to name liaison officers in "areas of concentrated settlement of outside personnel" to assist in their "*hukou* management."

In Shenzhen, the city instructed neighborhood committees to set up security squads to help manage the temporary population (Human Rights in China 2002a:43),[25] and because it is also a border area (with Hong Kong), the city has two guarded perimeters that can only be crossed with the proper permits (ibid.:90). In addition, a number of local migrant management bodies employ private security guards (ibid.:43).

An important function of the system is to ensure compliance with family planning rules. The 1994 "Temporary regulations on the management of interprovincial movement and employment of rural labor" makes employers and landlords responsible for checking family planning certificates, which register marital status and number of children of women migrants, and introduces fines to those who employ or rent accommodation to women who cannot produce valid certificates. In 1997, the State Planning Commission "reiterated the concern that migrants were slipping through the cracks of China's planned reproduction system," which "threatened to create a 'population crisis'" (Human Rights in China 2002a:104). Since 1998, women of reproductive age must also present their family planning certificates to obtain a business license. In Shanghai, women are supposed to have their temporary residence permits stamped annually to attest to their continued compliance with family planning rules (ibid.:69). In Canton, they are supposed to renew their family planning certificates once a year in their places of *hukou* registration, and if they want to give birth they must obtain a birth permit there (*Nanfang Dushibao* 2004); in addition, employment, rental contracts, and business licenses can be cancelled if family planning rules are violated (Human Rights in China 2002a:72). In practice, employers avoid fines by promptly dismissing all women who are "illegally" pregnant before the yearly inspection raids by the local family planning commission (Luan 2000:109–10).

Echoing citizenship tests for immigrants in Western countries, the Shanghai Transient Outside Population Management Leading Group has proposed that everyone applying for a temporary residence permit be tested on the contents of the handbook for migrants, *A Guide to Entering Shanghai: For Brothers and Sisters Who Come to Shanghai to Work* (Xu et al. 2000:13). But how well does the system actually work? An official survey conducted by the Ministry of Agriculture in 1996 found that 79 percent of migrants never registered their arrival in the cities (quoted in Human Rights in China 2002a:86), a conclusion seconded by many researchers (e.g., Solinger 1999; Murphy 2002). Employers and local officials are often reluctant to report the presence of "illegal" migrants, and in other cases are willing to issue permits to people without any documents in exchange for cash. One neighborhood committee in Peking "only registered those migrants who lived or ran shops within walking distance of the committee office, and only enough of these to 'keep the district government happy'" (Human Rights in China 2002a:87). Dorothy Solinger maintains that some police officers actually refuse to issue temporary residence permits to migrants who try to register because they prefer the repeated revenue from fines (ibid.). On the other hand, employers often keep their employees' residence permits as a way of ensuring that they do not run away, resulting in what Human Rights in China (ibid.:95) calls a system of bonded labor. In 1997, a Henan police official lamenting this trend proposed as a remedy the introduction of quasi-passports for outside workers that would contain a photo and a record of all their movements, beginning in their home village (Yuan 1997).

Limitations on Chinese citizens' freedom of movement were routinely justified in terms of the economic needs of "socialist construction" and the limited capacity of urban communal services, and sometimes in terms of social stability, referring to the fear that the urban population would not accept a claim suddenly staked by the rural masses on their privileges and living space (Dong Shaoping 2003:57). Yet underlying the measures was a concern for control. Lacking an effective system of monitoring human movement or reliable identification, authorities relied on village and neighborhood committees to track down those they wanted. With migrants, this became impossible, and if they did not register their place of origin and real name at their place of employment or new residence, finding them became very difficult and costly. From this perspective, any movement appeared a security risk. As police official Yuan complained (1997:4), "As long as they have an identification card, these people can travel far and wide, they are free to come and go; this gives crime suspects an opportunity to flee." In 1991, the "Decision on reinforcing the comprehensive control of social order,"[26] issued by the CCP Central Committee and the State Council, stressed the "management of the transient population" as one of the central tasks in maintaining social stability. Following this decision, Comprehensive Control Committees were established at all administrative levels and charged with coordinating crackdowns on migrants who lack the required permits (Human Rights in China 2002a:41). In 1995, a national conference on the "transient population" "urged local governments to put combating migrant-related crime . . . at the top of their agenda for safeguarding the socialist order and . . . political stability" (L. Zhang 2001:166).

The 1990s and early 2000s saw a series of highly publicized raids on migrant settlements in major cities, involving the demolition of housing and closure of businesses. The best known of these raids was the 1995 demolition of Zhejiang Village in Peking, ordered personally by Premier Li Peng and documented in Li Zhang's *Strangers in the City* (2001). Thirty thousand migrants—mostly petty traders—were evicted, which, as authorities boasted, resulted in the shutting down of 1,432 unlicensed businesses and the confiscation of 700 unlicensed rickshaws in addition to the arrest of alleged criminals and the confiscation of drugs, weapons, and pornography (Human Rights in China 2002a:46). Canton also conducted large-scale sweeps in 2000 and 2002, vowing to detain and expel those who did not have "legitimate reasons" to stay in the city (ibid.:47).

But in the 2000s, along with further *hukou* reforms, a new discourse appeared in newspapers as well as in scholarly and official publications, which, in a series of articles, explained the inevitability of lifting the rural/urban barrier and reuniting town with country (*chengxiang yitihua, chengxiang ronghe*) for both economic development and social equality.[27] These articles stressed the contribution of migrants to economic development and urbanization—a key goal of the Tenth Five-Year Plan issued in 2001—as the basis for the need to reform the system. In 2002, the Central Committee of the Communist Youth League published a damning study documenting the excessive working hours, abuse, and nonpayment of wages migrant workers were subjected to (cited in Li Peilin 2003). A 2004 editorial in the popular Peking newspaper *Xinjingbao* called for the granting of local *hukou* to all residents who had stable income and housing, equal treatment to all citizens, and the abolition of all discriminative regulations distinguishing between permanent and temporary *hukou*. A representative to the National People's Congress proposed a resolution entitled "Include citizens' 'freedom of movement' in the constitution as soon as possible" (Liu Bowen 2004). An editorial of the Xinhua News Agency—a key outlet of official opinion—criticized Peking's green card scheme for its principle of differential treatment, stating that "physical laborers . . . must enjoy equal rights to free movement and residence" (quoted in *Lingdao juece xinxi* 2003b). In a couple of years, even Public

Security officials were publishing articles condemning the "two-tiered society" in the name of the constitutional freedom of movement (e.g., Wang Gan 2001; Hu Zhigang 2003; Hu Xuequn 2004).

No one, however, went as far as suggesting the abolition of the household registration system. On the contrary, many authors argued that once the *hukou* shed its inappropriate functions of migration control, it would be better suited to serve its original role of population control and management (e.g., Ai 2004). Concurrently, official explanations of why limits on mobility had to remain in place shifted toward the cultural, drawing on popular media discourse. Thus, in 2001, when explaining why *hukou* limitations were being lifted in small towns but not in big cities, officials argued that this was necessary to reduce culture shock, as the "culture and quality" of people in small towns was closer to that of migrants.

This shift indicated the Party's new willingness to address social inequality, particularly across the rural-urban divide (Froissart 2005). The new rhetoric was manifested in a series of slogans promoting attention to the individual *(yi ren wei ben*, a phrase that can also be understood as "humanitarianism"), and the idea of a residential community (*shequ*). Some slogans were reminiscent of the transition to "governance through community" in Western liberal democracies that, according to Nikolas Rose (1999), is an essential characteristic of neoliberalism. Practically, the new language signaled the emergence of measures promoting the social integration of locals and "outsiders." In 2003 and 2004, the State Council issued a decree directing city governments to begin designing workplace injury and medical insurance systems for it what it called the outside population.[28] By 2005, several major cities, including Peking, Shanghai, and Canton, had done so, and the Ministry of Labor and Social Security began a so-called Spring Wind Campaign to provide free job placement services for migrant workers. Importantly, however, despite the new discourse of breaking down the rural-urban barrier, these schemes did not extend existing urban welfare provisions to migrants but introduced a separate system for them, with a narrower scope, lower benefits, and no state contribution, thus further cementing the division of urban society into two classes.[29] A number of smaller factories and service enterprises highly dependent on migrant labor have not implemented any insurance scheme in order to keep costs low, and city officials keen on economic growth tolerate this practice (Froissart 2005). Even in the plans of the central government, the full integration of urban and rural social welfare is not scheduled until 2020.

Nonetheless, at least in rhetoric, the move to address some of the inequalities was evident. For the first time, the 2003 State Council document acknowledged arrears in the payment of wages of migrant workers as a problem and threatened major wage withholders with legal action and exposure in the media. It ordered enterprises to sign contracts with workers, calling on labor protection offices to ensure that this was done and that employers did not wantonly extend working hours, deduct fees from wages, or use child labor. (More importantly, in 2005, the Ministry of Labor expanded the definition of a legal labor relationship to provide legal protection to workers who are employed without written contracts.[30]) The document expressed support for organizing migrant workers into branches of the state labor union. (According to Froissart [2005], labor unions in Chengdu have begun to recruit migrant workers, but because of worker distrust, have largely been unsuccessful. In her study, fewer than 20 percent of the workers were union members.) In addition, it called for ending "unreasonable limitations" and discriminative regulations governing migrant workers' employment, calling them an "interference with the sovereign right of enterprises to legally employ migrant workers." It also instructed local governments to ensure that migrant children have the same access to compulsory education as locals, that they are charged no extra fees, that migrant-run schools are directed to improve their quality but not summarily closed down, and that special funds are set aside to support migrants' education. (As already noted, some city governments have responded to this by moving all migrant children to special schools with no government funding [Shen Ying 2004].) At the same time, the document called for the implementation of a group responsibility system, making employers and community organizations responsible for crimes committed by migrants.

Under Mao, the *hukou* system, combined with the rural system of people's communes and the urban systems of work units and neighborhood committees, provided effective and multiple means for the state to control the activities of every individual with a relatively small apparatus. A person's file (*dang'an*), created in the first official institution she encountered (often kindergarten), traveled with her to every place of study and work, becoming fatter with records entered in each place. This system, however, was premised on the absence of spontaneous mobility. Migrant workers travel without their personal files. The lament of Public Security official Yuan that migrants are "free to come and go" reflects the frustration of law enforcement organs with a situation in which mobility denies them the familiar means of tracking individuals' economic, political, and reproductive activities. The infrastructure to monitor their movement in a vast country without a reliable system of identification is simply not there. Personal identification cards (*shenfenzheng*) were introduced only in 1985, and as Yuan (1997) pointed out, many people still did not have them in the late 1990s.

If the illegal status of non-*hukou* migrants has deprived them of rights and created, as many Chinese authors write (e.g., Li Peilin 2003), an invisible wall between them and the locals, it has also rendered them far harder to control. Some city governments have made moves to shift from a *hukou*-based population management regime to a residence-based one. These moves are based on the 1999 directive that requires urban neighborhoods to elect community committees (*shequ weiyuanhui*)—distinct from, though effectively controlled by, the Party's neighborhood committees (*jiedao weiyuanhui*)—that are charged with a range of tasks from enforcing family planning to ensuring the delivery of communal services (Shi Fayong 2004). But these committees have not gone far in achieving control of compact colonies of migrants such as Zhejiang Village, where control through the workplace was also hard to implement since most migrants were self-employed or employed by fellow migrants (Li Zhang 2001; He 2003; Xiang 2005). These colonies and their parallel institutions, such as schools and clinics—Zhejiang Village effectively had its own law enforcement—are a product of necessity, but they are also beyond the reach of normal state structures and thus subject to periodic crackdowns (Li Zhang 2001). Authorities in Shanghai have reported setting up Party and Communist Youth League branches at Outside Population Service Centers (Xu Deming 2003:162), but according to Jacka (2006), similar centers in Peking do little beyond processing temporary residence permits.

At the same time, driven by economic as well as political interests, local governments in the residence areas and those in the home areas compete for access to migrants, resulting in a breach of China's strict hierarchical system of political power. More often than not, their interests are in conflict, with governments of poor rural sending areas benefiting from remittances generated by increased migration, and receiving areas attempting to limit it (see He 2003). In 2003, Sichuan received 17.7 billion yuan in remittances, equivalent to a third of the peasants' income in the province (Froissart 2005). The eventual return of migrants to their native villages is one outcome that appears to satisfy both sending- and receiving-area governments—provided they have made money. The migrants often strive—though do not always succeed—to come back as entrepreneurs, and sometimes assume leadership positions in the villages, including participating in elections for village head (Zhou Daming 2003). For a woman in particular, returning as an independent entrepreneur can dramatically change her position in local society. The central government, including former Premier Li Peng, has made statements supporting such entrepreneurship by skilled returning migrants, and some local governments provide a variety of incentives to "bring-back projects," including reintegration aid, tax breaks, simplification of administrative procedures, help with land acquisition, information and credit, and cooptation into the local political hierarchy (Murphy 2002:124–43).

In her study of Zhejiang Village in the first half of the 1990s, Li Zhang (2001) concluded that part of the reason for the state's failure to penetrate the "transient population" was the absence of migrant organizations that could broker the power relations between migrants and the state. In fact, settlement-area governments have increasingly taken to cultivating leading figures in migrant communities—such as successful entrepreneurs—in the hope of exercising control over migrants through them (Xiang 1999). At the same time, in a process paralleling the Chinese state's efforts to retain the loyalties of overseas migrants, sending-area governments have encouraged the formation of native-place associations and cultivated them as constituent communities that can be mobilized to further native-area interests in major cities. For instance, in 2003, Xinyang Prefecture, the home of over 1.5 million migrant workers, ordered county and township governments to set up Leading Groups for the Protection of Legal Rights of Out-migrating Workers as well as Migrant Worker Associations, and succeeded in recruiting more than 200,000 members during the first five months (Wang Minghao 2003). Continued ties with the home area have been facilitated by exclusion in the place of settlement; as Murphy (2002:43) writes, migrants "are able to come to terms with their lowly status in the cities because the host society is not the social and spatial reality in which they define themselves."

For their part, native-place associations attempt to leverage their connections, not just in the home area and the place of residence but also with fellow migrants elsewhere in China and especially abroad. For example, the Fu Tsing World Friendship Association is a Hong Kong–based organization of migrants from Fuqing Municipality, Fujian Province, with a mainly Southeast Asian membership and founded by the Indonesian tycoon Liem Sioe Liong. It now has several member associations in China itself, including in Peking, Shenzhen, and Canton, as well as Hong Kong and Macau. Leaders of these associations frequently travel to meet with their counterparts abroad, and Fuqing officials attend these meetings. For instance, they were invited to attend the 1999 handover ceremony in Macau by the Association of Fujianese in Macau. Although new, this association seems to have clout with the Macau government because of the large number of Fujianese in the ex-colony and the importance of their economic ties.

Various ministries in the central government have also attempted to expand their respective turfs by extending their control to migrants. For example, the Ministry of Agriculture has organized a China Rural Labor Association that lent some support to migrant workers (Woronov 2004:310n15).

The central government has tried to assert its control over these divergent interests by requiring sending- and receiving-area governments and employers to cooperate. For example, back in 1995, it imposed a month-long freeze on the employment of new workers after the Spring Festival holiday period each year (when factories stop production and most workers go back to their home areas), requiring employers to encourage the rehiring of old workers and sending-area governments to stop the outflow of new migrants.[31] But the decree, intended to reduce the yearly peak in population movement, is reported to be widely ignored because it contradicts both the interests of sending areas and the economic rationality of the "dormitory labor regime," which favors a high turnover of workers to keep wages low (Pun 2005b). In 2005, Guangdong Province lifted the ban altogether (Leu 2005).

In sum, despite relentless efforts to do so, most authors agree that the Chinese state has failed to extend its usual forms of administrative control to internal migrants. Instead, there has been a shift toward a "community management" approach, where migrants are supposed to be subjected to the beneficial influence of their more "civilized" urban neighbors, who in turn are encouraged to recognize migrant workers' contributions to their own well being. This shift reflects a recognition of the state's failure to penetrate the "non-state spaces" (Xiang Biao 1999) and an attempt to co-opt, rather than combat, the forms of spontaneous migrant organizing that Solinger (1991) earlier called "a form of civil society." As Jacka (2006:54) points out, the reportings both of migrant criminality and migrant victimhood "lend legitimacy to the role of the state in maintaining social order": in the former case to protect society from migrants, and in the latter to protect migrants from exploitative (often foreign) employers.

Incidentally, factory owners and managers from outside mainland China—mostly Hong Kong, Taiwan, and South Korea—are another kind of "outside population" whose management poses challenges not entirely unlike that of rural workers, despite the vast differences in their social status. Before the 1990s, the only foreign residents in China tended to be students and a few "experts" or technicians, residing in special dormitories or compounds with restricted access for Chinese citizens. Since then, however, China has made it easy for foreign investors and skilled corporate personnel to reside in the country, and their numbers have been growing steadily. Estimates put the number of Taiwanese residents in Shanghai at over 100,000; the city is also home to tens of thousands of Japanese. According to one source, a stunning 600,000 South Koreans are now living in mainland China (Harajiri 2008), and the number of Hong Kong residents either residing in or commuting to the Pearl River Delta must be no less than 100,000. Large numbers of European, North American, and African managers and businessmen also live in Shanghai, Peking, and the trading and manufacturing cities of Guangdong, Zhejiang, and Jiangsu Provinces.

These expatriate businessmen and managers almost invariably reside in gated condominium-type estates and often form compact, sometimes largely monoethnic, expatriate neighborhoods. Thus, Peking's Wangjing West Garden, with reportedly more than 20,000 South Korean residents, has been known as "Koreatown" (*Hanguocheng*) since 2002 (Yeo 2008). Helen Siu (2005:84) describes a condominium near Canton where 65 percent of residents are from Hong Kong. Such enclaves are a headache to the Public Security Bureau because they hinder setting up the usual structures of community management/surveillance. Although some of the heavily foreign-inhabited housing occasionally displays banners, with slogans such as "Chinese and Foreign Residents, Create a New Internationalized Community Hand in Hand,"[32] and some foreign residents are praised in the media for their active participation in community committees, the smooth operation of the committees and their cooperation with the PSB cannot be taken for granted. Fears of being unable to control foreigners' activities came to the surface before the 2008 Peking Olympics, when the PSB began telling visa applicants that they could not apply for a visa to enter China during the games unless they had a ticket to an Olympic event. Rules requiring foreigners not staying in hotels to register with the police, formerly rarely enforced, now began appearing, in English, on announcement boards in apartment buildings with foreign residents (Jacobs 2008). According to some reports, China was planning to "order all foreign students to leave the country before the Olympic Games in August . . . and deport refugees. 'Even if you have to continue your studies in September, you need to leave Beijing in July and August,' a spokeswoman for Beijing University" reportedly said.[33] Moreover, a manager of a luxury hotel in Peking reported that citizens of certain Western countries employed as front-office hotel staff were told their contracts would be terminated, apparently for fear that they might offer negative views on China if interviewed by Western journalists during the Olympics.

China also receives an increasing number of nonelite foreign migrants: entertainers and prostitutes from the former Soviet Union, North Koreans who cross the Yalu River to escape hunger, and brides from Vietnam who marry Chinese men. Some of these migrants are illegal and are usually deported if found by the police. But Zhang Juan's research in Hekou, Yunnan, indicates that local authorities in a small border town may be willing to tolerate the presence of foreign traders and prostitutes because they are seen as contributing to economic growth.[34] How the state exercises control over such fledgling colonies is a question that needs researching, but the neighborhoods occupied by Vietnamese traders and sex workers in Hekou may well be easier for PSB officials to control than the gated communities of wealthy expatriates in Shanghai, where policemen may feel uncertain in applying their usual scripts for interacting with residents.

2
International Migration from China

Under Mao Zedong's rule, China, like other state socialist regimes, restricted travel abroad to high-level government delegations, sports teams, and art troupes (although a small number of individuals with relatives abroad were permitted—or forced—to leave China to join them even at the height of the Cultural Revolution). After 1977, however, this policy changed. Deng Xiaoping declared that "foreign connections," condemned during the previous decades as "reactionary political connections," were a "good thing" (*Renmin Ribao* 1978). At first, four categories of individuals were permitted to go abroad: "experts"—largely in engineering and the natural sciences—who were to study and bring back advanced technologies and set up cooperation projects to aid modernization; workers going abroad on government-brokered contracts, mostly in construction projects; students, many of them government-sponsored to undertake advanced degrees in the natural sciences and engineering;

and overseas Chinese who had moved to China after 1949 and wanted to go back, or family members of overseas Chinese sponsored by relatives abroad.

Students and Contract Workers

Although at first family migration outnumbered other categories—between 1978 and 1996, 378,000 people migrated abroad from Guangdong, the home province of the largest number of overseas Chinese (Nyíri 1999:23)—the rapid rise in the number of students going abroad was no less striking. When the TOEFL examination—necessary to be admitted to a university in the United States—was offered in Peking for the first time in 1981, 285 students sat for it. By 1987, this number had grown a hundredfold to 26,000. At that time, only nine years since the first students had left mainland China, there were already 30,000 in the United States alone (Hu and Zhang 1988). The "study abroad fever" was so high that in 1988 and 1989, much to the consternation of city authorities, students in Shanghai demonstrated in front of the Japanese and Australian consulates, protesting new restrictions on student visas (Fang and Chen 1991).

According to a study by the Chinese Academy of Social Sciences, more than one million Chinese went abroad for study and research by 2007, and only 276,000 have returned (Watts 2007). When obtaining student visas to the United States became difficult after 2001, more Chinese students went to Australia, Germany, and Britain. In Australia, by the early 2000s, student migration significantly outweighed other channels. The country received just under 60,000 skills-, investment-, and family-based settler immigrants from China between 1995 and 2004, but almost 50,000 Chinese students in the 2003–4 academic year alone (Hugo 2005). In Britain, the number of Chinese students rose from under 3,000 in 1997–98 to 50,000 in 2006. The United States, despite stagnating growth, continues to have the highest number of Chinese students: 93,000 in 2006 (Campus France 2008:6–9). In all of these countries, Chinese are the largest group of foreign students.

The initial dominance of science and engineering students in advanced degree programs on government scholarships gave way to a majority of self-financed students, largely in business, and in the 2000s, to a rapidly rising contingent of secondary-school students as well. (Australia alone received nearly 27,000 pre-tertiary students from China in 2003 [J. Gao 2006:155]). According to a 2001 household spending survey in four Chinese cities, 0.7 percent of households had a child studying abroad (Ma and Zhang 2004:15).[1] Ironically, while most of the government-sponsored students who were sent abroad with the injunction to bring advanced science and technology back to China did not return, more students going abroad now do so as a means to social advancement in China rather than with the intent to settle abroad. I have often heard Chinese parents explaining why they sent their child abroad to study say that the child was unable to enter a "brand-name" university in China, and a degree from a "common" university—not to mention no degree at all—provides little in terms of opportunities. To have a graduate "degree from an overseas university is going to be a basic requirement in China's job market in the future," wrote He Jianming (2000) with some exaggeration. As the competition to enter "brand-name universities" expands overseas, wealthy parents are increasingly sending their children abroad while still at secondary school, in the words of one father, "in the hope that [they] can later get into Harvard or MIT" (He Jianming 2000). This would then, in the father's reckoning, enable the child to make a lot of money overseas before eventually returning to China and enjoying it: "Wasn't there that report about that Chinese student in America who . . . returned with $2 million—that's 17 million yuan!" (ibid.).

Self-help and testimonial literature on American universities—with titles like *Harvard Girl Liu Yiting: A Chronicle of Quality Cultivation* (Liu and Zhang 2000), which reportedly sold nearly 2 million copies (Kipnis 2006); *Love at Harvard* (Wang Zhengjun 2004); *An Ordinary Family's Path to Sending Their Child to Study Abroad* (Song Zhida 2004); *Let Your Friend Be Truth: My Harvard Experience* (Yue Xiaodong 2004); or *Our Dummy Goes to Cambridge* (Zhang and Du 2001)—enjoys unbroken popularity. Even as the ideal of pedagogy among the Chinese elite shifts away from top exam results and toward fostering "creativity" and "cross-cultural skills," study abroad remains a necessary component of success.

During the 1980s, students wishing to go abroad had to secure permission from their university, and postgraduate students were usually not granted permission unless they were sponsored by the government. In 1986, the government's overseas student work conference announced that students should return "to contribute to the Fatherland's construction" as soon as they finished their studies (Cheng Xi 2003:273). In particular, students on government scholarships were required to work in government-designated jobs for two years after finishing their studies. In 1992—in recognition of the fact that most students had secured permanent resident status overseas after the Tiananmen Square massacre—this policy was revised, with the State Council issuing a note stating that the principles regarding students overseas were to "support study abroad, promote return, [uphold] freedom of movement."[2] At the same time, the Communist Party, in a "Decision on some questions of establishing a socialist market economy," exhorted "overseas individuals [to] serve the country."[3] From then on, "serve the country" (*wei guo fuwu*) became the standard slogan for overseas students, replacing "return to serve" (*huiguo fuwu*; see Cheng Xi 1999). In practice, this meant that students wishing to stay overseas could get the validity of their passports extended, those who wished to relinquish their Chinese citizenship were able to do so, those who returned home for a visit did not have to reapply for permission to go abroad again, and relatives of overseas students were allowed to join them abroad. Nonetheless, government-sponsored students still must sign a contract with their employer or the government, and their personal files are held by the Chinese embassy in the destination country. The contract stipulates that if the student does not return to China on the completion of his or her education, he/she has to pay a large fine. Until 2003, those who decided to interrupt their study at a Chinese university and go abroad without a government scholarship had to secure the university's permission to do so and, if successful, were charged a fee to cover the costs of the higher education they had received in China (Cheng Xi 2003:284), a fact that discouraged many students considering going abroad from applying to a domestic university in the first place.

Another early channel for going abroad was government-organized labor export, which started in 1979. According to official data, there were 58,000 Chinese working on contracts abroad at the end of 1990 and 600,000 at the end of 2004, mostly working in construction in Japan, Korea, Singapore, Israel, but also in the Middle East, Africa, and South America, as well as in the (mostly Taiwanese-owned) garment industry in Mauritius, Saipan, and Cambodia, hotels in Singapore, and on ships belonging to Singaporean and Korean companies (Sun and Yang 2001; Li and Hao 2003; Liu and Luo 2004; Xiang Biao 2007). In 2003, the liberalization of the passport regime brought further growth. For instance, the number of people departing on work contracts from Nantong, the largest labor exporting region in Jiangsu, grew to nearly 11,000, a 20 percent increase over 2002 (Zhao and Geng 2004). In 2003, when the death or injury of nine Chinese in a terrorist attack in Tel Aviv attracted attention to Chinese workers in Israel, Chinese sources quoted a figure of 20,000—though most had overstayed their visas and were now working unofficially (Li and Hao 2003). Chinese construction workers are also beginning to work on Chinese-financed construction projects in Europe (He Yifan 2007), but there workers who are paid as little as one-tenth of local wages and work much longer hours are likely to stir strong resistance. Finally, there is a rapidly growing (though still small) number of Chinese agricultural workers on Chinese-managed rubber plantations in Laos (Shi 2008).

Both the Ministry of Commerce and the Ministry of Labor allocate quotas for the recruitment of overseas work by province. Provinces, in turn, allocate these by prefectures, counties, and so on. In a number of areas, local governments have set up special bodies and service centers to assist and control recruitment for overseas contracts. Thus, several county-level governments in Jilin Province, one of the major sending provinces, have set up networks of township- or village-level labor service stations to put prospective migrant workers in touch with the provincial labor export corporation (Cao and Shuangshuang 2004; Luova 2007:166–69). Under a government directive, a number of local governments have also set up courses to "improve the quality" of overseas workers. Courses in Nongan, Jilin, include training in twenty-two professions, including lathe work, tailoring, and agriculture (Cao and Shuangshuang 2004). In addition, workers are required to attend "general training" that includes "information about the intended country, basic language training as well as political and ideological education" (Luova 2007:176).

Workers going abroad on official labor contracts typically have contracts for up to three years. They have to pay a percentage of their wages to the labor export agency and they are obliged to return home after (but not earlier than) their contract is over. Moreover, until 2004, contract workers had to pay a guarantee deposit that was forfeited if they did not return. (In 2004, the Ministry of Commerce replaced the deposit with a written guarantee, but the new system was not immediately implemented [see Luova 2007:180]). The effectiveness of these measures varied, in part because Chinese migrants find it more difficult to find lucrative work on their own in some destination countries than others. Thus, Chinese workers in Korea and Israel reportedly often overstay their contracts (Li and Hao 2003; Luova 2007).

Opportunities for going abroad expanded beyond these groups after 1985, when the government passed the Law on the Management of Citizens' Exit and Entry,[4] enabling citizens for the first time to apply for passports as long as they could provide invitation letters and sponsorships from overseas. The effect of the liberalization was dramatic: according to the state news agency, Xinhua, the number of exits rose from 80,828 in 1986 to 248,689 in 1989 (*Renmin Ribao* 1990). Nonetheless, the liberalization was far from complete. Passports were only valid with an exit visa, which had to be applied for prior to each journey. In 1990, in Shanghai, rejection rates for passport applications were around 20 percent (Zhang Zhiye 1990:7). Exit visas were abolished in 1996, but the police retained multiple instruments to control who went abroad for private reasons. In the late 1990s, an application to travel abroad on private business (such as for a trade fair) typically had to be accompanied by four documents: notarized invitation from a foreign entity, legal proof of the existence of that entity, proof of the applicant's planned participation in an event held by the entity, and proof of payment of the participation fee. A 1996 document stipulated that applications had to be accompanied by a letter of support from the employer, from the local branch of the Association of Individual Laborers Association of Private Enterprises or the Federation of Trade and Industry for self-employed individuals, and from the Chinese partner in the venture for those working on joint ventures.[5] Yunnan Province further stipulated that executives (*faren*) of private enterprises must have the approval of the Private Enterprise Leading Group above the prefectural level, while owners (and in the case of share companies, executives) of enterprises must have an approval signed by the members of the board (*dongshihui*).[6] Artists going abroad to perform had to supply a letter of support from the cultural bureau at the provincial level or above.[7]

The approval of applications was far from automatic. A Hunan police official explained that he followed a policy of "four stricts and four lenients": (1) "lenient on business activities, strict on ideology," such as "cultural discussions" and religious training; (2) "lenient on developed countries, strict on developing countries"; (3) "lenient on groups, strict on individuals," subjecting the latter to tests determining if their "participation in that event was really necessary," and (4) "lenient on invitations, strict on employer consent," that is, being willing to overlook a suspicious-looking invitation as long as the employer agrees (Gao 1999:121).

Further liberalization took place between 2002 and 2005, eventually allowing all citizens—except those banned from leaving the country[8]—to obtain passports simply by applying and presenting their identity cards and residence documents. (The provinces of Fujian and Zhejiang, from which most illegal Chinese entrants in Europe and North America originate, are excluded.) The 2005 Passport Law made obtaining a passport a legal entitlement of Chinese citizens (Xiang 2007:70).

There is little doubt that millions of new migrants—including tens if not hundreds of thousands of migrants benefiting from a semi-legal network of migration brokers, some of them ending up caught as undocumented "boat people" or asylum seekers in North America and Europe—have left the Chinese mainland since 1978 to study, join relatives, work, or trade abroad. Official figures and unofficial estimates range from several hundred thousand to around 5 million (see, e.g., Xiang 2003). No matter which figure is closest to the truth, it is still very low compared to China's population and the volume of domestic migration. Nonetheless, both Chinese and Western governments and media have assigned international migration an importance far beyond what the numbers suggest. While concerns in the West have focused on illegal migration (e.g., Smith 1994), the Chinese view has been more holistic, considering everyone who settled abroad, from illegal workers to students, as "new migrants" (see Nyíri 2005a). Ever since the publication of Glen Cao's bestselling novel *The Chinese Woman of Manhattan (Manhadun de Zhongguo nüren)* in 1991, "new migrants" have captivated the imagination of soap-opera scriptwriters as much as that of government officials.

Entrepreneurial Migrants

While migration to the traditional destinations of Western Europe, North America, and Japan, as well as Australia and New Zealand, mainly took the shape of overseas study, family unification, and contract-labor migration, entrepreneurial migration emerging in the late 1980s was directed at destinations with no existing Chinese population. The normalization of Sino-Soviet relations, which closely followed the liberalization of the PRC's rules governing travel abroad, made it possible for Chinese citizens to engage in trade across the Soviet border.[9] Starting in 1987, Northern

Chinese began to take advantage of the simplified passport procedures to engage in shuttle trade with the Soviet Far East and Siberia. Many of the first shuttle traders were moonlighting Chinese contract laborers who were invited to Russia on contracts. After the collapse of the Soviet Union and especially after the 1992 signing of the Sino-Russian treaty waiving the visa requirement for overland group tourism in the bordering provinces, crossing the border became even easier. Russian news agencies reported a million border crossings by Chinese citizens into the Russian Far East in 1992, rising to 2.5 million in 1993 (Nyíri 2007).

Informal shuttle trade was a feature of the economies of scarcity in Eastern Europe since at least the 1960s, but Chinese traders expanded it on an unprecedented scale, stepping in to fill the market vacuum created by nonexistent or broken-down retail networks of low-price clothing and shoes. Venturing farther and farther by train and spending more and more time at their destinations, they first reached European Russia and then Hungary, which in 1988 signed a treaty waiving the visa requirement for Chinese tourists. According to a Chinese source, nearly 10,000 Chinese traders were registered as Moscow residents in 1992 (*Huaren jingji nianjian* 1994:210). According to the Hungarian Ministry of the Interior, the number of border crossings by Chinese citizens entering Hungary jumped from nearly zero in the mid-1980s to 11,621 in 1990 and 27,330 in 1991 (Nyíri 1999:32). From Russia and Hungary, Chinese traders spread across Eastern Europe, with perhaps the next most important destination being Romania, which experienced 14,200 inbound border crossings by Chinese in 1991.

Data on the actual number of Chinese in the region is very unreliable for two reasons: wildly contradictory official figures and the high mobility of migrants. Gelbras (2002) estimates the number of Chinese in Moscow to be between 20,000 and 25,000, and between 200,000 and 400,000 across Russia. Chinese in Hungary probably number between 10,000 and 15,000. In Romania, Border Guard data in 1999 showed 14,200 Chinese residents. In all, some 50,000 to 70,000 Chinese may have migrated to Eastern Europe excluding Russia.

The expansion of Chinese investments and exports, particularly low-price consumer goods, also fostered the migration of hundreds of thousands of Chinese to Cambodia, Thailand, the Philippines, Burma, Central and South America (including an estimated 60,000 in Argentina), and Africa (e.g., Nyíri and Saveliev 2002; Chin 2003; Zhou and Yang 2006;

Mengin 2007). According to some estimates, the number of Chinese grew by 200,000 to 300,000 between 1998 and 2006 in South Africa and by 100,000 in just two years, from 1999 to 2001, in Cambodia (Zhuang n.d.).

In several places, Chinese migrants encountered hostility. The new Chinese presence in Africa suddenly became a focus of a worldwide media debate in 2006, when a China-Africa summit was held in Peking just after the challenger in the Zambian presidential election denounced the presence of an estimated 30,000 Chinese for exploiting local labor and dumping inferior goods (Blair 2006). The challenger lost, but some of his allegations were repeated by South African President Thabo Mbeki, a traditional ally of China (Alden 2007:120), and African media was divided over the balance between benefit and harm brought by Chinese immigration (see also Alden and Davies 2006; Wines 2007; Dobler 2008). In Zambia, China canceled plans to launch a copper smelter, and merchants fearing attacks reportedly painted over Chinese shop signs in Lusaka's Kamwala market (McGreal 2007). Disaffected locals have attacked Chinese workers in Sudan, Niger, and Ethiopia, killing nine in a 2007 incident (*Financial Times* 2007). Conflicts about the working conditions of local laborers hired by Chinese construction teams also occurred in Tanzania (Hsu 2007), Namibia (Dobler 2008), and Angola (Johnson 2007), where President Eduardo dos Santos reportedly said that up to 3 million Chinese could migrate to the country (Davies 2007). In the Russian Far East, the "demographic threat" of Chinese immigration has long been a prominent topic of local politics (Nyíri 2007), and similar fears are reported to be rising in Laos (Gray 2008).

In many of these countries, Chinese merchants have established nationwide networks of wholesale and retail shops catering to urban and rural populations (Nyíri 2006c; Østbø Haugen and Carling 2005; Dobler 2008). Similar to Chinese and Indian shops in colonial Southeast Asia and Africa in the early twentieth century, Chinese markets and shops have emerged as the main suppliers of certain consumer goods, including clothing, to large segments of the rural and low-income urban populations in Eastern Europe, Africa, and South America whose needs local retailers working with higher costs were unable or unwilling to meet. In 2001, a market research survey in Hungary concluded that in clothing retail the share of open-air markets—where the merchandise and most vendors come from China—was as high as 39 percent (*Heti Világgazdaság* [March 31, 2001], 65), though it later declined. By the mid-2000s, Chinese-made clothes were pushing out local manufacturers and secondhand European and Brazilian imports from the low-end fashion market in Africa (Bredeloup and Bertoncello 2006:218; Traub 2006). In Cape Verde, the opening of Chinese shops has resulted in "a rapid transformation of home interiors" because of the availability of cheaper household electronics and decoration ranging from household textiles to Christmas figurines (Bredeloup and Bertoncello 2006:220). In Oshikango, a Namibian border town of around 5,000 inhabitants, there were nearly one hundred Chinese-owned shops by early 2008 (Dobler 2008).

In 2002, the Hungarian Ministry of the Economy reported that the number of Chinese-owned businesses had risen to around 10,000, and Chinese shops reached practically all towns and villages with populations over 2,000 (Nyíri 2006c). In Argentina, according to Chinese sources, there were 3,000 Chinese-owned groceries in 2006 (Chen Guohong 2006). In 2005, there were around 150 Chinese shops in Dakar, the capital of Senegal, and around 70 in Praia, the much smaller capital of Cape Verde, where they occupied "practically all [the] space" of a central area "so that they overshadow[ed] the impact of the buildings that embody national economic, political and cultural power" (Bredeloup and Bertoncello 2006:209–12).

While some of this development took place in countries that were in transition from planned to market economies, others offered different sorts of market opportunities. Post-apartheid South Africa saw an abrupt change in consumption and retail patterns formerly governed by strict segregation. In Argentina, the economic position of Chinese migrants' improved following the late 1990s currency crisis and ensuing retail bankruptcies. Chinese importers and shopkeepers moved to Kosovo and Afghanistan soon after the wars there ended; a large store selling construction materials reportedly opened in Kabul in 2003 (Dongfangming 2004).

Managing Overseas Migrants:
The Politics of Transnational Mobilization

The new ethnic economy created by entrepreneurial migrants depended on imports (as well as capital and business information) from China. This meant that the migrants had to maintain social networks with China through frequent communication. Networks were maintained through regular travel back to China and inviting and entertaining visitors from there, as well as over fax, telephone, e-mail, and later Internet relay chat. Given that the separation of economic and political power—even formally—has proceeded slowly in China, the contacts that had to be cultivated included government officials. Particularly in the first half of the 1990s, entrepreneurs with connections to state enterprises had privileged access to merchandise, often at highly favorable credit terms. In addition, those who migrated with the informal consent of their state work units were also allowed to maintain their employee benefits without actually drawing a salary. Such migrants not only enjoyed preferential access to sources of merchandise but frequently received seed capital and favorable credit arrangements from the state enterprises with which they were affiliated (Nyíri 2006c).

In the early nineties, managers of state enterprises wanted to get rid of stockpiles of goods that clogged up the domestic market. They were eager to show their government minders that they were developing overseas markets and they counted on private kickbacks from the capital they were cheaply transferring overseas. As the owner of Hualu, one of the largest Chinese-owned businesses in Hungary in the early 1990s, put it: "The main source of capital for Hungarian Chinese enterprises is the support of . . . various foreign trade companies in China: without it, Hungarian Chinese could not have achieved their current level [of economic success] even in ten years" (Li Qiang 1996:1).

These arrangements resulted in a large number of bad loans in the state sector (soon after this interview was published, Hualu itself suddenly collapsed and its owner moved to Sierra Leone), and in the second half of the 1990s, the Chinese government under Zhu Rongji ordered state enterprises to require a surety for exports and to limit their investments abroad. During the 1998 Asian currency crisis, this was followed by a new decree requiring state enterprises to liquidate most of their overseas investments. This devalued contacts with state enterprises, but at the same time, migrants were becoming increasingly interested in moving beyond relatively small-scale trade in consumer goods and acting as middlemen for a range of large players in the expanding Chinese economy, from emerging electronics brands like Haier, Lenovo, and Hisense to fuel and raw-materials corporations. Rather than just sales, these corporations wanted to create brands, set up manufacturing, and scout for suppliers, but because of the strategic and high-profile nature of some of their deals, their decisions were also embroiled with politics. Thus, after visits to China by two Hungarian prime ministers in consecutive years, at the end of 2005 the Chinese government announced its intention to purchase Asia Center and ChinaMart, two wholesale centers developed by Chinese entrepreneurs in Hungary, for the purpose of setting up a European exhibition center for Chinese-made goods. The choice was clearly a gesture to the Hungarian government's courtship of China, but at the same time, both corporate managers in China and Chinese in Hungary attributed it to the existence of a well-established entrepreneurial community that had received relatively wide publicity and maintained extensive ties in China. Similarly, existing Chinese-run garment factories in Mauritius undoubtedly played a role in attracting further capital and making the Chinese government choose Mauritius as the site for a $500 million manufacturing zone (Davies 2007:5). Thus, in this second wave of China's economic expansion overseas, migrants again played an important role.

In addition to maintaining contact with China, a number of entrepreneurial migrants expanded their businesses in countries outside of their country of residence. Successful entrepreneurs in Hungary set up branches in other Eastern European countries, and to a lesser degree in Africa and South America as well. In doing so, they relied on networks of relatives and acquaintances from home who had migrated to different places. An added advantage of doing business in those countries was that winter or summer stocks unsold in Eastern Europe could be shipped to the Southern hemisphere, where the season was just starting (Nyíri 2006c).

While entrepreneurial migrants pioneered economic transnationalism, beginning in the mid-1990s many overseas graduates jumped on the bandwagon as business intermediaries for Chinese and foreign companies. Being highly trained, they generally occupied positions in financial services and consulting, as well as high-tech engineering and research. In 1996, the government unveiled Project Parental Love (*Chunhui Jihua*), which offered financial incentives to scholars employed overseas who agreed to offer courses in China. Between 2001 and 2002, it set up over sixty Overseas Student Enterprise Parks (*liuxuesheng chuangyeyuan*), providing special advantages to some 14,000 overseas graduates who invested in high-tech industries, including 6,000 at the Zhongguancun Science Park in Peking (Cheng Xi 2003:283). Over half of the investors maintained their primary residence overseas (Zweig and Chung 2004).

In addition, a number of major cities have passed a series of measures including tax breaks, interest-free loans, and *hukou* provisions to attract returning graduates. Canton has been holding an annual Overseas Graduate Science and Technology Fair since 1998.

The Returned Overseas Student Service Centers under the Ministry of Personnel are dwarfed, however, by the overseas Chinese affairs bureaucracy that was resurrected and has grown on an unprecedented scale since 1977. The so-called *wu qiao*, or five overseas Chinese affairs bodies of the Chinese government, are the Overseas Chinese Affairs Office (Qiaoban) of the State Council; the National Association of Overseas Chinese, Returned Overseas Chinese, and Dependents of Overseas Chinese (Quanguo Huaqiao Guiqiao Qiaojuan Lianhehui, abbreviated as Qiaolian); the Overseas Chinese Commission (Huaqiao Weiyuanhui, abbreviated as Qiaoweihui) of the National People's Congress; the Hong Kong, Macau, Taiwan, and Overseas Chinese Committee of the People's Political Consultative Conference;[10] and the Zhigongdang, the remnant of a pre-1949 political party that supposedly represents the interests of the "patriotic overseas Chinese." Each of these bodies commands a network of provincial-, prefectural-, county-, township-, and sometimes village- or district-level branches, as well as a parallel "mass organization" such as the China Overseas Exchange Commission affiliated with the Qiaoban or the China Overseas Friendship Association, the alter ego of the Hong Kong, Macau, Taiwan, and Overseas Chinese Affairs Committee of the People's Political Consultative Conference. Such organizations are typically run by the head of their parallel government organization but are deployed in situations where "people's diplomacy" is preferred. For example, a rule issued by the State Council in 1980 stated that in key overseas Chinese sending areas (*qiaoxiang*), the township (*xiang*) governments must put in place a set of cadres for the local Qiaolian and pay their salaries out of the government budget or the revenue from the collective enterprise of the Qiaolian.[11]

By 1994, the Qiaolian already had more than 8,000 branches and affiliated mass organizations at various levels (*Guangdong Qiaobao* [18 June 1998], 1). In the first decade of the twenty-first century, the Qiaolian accelerated its expansion, and today, major migrant sending areas tend to have a branch in each village, with "an important role in rapidly liaising with new migrants, discovering and solving problems" (Li, Jiang, and

Yu 2003:9). By keeping in touch with the families of migrants, branches of the Qiaolian are supposed to keep track of who leaves the village to go abroad, who obtains permanent residence or citizenship outside China, and other key information. In addition to such informal data gathering, the Qiaolian administers a periodic "overseas Chinese census" (*qiaoqing pucha*) of migrant households. The function of these data is to keep track of the state's "overseas Chinese resources" and to be able to mobilize them rapidly when the interests of the economy or diplomacy demand it.

In key *qiaoxiang*, other organs also deal with overseas Chinese. For example, in the famous *qiaoxiang* in Guangdong Province, Xinhui County, in addition to the United Front Work Department of the city Party committee, the city Qiaoban, Qiaolian, and Overseas Chinese Commission, a People's Association for Friendship with Foreign Countries, the trade union, the youth federation, the women's federation, and the departments of culture, education, propaganda, civil affairs, foreign trade, customs, etc., also engage in overseas Chinese work. In another important *qiaoxiang*, Jinjiang in Fujian, the Qiaoxiang Construction Commission and the Leading Group on Overseas Chinese Donations for Welfare Facilities, headed by Party and city government leaders, also deal with overseas Chinese (Cheng and Ngok 1998).

The main task of the bodies in charge of overseas Chinese was attracting overseas Chinese investment and, inseparable from this, winning back the confidence and loyalty of overseas Chinese. In the 1990s and 2000s, the priorities of "overseas Chinese work" expanded from attracting capital to include exploiting the skills and human networks of more recent migrants as "overseas Chinese resources" of development (Shi Hanrong 2004). Zhuang Guotu (2000:45), a senior scholar of overseas Chinese in the PRC who is also involved in various overseas Chinese affairs organs and can be seen as representing the official point of view, wrote that "two . . . changes . . . have attracted the attention of the Chinese government from 1978 onward. One is the Overseas Chinese wealth, and the other is the new Chinese emigrants." People who left China since 1978, regardless of the purpose of their departure, their status as foreign or Chinese citizens, or if they were students returning from abroad, are now often referred to as "new migrants" or "new emigrants" (*xin yimin*) in official parlance. This pragmatic usage assumes that once a person has left the PRC, she is unlikely to return permanently, at least not without having established a social space abroad to return to in the future. While such a use of the term migrant reflects the reality of modern migratory phenomena better than official Western usage, it also shows the long way the Chinese Communist government has come from the earlier paradigm of state socialism that considered talking about emigration in terms other than defection tantamount to admitting its own failure.

Migrants as a Resource for the Nation

Today, new migrants are recognized by the government as a highly useful resource for economic construction in China, attracting foreign investors and business partners and providing leadership to overseas Chinese communities in Japan, the United States, and Europe, which are judged as losing touch with the homeland and Chinese culture. This approach is reflected in a series of publications in the overseas Chinese studies journals *Huaqiao Huaren Lishi Yanjiu* and *Bagui Qiaoshi*, as well as other periodicals and interviews by officials of the Qiaoban, Qiaolian, and the Overseas Exchange Commission (the "NGO" that duplicates the Qiaoban) (Cheng Xi 1999; Tan Tianxing 1997; Zhu Huiling 1995; Shanghai New Migrants Research Project Team 1997; Shi Hanrong 2004). While on paper, China's overseas Chinese policy continues to define *huaqiao* (overseas residents who have retained their Chinese citizenship) as its only target, the media and government officials nowadays treat migrants with temporary residence permits (such as students) as well as naturalized foreign citizens as part of the same community, defined more by common descent than by legal status. As a Chinese consul in Cape Town recalled telling a Chinese association there in 1999: "As long as [we are of] 'the same blood [and] the same kind [race],' all of us share an ardent love for the Chinese nation-race with its five thousand years of history" (Lu Miaogeng 2004). This frequently voiced assumption, which extends the Chinese nation beyond the state's territorial confines, means that migrants who acquire the citizenship of their country of residence—and, since China does not recognize dual citizenship, are expected to give up their Chinese passport—remain a legitimate object of "overseas Chinese work."

The Chinese government has been building its contacts with new migrants and overseas Chinese through a strategy known as "going out and inviting in" (*zouchuqu-yingjinlai*), that is, sending delegations overseas and inviting migrants to visit China. According to one study, overseas Chinese affairs authorities in Guangdong Province dispatched 526 delegations involving 21,966 people and received 3,087 groups of overseas Chinese and Chinese from Hong Kong, Taiwan, and Macau, totaling a staggering 270,514 people in 1995 alone (Cheng and Ngok 1998). The legitimacy of both of these forms of interaction relies on the participation of migrant organizations. In the mid-1990s, the leadership of the Qiaoban intensified its focus on building contacts with new migrant organizations as well as with "key personalities" (*zhongdian renwu*). In its "Opinion on stepping up new migrant work" (*Guanyu kaizhan xin yimin gongzuo de yijian* document no. 03 [1996]), the Qiaoban formulated the task of training a "core cadre" of new migrants "to actively assist in accomplishing the country's three great tasks." To this end, it recommended "promoting them in our domestic and foreign media to increase their fame overseas." At the same time, it stated the necessity of strengthening "thought guidance" of new migrants, as they were susceptible to the influence of Western media, and recommended more frequent communication as well as encouragement for establishing organizations of migrants' relatives. One of the consequences of this directive was the publication of patriotic literature on Chinese history specifically for overseas Chinese (Callahan 2003:492). In compliance with this policy but also as a means of competing with each other, an increasing number of prefectures, counties, and even villages have been forming their own overseas Chinese associations (*Fujian Qiaobao* 2004a). These in turn search for and encourage the formation of migrant organizations based on migrants' location of origin. Simultaneously, professionals to whom the idea of a rural homeland does not appeal are encouraged to set up alumni and professional organizations (Zhuang 2000:48, 49). For example, in 2004, the Shanghai Qiaoban offered to strengthen alumni associations in the United States for all its universities "in order to disseminate information about business and scientific opportunities" (Zweig and Chung 2004).

Chinese businesspeople are encouraged by embassies to form chambers of commerce and are expected to join them, so that embassies can delegate matters such as conflict mediation or requests for help with commercial affairs to these associations, turn to them when they feel a need to intervene with the activities of Chinese businesses, and generally "keep an eye" on what is going on without having to expend embassy resources or expose themselves to allegations of interference by the host country. It was at the initiative of the Chinese embassy, for example, that an informal association of Chinese enterprises present in Laos was transformed in 2005 into the Lao-Chinese Chamber of Commerce.[12] The organizations also function to disseminate political messages from the embassy. For example, at the preparatory meeting of the Kenya Chinese Association, which was held at the Chinese embassy in Nairobi in 2005, the not-yet-existing association enthusiastically approved China's new "Law against splitting the Fatherland" and swore to "contribute its strength to realize the complete reunification of the Fatherland and the great renaissance of the Chinese race." While the embassy had reportedly "long wished that overseas Chinese in Kenya be more closely united" and had "provided timely and full guidance" (Lin Zhishen 2006) to forming the association, it is hardly a coincidence that it was finally formed in haste at a time when Chinese embassies worldwide were encouraging Chinese organizations to lend their support to the anti-separatism law (especially in Africa, where some countries still maintain diplomatic relations with Taiwan).

In this way, larger Chinese migrant organizations acquire a semi-official status, not unlike their predecessors had under the Kuomintang government in the first half of the twentieth century. They are also interpellated by overseas Chinese affairs authorities when they wish to strengthen contacts with migrants in a particular foreign country for diplomatic or economic purposes, or simply to organize a visit. The Chinese Finance Association in New York, consisting of Wall Street investment bankers and financial analysts, frequently hosts visits by top Chinese government officials. But, far from the glamour of Wall Street, former illegal migrants in Italy, who at most run small garment workshops, are also sought out by government delegations. The chairman of the Fujian *tongxianghui* (native-place organization) in Italy told me that one of the reasons for setting up the organization was that it was becoming increasingly awkward that there was no organization to formally receive the growing number of Fujian delegation visitors (Nyíri 2001:646). Many leaders of this *tongxianghui*, and most other Fujianese organizations in Europe, are irregular immigrants who only recently acquired legal status and relatively modest businesses (see Pieke et al. 2004), and while visits of official delegations can bring considerable benefits to those of them who wish to do business in China, not everyone is happy with the costs of these visits. In Cambodia, the acting chairwoman of the Zhejiang *tong-xianghui* complained that with the expenses that went into sending gift baskets and taking out congratulatory advertisements for each activity organized by the embassy or by other Chinese organizations, her association lacked the money to invite official delegations from Zhejiang Province (though she was nonetheless proud that such a delegation had once visited them).[13]

By far not all new Chinese migrants think highly of these organizations and their leaders, let alone wanting to join their ranks. In fact, they are commonly derided for being interested only in their own personal profits rather than the benefits of the community, and most have no real membership apart from the numerous vice presidents and board members. Even some organization leaders see their activities as a waste of money, and though there are always scores of businessmen eager to join in the hope that these activities will open doors for them in China, many of the most successful businessmen in fact stay out of them. On the other hand, in some countries—such as Laos—where there are many small traders with unlicensed businesses, such traders are not allowed to join chambers of commerce. Yet overall, the reach of such organizations has increased sharply since the 1990s as the threshold for becoming an association leader has been lowered. This is due both to the Chinese government's efforts to seek contacts and promote patriotism and to the potential financial benefits of organizational roles as Chinese business overseas becomes increasingly tied to economic contacts with China. Even for migrants who have no interest in being involved, the events organized by the embassy-organizations nexus—celebrations, meetings, banquets that remind migrants of how the Fatherland sees them and their relationship to it—nonetheless punctuate their daily lives and define the public expressions of national identity. This is particularly so when—as in most countries where Chinese immigration is a recent phenomenon—the local Chinese-language press is linked to the organizations set up by new migrants. For example, the first Chinese newspaper in Nigeria, launched in 2005, is called *Xifei Tongyi Shangbao*, which can be translated either as "United West African Commercial News" or as "West African Reunification Commercial News," referring to reunification of Taiwan with China. That the *double entendre* is deliberate is made clear by the characters of the masthead, which have been written by the chairman of the China Association for the Promotion of Peaceful Reunification, Wan Guoquan, who is also a vice-chair of China's National People's Political Consultative Conference (Dai and Lin 2005).

Organization leaders often sound like Chinese government officials, both to emphasize their identification with the official project of the nation and to display their social capital to other Chinese, as if, through this metonymy, they actually *become* officials. In this way, they help disseminate the Chinese state's discourse of nation-building and modernization abroad. The president of the Buenos Aires Chinese Supermarkets Association uses a Party formula when he speaks of "uniting under the leadership" of the four Fujianese associations in Argentina to "enthusiastically participate in . . . activities to oppose Taiwanese independence and promote the Fatherland's unity" (Chen Guohong 2006). The secretary-general of the West African Assocation for the Peaceful Reunification of China describes his strategy of "developing" (recruiting) new members with the vocabulary of a rural Party secretary talking about "united front work:" "We have to give them business opportunities; after all, we can't expect overseas Chinese to do (*gao*) reunification on empty stomachs" (Mao and Zhou 2007:472). Similarly, when the Vientiane Chinese Association states in its programme that "Our life-breath and our fate are one with the Fatherland's" (*women he zuguo tong huxi gong mingyun*), using a phrase that is normally applied to the relationship between the Chinese Communist Party and the Chinese people, it is not simply expressing its patriotism but tying it to the CCP (Association Chinoise Vientiane 2007:5).

As already noted, in the years of the Chen Shui-bian presidency in Taiwan, during which pro-independence sentiments were frequently voiced, new migrant organizations (and many other Chinese organizations) worldwide held meetings and issued statements supporting the Chinese government's policy. For example, the Mozambique Association for the Promotion of China's Peaceful Reunification (founded in 2002) launched an on-the-spot signature and fundraising drive to oppose Chen Shui-bian's attempt to organize a referendum on Taiwan's joining the United Nations at a Chinese New Year's reception hosted by the Chinese embassy in 2004 (Chinese Embassy 2005). In Cambodia, a meeting about "resolutely opposing Taiwan independence" was held in September 2007. In the following year, the rioting in Tibet and the failure of the subsequent talks between the Chinese government and the Dalai Lama's delegation appeared to put a new item on the agenda. During my visit to Laos in December 2008, the Vientiane Chinese Association—whose 2007 brochure already listed "peaceful reunification" as one of its priorities—was planning a meeting to oppose Tibetan independence and "to explain it to people," although, as the association's secretary-general admitted, "we can't explain very much."[14]

Chinese authorities encourage the formation of regional and global federations comprising Chinese associations in different countries, ranging from the Fu Tsing World Friendship Association (based on Fuqing County as place of origin) to the World Chinese Chamber of Commerce and the World Association of Peking University Alumni. Every two years since 2001, a Congress of World Chinese Associations has been held in the Great Hall of the People in Peking and attended by China's top leaders.

In 1992, the European Federation of Chinese Organizations was set up in Amsterdam after European association leaders received a positive response from the Qiaoban leaders in Peking; Vice-Premier Qian Qichen attended the founding ceremony (Li Minghuan 2004). In October 2001, a World Federation of Overseas Chinese Organizations was set up in Hong Kong "to work on the achievement of China's complete reunification, on the promotion of the outstanding culture of the Chinese nation and the promotion of the unity of overseas Chinese and foreign citizens of Chinese origin all over the globe."[15] The congresses of these organizations are elaborate affairs attracting thousands of people and serving as occasions for interaction with Chinese officials. They also communicate the PRC's political messages to Chinese audiences worldwide, particularly with regard to Taiwan and the suppression of the Falun Gong religious movement. In response to the Overseas Chinese Affairs Bureau's policy to put support of Taiwan's reunification with the mainland at the top of its priorities, some 160 Societies for the Promotion of the Peaceful Reunification of China were organized worldwide in the early 2000s, headed by new migrant association leaders and supported by the United Front Department of the Chinese Communist Party (the Party organ that supervises overseas Chinese affairs). The Association for the Promotion of China's Peaceful Reunification in China itself, headed by a vice president of the National People's Political Consultative Conference, provides "guidance" to the other Associations, which are organized into regional federations and a World Federation, which organizes regular world congresses. While these Associations seek and receive very little publicity outside China, they form a highly structured network spanning the globe and directly connected to the Chinese Communist Party, somewhat like overseas branches of the Kuomintang in the 1930s, and occasionally carry out political missions that Chinese diplomats are unable to. Although in places with large and diverse Chinese populations they tend to be relatively obscure, in some countries they have become umbrella organizations, with leaders of large Chinese associations becoming their chairmen and vice chairmen. Thus, top leaders of the Cambodian Association for the Promotion of the Peaceful Reunification of China (CAPPRC) are delegated by the Chinese Chamber of Commerce in Cambodia, the China Hong Kong and Macau Expatriate and Business Association, and the Association of Khmer Chinese in Cambodia, which itself is the umbrella organization of traditional Sino-Khmer (Cambodian Chinese) kinship and native-place associations. The latter's president, who is also the chairman of CAPPRC, has been granted a title by Cambodia's king and thus accumulates positions of honor in both the Cambodian and Chinese political hierarchies; he is also the publisher of one of Cambodia's three Chinese dailies, *Jianhua Ribao*.

Hu Jieguo, the secretary-general of the West African Association for the Promotion of China's Peaceful Reunification, is an advisor to the office of Nigeria's president and holds the title of chief; he is also an honorary president of the Chinese Chamber of Commerce in Nigeria and a member of the board (*lishi*) of the China Association for the Promotion of Peaceful Reunification. Hu says that his family and the Chinese embassy "rely on each other, support each other in gooddoing overseas Chinese affairs work." For example, he claims that when Taiwan opened a consulate-general, he and the Chinese ambassador hurried together to the Nigerian foreign minister's home and persuaded him to have it closed. "There are some Taiwanese who want to do 'money diplomacy' here; once we find out, we stop them straight away; we liaise with the Nigerian government and have them deported." Hu has taken it as his personal mission to organize Associations for the Promotion of Peaceful Reunification in the war-torn countries of West Africa, using trade ties to build his organization and to "attack green [pro-independence] Taiwanese businessmen. . . . The Taiwan Trade Representative Office dares not wriggle too much, because their business needs my support." He also claims to have persuaded a wavering minister of defense in the Liberian government headed by Charles Taylor—later indicted for war crimes—not to switch diplomatic recognition to Taiwan (Mao and Zhou 2007).

The Qiaoban's 1996 "Opinion on stepping up new migrant work" called on Chinese officials to increase friendship with and strengthen guidance for publishers of overseas Chinese newspapers. The Qiaoban answered its own call by investing in overseas Chinese television stations through two of its Hong Kong–based companies. More commonly, however, its involvement with overseas media has been indirect, providing articles or television programs, often specially produced for overseas broadcasts, as well as extending invitations to and cultivating relationships with media producers.[16]

Since the mid-1990s, Chinese-language media—especially satellite television—has become a contiguous worldwide mediascape that contributes to the construction of a global Chinese identity, raising cultural Chineseness and transnational modernity in importance above the immediate environment the viewer or reader happens to be in. This takes place through the broadcasting of reports and soap operas portraying the lives of Chinese migrants in other countries, as well as simply by spreading shared entertainment programming, language, and style (Nyíri 2005a). This is helped by the fact that Hong Kong and overseas private satellite stations have little political programming, and the language of their news programs is not all that different from state-owned CCTV. (The exception is New Tang Dynasty Television, which is close to the Falun Gong and claims the Chinese government has "used threats, financial pressure and blackmail" to coerce satellite operators into refusing to transmit its programming [see Matisoff 2004:10].) To a lesser extent, the same trend of visual and textual homogeneity and shared content—often based on unacknowledged cross-borrowing—can be observed in print media published by new migrant entrepreneurs (see Nyíri 2005a), but the distinct political and linguistic positions of traditional newspapers remain stronger in this sphere (see Li Minghuan 2005). The spread of global Falun Gong (*Epoch Times*) and Christian newspapers contributes to a more diverse print media landscape.

The Central Television's Spring Festival Gala, in particular, is a worldwide master recital of national imagery (Sun 2002:159–63). The Spring Festival is traditionally celebrated with family in one's ancestral village, and the gala, a sequence of songs, dances and skits, is broadcast worldwide on satellite television as a ceremony that reconnects Chinese around the world with their "roots." The *People's Daily* has described it as a "new folk celebration" that unites 100 million "sons and daughters of China, no matter whether at home or abroad, to the north or south of the Great River," and "with plenty of inspirational force, naturally expresses . . . the spirit of the Party's 16th Congress" (Zhong 2003). The reporter for the *People's Daily* approvingly analyzed the show as a ritual affirming the affective bonds of the Chinese people, structured by the hosts' calls to "Embrace your family!" "Thank your friends!" "Greet your neighbors!" and finally "Eulogize the Fatherland!" This last call cues the culmination of the ritual by starting the final massive performance entitled "Coming together of the nation's soil" (*guotu huiji*), in which soil from China's provinces, Taiwan, Hong Kong, and Macau are poured into a ritual *ding* vessel under the solemn guard of army generals. During the performance, the song "Love of the Old Soil" (*Gutu qing*) "transports the sons of China and millions of viewers into the great national sentiments, the great racial goals (*guojia da qing, minzu da yi*) of unifying the Fatherland, uniting the nation, developing the economy, and making the people happy" (ibid.). Recently, songs and dances from neighboring countries such as Vietnam, Burma, and Cambodia, performed by individuals from these countries, have been included in the program, which in this context can be seen as a symbolic expression of China's central role in the region.

The Internet, of course, is another space where transnationalism is reinforced. Although overseas involvement in Chinese cyberspace has yet to be seriously studied, it is clear that popular discussion sites such as Tianya and Qiangguo attract lots of postings from overseas. A cursory look at Chinese-run Internet cafés in foreign cities with substantial Chinese populations, from Budapest to Sydney, suggests that recent migrants and their more computer-literate children, even if born abroad, often use China-based portals (such as Sina.com.cn, Sohu.com, and numerous others) to download music, browse entertainment features and news, chat, blog, search, and e-mail. A number of China-based commercial portals specifically cater to overseas migrants and students. Given that Internet content providers in China may only use the news service of the official news agency, Xinhua, none of these popular portals carries content of a politically controversial nature. Bulletin board systems that are based in China but are popular among migrants (such as Tianya.cn) do carry posts critical of the government, but differ little from it in their view of the Chinese nation and are often stridently nationalistic in tone. Popular portals often serve as vehicles through which individuals seen as standing up for

China's dignity overseas become national heroes, as with a Chinese professional who painted graffiti on the Yasukuni Shrine in Tokyo in 2001 to protest Japanese imperialism (W. Sun 2006:13). In 2008, Jin Jing, a paralympic athlete from whose hand a Tibetan protester snatched the Olympic torch in Paris, became China's first hero of the Peking Olympics, and people who turned out to protect the torch on subsequent stations of its world tour were celebrated on the Internet as defenders of China's honor.[17]

As Chiu and Tan (2004) note, many Web sites set up by recent migrant entrepreneurs and organizations, mostly in North America, Europe, and Japan, are primarily dedicated to fostering connections with China. (This contrasts with more traditional overseas Chinese organizations' sites, which focus more on documenting local overseas Chinese history and preserving local traditions.) For example, Fujianese.com, launched in 2004, is dedicated to promoting "the positive image of American Fujianese, one of the largest recent immigrant groups from China." It also "provides survival tips" and assists "information exchange between immigrants and their relatives back home" (Chiu 2005). Along with business-oriented links, these sites feature links to government and official news sites in China, notably those set up by various branches of the Qiaoban and Qiaolian. They also link to national news sites such as *Zhonghua Qiaowang* (Overseas Chinese Net), *Zhongguo Qiaowang* (idem), and *Huaxia Liantong* (The China Connection), and provincial or local sites such as *Guangdong Qiaowang* (Guangdong Overseas Chinese Net) and *Fujian Xiangyin* (Fujian Homeland Voice). As Chiu and Tan (2004) write,

> New Chinese migrants from Wenzhou and Qingtian [in Zhejiang Province] can read [the] online newspaper *Nouvelles d'Europe*, then link to *Wenzhouwang* (Wenzhou Net) and *Qingtian Zaixian* (Qingtian Online) to update their knowledge of hometowns without much effort or concern about negotiating their roles of being Chinese in a non-Chinese land.

Some of the migrant-run sites also list job opportunities in China, sometimes with the comment that "China needs their talents to support her national construction" (ibid.).

Of course, these sites exist side by side with numerous others that are based on alternative formulations of Chinese identity, from political and religious sites opposed to the PRC government (of which the Falun Gong's cyber-empire is of particular note) to those promoting alternative, though not necessarily oppositional, cultural identities. These in turn cover a broad range, from those run from Taiwan and Hong Kong or by overseas-born Chinese and promoting alternative political or "hybrid" ethnic identities (such as huaren.org or *Chinatown Online*) to those promoting regional Chinese identities or languages, such as Wikipedia's Cantonese, Hokkien, or Shanghainese sites. Significantly, most of these sites either do not offer the popular entertainment, search, and chat functionalities, or migrants from the mainland are unaware of them. In the PRC, a number of them are either blocked or unknown, making them inconvenient for communicating with friends in China. This is especially significant because the use of chat, bulletin boards, and other direct communication functionalities of the Internet is much more common in China than in the West (Giese 2005), and Chinese users tend to see the Web primarily as a place to form personal relationships and exchange opinions. Thus, despite the theoretical accessibility of alternative Chinese-language discursive spaces produced outside the PRC, their influence on recent migrants appears very limited, while popular PRC-produced Web sites, as tools of communication and sites of leisure, increasingly constitute part of migrants' social spaces.[18]

In sum, since the 1990s, new patterns of migration from the PRC have resulted in the merger of traditionally distinct translocal migration flows—ones that had linked, for example, Guangdong Province with the West Coast of North America, Fujian Province with Southeast Asia, or Zhejiang Province with Europe since the late nineteenth century—into a global migration system. This system links new migration spaces in Eastern Europe to traditional ones in Southeast Asia and China through trade, media, and organizations. It is also characterized by increased mobility between destination countries as well as increased interchange between different social strata of migrants, from students to illegal workers. Increasingly, the social, economic, and political practices of these migrants are characterized by transnationalism, that is, sustained structural embedding and accumulation and expenditure of various forms of capital both in China and in one or more countries overseas. This is a result of a range of circumstances: the personal histories of new migrants in an intensely modernizing China that is more open, capitalistic, and nationalistic; the increased global importance of China's economy; advances in communication technology; and the nature of the Chinese government's control over both economy and communications. The intertwining of transnational business with transnational politics is captured in a couplet on a temple gate in Shaxi Township in Mingxi County, Fujian, built by new migrants' donations and recorded by Li Minghuan (2005): "Opening the door to [ac]quire wealth in Europe by migrating and establishing business there; building the road to create glory in [the] native place by highlighting patriotism and solidarity here."

3
Tourism in Contemporary China

n Maoist China, tourism was seen as an element of bourgeois lifestyle and was therefore, in principle, taboo (Zhang Guangrui 2003a:15). But soon after Mao's death, the goverment began promoting incoming tourism as a way to earn foreign currency. The policy toward domestic tourism at the time was known as the three don'ts (don't support, don't promote, don't oppose). This ambivalent attitude reflected a fear that domestic tourism bred immoral behavior, wasted resources, and distracted the population from productive activities; in particular, there was a belief that official "study and inspection trips" served as cover for tourism funded from state coffers and involving lots of banqueting, prostitution, and gambling.

The precipitous decision in 1998 to designate tourism a new key growth area of the national economy (*guomin jingji xin zengzhangdian*) and, the following year, to create three weeks of public holidays was triggered by the Asian financial crisis and the government's urgent need to increase domestic consumer demand (Wei Xiaoan 2001:246). In 1999, the Policy and Regulation Division of the National Tourism Authority even proposed a National Tourism Plan with the aim to "truly make tourism a part of the people's common consumer practices."[1] Although no Tourism Plan was enacted, the introduction of the three-week holidays (around the state holidays of May 1 and October 1 and the traditional Spring Festival holiday) resulted in a revolution in Chinese leisure. The holiday periods, which came to be known as golden weeks, became times for the urban consumer class to travel. In a 2002 survey of more than 4,200 residents in ten cities—Peking, Shanghai, Canton, Wuhan, Chengdu, Shenyang, Xian, Zhengzhou, Jinan, and Xiamen—24 percent of respondents said they had traveled at least once during the golden weeks in the year before (Horizon Research 2002).

All of a sudden, tourism gained prominence as a lifestyle attribute of the higher-income, urban population and began spreading to an increasingly large part of Chinese society.[2] The state's role, both administrative and pedagogical, in engineering this change cannot be overestimated. While the crucial 1998 decision to promote tourism was justified in terms of economic development (Wei et al. 1999:4), it coincided with the appearance of the term "leisure culture" (*xiuxian wenhua*) in the government's "civilization campaigns" as an attribute of the "modern and civilized citizen/bourgeois (*shimin*)" (J. Wang 2001:39–41).[3]

Unlike in the West where hotel nights are the most common tourism indicator, Chinese tourism authorities use ticket sales data from tourist sites, or scenic spots (*jingdian*, also *jingqu*), recognized and classified by the state, to gauge the volume of domestic tourism. As far as the state and the tourism business are concerned, the map of China consists of a network of scenic spots ranging from imperial palaces and revolutionary memorials to nature reserves and fenced villages. Ticket sales from scenic spots constitute the backbone of state-owned tourism corporations' income, and many local governments see the sale of management rights of scenic spots to investors—all land in China being the "property of the people"—as the brightest prospect of generating revenue. By contrast, domestic travel to other locations, or travel that does not engage these state-sanctioned sites, falls outside tourism statistics. Thus, tourism in China is understood by its managers as the consumption of bounded and controlled zones. As I have argued (Nyíri 2006a), this understanding is based on the premodern tradition of literati travel, which consisted of revisiting nature sites, literally and figuratively inscribed with the poetry and essays of cultural heroes and canonized for their cultural and historical significance. The image of the tourist as self-educating explorer, self-bettering sportsman, or romantic flâneur, characteristic of the Western evolution of tourism, is not part of Chinese cultural history and was not accessible to fledgling Chinese tourists in the 1990s.

The reconstruction of key tourist sites after the depredations of the Cultural Revolution and their rehabilitation as part of national culture began right after Deng Xiaoping's accession to power. For many buildings, this meant constructing them anew. Some structures of iconic cultural significance were "restored" even though they had disappeared long before and their site was no longer exactly known. Reenactments of historical ceremonies at famous sites became widely popular (Sofield and Li 1998:378). Traditional views of landscape and architecture spread by means of wall calendars, postage stamps, and—not least—banknotes, reaching the entire population (Petersen 1995:149). In the nineties, for the first time, television began conveying the same images to the majority of the Chinese population, and today they are reproduced on countless Internet sites. As a result, recognizing representations of scenic sites and identifying some cultural references associated with them once again became part of a shared cultural grammar. The desire to travel could once again be the desire to validate one's knowledge of canonical representations, this time for a much larger part of Chinese society, but one which was poorly versed in the literati tradition beyond its superficial signs and had no code of travel behavior at its disposal.

While many of the revived scenic spots were part of the literati travel canon, others were reinterpreted or added in accordance with the government's ideology of modernization, nationalism, and socialism. Some were named Patriotic Education Sites. Mount Tai, historically one of the most-traveled sacred mountains, was reinterpreted as—in the words of a 1993 gazetteer—"a base area for people's resistance against oppression, tyranny, and invasion" (quoted in Dott 2002). New catalogues and encyclopedias of scenic spots (e.g., China Cultural Relics Research Association et al. 1998; Yong 1999) expanded the list from traditional landscapes of literati travel (reconfigured as proof of a rich national culture) to landscapes symbolic of the Communist victory and the birth of New China, and landscapes expressing China's reform-era economic modernization and rising standing in the world (e.g., theme parks), into a seamless whole. As Tim Oakes (1998:48) wrote in his pioneering study of tourism and modernity in Guizhou, southwestern China, the state took an active role in shaping and promoting the new canon as it attempted to "fix the boundaries of a unique and essential China, a nation equal and unique among a modern community of nations." In 1982, it created a system of National and Provincial Key Scenic Areas (*zhongdian fengjing mingshengqu*). The National Tourism Administration's current Tourism Development Plan reaffirms that "patriotic education should be part of tourist activities" and that "the construction of memorials and scenic spots with patriotic content should be strengthened" (National Tourism Administration 2001:7, 64).

The appearance and popularity of theme parks in the 1990s—beginning with the first and best-known, Splendid China in Shenzhen—played an important role in creating a new popular canon of China's scenic spots. Most of the estimated 2,000 to 2,500 amusement and theme parks were based on themes from Chinese history and folk customs (Ap 2003:195–97). Visiting them became a proto-tourist activity for many people: it familiarized them with representations of traditional scenic sites and taught them to see these as parts of a national landscape. Splendid China, which served as a prototype for many other theme parks, displays twelve miniaturized landscapes from the traditional canon plus forty-eight famous man-made structures, from the Great Wall to the Potala in Tibet. It also contains ensembles of 65,000 terracotta figurines, ranging from a memorial ceremony for Confucius to Mongol archers on horseback. Ethnicity became the main theme at the Shenzhen theme park China Folk Culture Villages, which opened in 1991. This theme is reinforced by regular performances featuring members of minorities who live in their respective villages within the park and wear their putative ethnic costume. Visitors can rent "ethnic clothing" and participate in the "ethnic dances" (Stanley 1998:68).

Parts of China's landscape were thus reinterpreted as both national and ethnic. In this process, Oakes (1998:36–37) argues, "parts which contribute to the construction of an imagined multicultural community get salvaged and preserved," whereas, Oakes goes on to quote Picard (1993:93) writing on Bali, "those deemed too primitive or emphasizing local ethnic identity should be eradicated." Since the 1990s, spectacles of "minority customs" have become almost *de rigueur* elements in any tourist itinerary aside from some metropolitan ones (Sofield and Li 1998:371–76; Oakes 1998:135–87; Tan et al. 2001:93–215; Hyde 2001).

In addition to reproducing *en masse* a national landscape canon and attaching new cultural references, such as ethnicity, to particular sites, theme parks also situated the national landscape in a global perspective. They did so in part by juxtaposing parks based on themes from Chinese history and ethnicity with others representing famous landscapes and buildings from other parts of the world—like Windows on the World in Shenzhen—or situating Chinese among other ethnic groups and nations. The World Primitive Totem Park (Shijie yuanshi tuteng gongyuan) in Peking displayed artifacts of foreign primitiveness, and the Foreign Lands Lore Village (Yiguo fengqingcun) that opened in Sipsongpanna in 2003 actually hired foreigners to live and perform in the village, as the Chicago World's Fair once had done. As a report in the *People's Daily* (9 February 2003, 2) affirmed, "Every day, border area residents from Burma, Thailand, Nepal, and India perform folk customs of their country."

In sum, the late socialist Chinese state reinscribed the national territory with a cultural canon that claimed historical continuity yet was modified in particular ways, notably by the ethnicization of the national geography and the nationalization of modernity. In doing so—and embracing the budding media of popular culture for the purpose—it prepared its citizens for being tourists in a number of fairly idiosyncratic ways.

Managing Landscapes

The literature on tourism that began to appear in the 1980s gave detailed instructions to Chinese readers about the proper consumption of scenic spots. The 1988 *Pocket Tourism Encyclopedia* (*Lüyou xiaobaike*), for example, devoted an entire chapter to taking proper photos. The emphasis here was as much teaching readers the appropriate content of the photos as the technical skills of taking them:

> Each famous mountain and great river has its specifics. . . . One should pay detailed attention to what angle of photography can bring out the representative, typical photo. . . . For example, taking a picture of Yueyang Pavilion (on the Yangzi) can make people think about the . . . ancient quatrains; taking a picture at the Yue Temple in Hangzhou can conjure up

people's admiration for the national hero, Yue Fei, and their contempt for the shameless traitors. . . . At Sun Yat-sen's Mausoleum in Nanjing, taking a picture of the thousand steps carved in stone, symbolizing Sun Yat-sen's untiring, lifelong struggle for country and people, is preferable to taking a picture of the heroic and imposing architecture. (Shandong 1988:493, 498)

Learning to reproduce the correct representation of a site was important: at stake was one's ability "to express the infinity of one's feelings towards the rivers and mountains of the Fatherland. . . . Only having mastered the skills and rules" of photography could one "get better at expressing these feelings" (Shandong 1988:495). The book also defined the role of the tour guide: the guide's narrative was supposed to "reflect objective facts," yet also "express approval or disapproval, praise or opposition, pleasure and contempt" (ibid.:506–8). At the time, this information was of purely theoretical value in a country with almost no holidays. But it was clearly intended to shape the behavior and consciousness of fledgling tourists, impressing upon them the importance of their future travels for modernization by invoking the example of "advanced" foreign countries: "In America and other Western countries, people have become used to hopping on airplanes on weekends or traveling in individual cars. This shows that . . . tourism is closely linked to the results of modern social development" (ibid.:4–5).

The lack of a cultural tradition of the wilderness may explain the tendency toward the encasement of nature into scenic spots. But the sensory and narrative uniformity of tourist sites requires other explanations. One reason for it is the strong and continued involvement of the highly centralized Chinese state in defining tourism itineraries. Unlike in European tourism, the development of both pilgrimage sites and literati-favored scenic spots in China was influenced by imperial pilgrimages and the routes of the official courier. Mass tourism emerged not with industrial modernization but as part of the emerging state-promoted service sector, at a time when the "modern citizen" was being recast as consumer. In the post-1978 era, the state chose to retain a defining presence in the tourism sector even as it proceeded to privatize the economy.

Tourism development can be initiated by the local, prefectural, provincial, or central government, or by a private investor, but because of the public ownership of all land and absence of a land market, it can only take place with state approval. Invariably, this involves a (usually county-level) government body taking responsibility for making the land available and subsequently becoming a stakeholder. In addition, despite policies of separating government from enterprise (*zheng-qi fenkai*) announced back in 1988 and the reaffirmation of state withdrawal from the management of tourism in 1998, government bodies retain control of scenic spots, travel agencies, transportation companies, and most hotels through full or partial ownership or through contracting them out to their employees, making travel one of the least free sectors of the retail economy (Nyíri 2006a:69–73).

At the same time as being owners, state actors—a hierarchy of provincial, prefectural, and county tourism bureaus with guidance from the National Tourism Administration—play a broader regulatory role than in Western countries. The government approves all changes to the infrastructure of scenic spots and controls ticket, and sometimes accommodation, prices. In Sichuan, changes to scenic spot ticket prices have to be approved three months in advance,[4] while in Zhongdian (renamed Shangrila), the government has prescribed a minimum room rate for three-star hotels to increase revenue (Kolås 2007:13). Governments approve tour routes (*lüyouxian*), scenic spots, hotels, restaurants, transport enterprises, shops, and entertainment venues as designated points (*dingdian*) authorized to receive tour groups.[5] (Without such designation, they may not receive such groups.) The authorities also approve "ethnic tourist villages" (Oakes 1998:159). By 2003, 210 villages had been approved as "demonstration objects of folk life, customs, and culture."[6] In principle, these designations do not mean that organized tours cannot be conducted in other places, but given the ownership structure of travel agencies, exceptions are rare. Therefore, although little or no state funding comes with the designations, they can have a profound effect on local development.

When the government decides to promote tourism in relatively small towns, the implications for urban design are often dramatic. In Wuzhen, a town on the Grand Canal near Shanghai, the Tourism Development Company is led by the township head, who is also Party secretary. Consequently, it has been able to impose a unified new look on the village and received high commendation from the National Tourism Bureau (Wei Xiaoan 2003b:106). At the end of the 1990s, the local government in Dali, Yunnan, promoted two theme projects based on a classic 1959 film and a Hong Kong martial arts novel set in Dali. These projects resulted in the construction of simulacra, including a temple, a palace, a resort island, and two theme parks, as well as the demolition and rebuilding of the main street. In the end, the tourist itinerary previously defined by backpackers was entirely reshaped (Notar 2006). Shanhaiguan, a town at the eastern end of the Great Wall near Qinhuangdao—which hosted part of the 2008 Olympics—demolished its old town with the exception of fifty-three protected buildings, relocating residents into seventy-two new high-rises. The old town will consist of newly built "Ming-and-Qing-style" buildings, complete with a new bell and drum tower and wall gatehouses. The master plan calls for one area of old town to be

> a "military experience zone," where tourists can dress as ancient warriors and ride horses. Another lantern-lit area will offer folk arts and include a bird market. A third will have cultural shows and include a rebuilt or newly built Confucian temple, governor's mansion and Korean culture center. Electric trams will carry tourists from area to area. (*The Age*, 2006)

In the Tibetan-inhabited areas of Zhongdian, Yunnan Province, and Songpan, Sichuan Province, the government mandated that residences and businesses remove tiles from facades and replace them with Tibetan-style patterns, put up signs in Tibetan, and replace shop shutters with "Tibetan-looking" iron doors. The old parts of both towns saw many buildings demolished and rebuilt in "Tibetan style" and their residents removed, with compensation to build new houses on the outskirts to make room for new shopping streets and ceremonial squares suitable for public events and reminiscent of official spaces in Peking (Hillman 2003; Kolås 2007:108–9). In Zhongdian, as part of a five-point program to "revive Tibetan culture," plans have been made to require villagers belonging to each ethnic group to build only houses in styles officially designated as traditional for that group. Even a new "Tibetan traditional standard" was developed by architects based on models in Tibet since such buildings had not previously existed in Zhongdian (Kolås 2007:108–9). Hohhot, the capital of Inner Mongolia, had all 184 buildings in its Muslim District renovated in "Muslim style" in 2006, primarily by adding tentlike domes to the usual concrete buildings. In contrast, the old garrison town was given "Mongol characteristics," a statue of Genghis Khan, a Mongol Customs Park, and a Zhaojun Cultural Festival under a master plan that called for marrying "the ethnic cultural essence with domestic and international architectural elements" of modernity (Li Mu 2007).

The reason for Zhaojun's prominence is that, as a Chinese princess who married a Hunnish chieftain, she is suited to represent the "harmonious relationship" between Han Chinese and Mongols, who like the Huns are regarded as martial horsemen. Songpan's touristic refurbishment also drew inspiration from an historical princess and her bridegroom. In 2004, a statue of the Tang Dynasty princess Wencheng and her Tibetan king-bridegroom was erected with a tablet stating *Han Zang he qin* (Han and Tibetan: harmony and amity). The number of domestic tourists has significantly increased and the statue has become one of the main photo-spots.

Managing Tourists Abroad

In 1990, traveling abroad from mainland China meant working (legally or illegally), studying, trading, or occasionally attending business meetings. Officially, tourism to foreign countries did not exist: Chinese citizens could travel abroad only on business or to visit friends or relatives. As a result, many officials and business people organized "delegations" to satisfy their curiosity about foreign countries. Many officials applied for passports through businesses set up by their government bodies to circumvent scrutiny for using public funds to travel. Businesses also sold sponsorships to people who wanted to travel abroad (Zhao Limei 1999). Although foreign governments never stated that Chinese citizens could not apply for tourist visas, their widespread fear of visa overstayers meant that the chance of such applications being approved was very low.

In 1990, bilateral government agreements with Singapore, Malaysia, and Thailand granted them "Approved Destination Status" (ADS) from China. This meant that Chinese citizens were now able to apply for tourist visas to these countries. Tourist visas were limited to groups organized by one of the nine licensed travel agencies (in reality, these agencies used over two hundred subcontractors), and passports were valid for a single trip and kept by the agencies' tour guides.

Foreign travel did not pick up until 1997, when the number of licensed travel agencies was expanded to sixty-seven (Li, Jin, and Zhuang 2003).[7] In the following year, the currency crisis throughout Southeast Asia and Korea resulted in more Chinese traveling abroad to shop. Some groups reportedly spent as much as 40,000 yuan (around US$4,500) per person in Hong Kong (Zhang Xiaoli 1998). That year Chinese tourists developed a reputation as big spenders so rapidly that the ADS became a trophy coveted by many countries, overriding the fears of being overwhelmed by overstayers. The arrival of low-fare airlines connecting China with Southeast Asia, the introduction of on-arrival visas in some countries by the mid-2000s, and the opening of group cruises to Vietnam requiring no passports (only national identity cards) provided further incentives for Chinese travelers.

In 1999, Australia became the first Western country to be granted ADS. And in 2003, the first European countries—Germany, Hungary, Croatia, Cyprus, Malta, and Switzerland—were added to the approved list, joining all of Southeast Asia, Japan, South Korea, India, Nepal, Sri Lanka, Turkey, Egypt, South Africa, Jordan, Australia, New Zealand, and much of Latin America. ADS meant that tourists to these countries were no longer required to masquerade as delegations, and the real costs of joining such tours went down. A memorandum of understanding with the European Union in 2004 paved the way for the expansion of ADS to most remaining European countries. An agreement with Britain followed in 2005, and with the United States in 2008. All these agreements are limited to group tourists, with heavy liabilities imposed on travel agencies in case a tourist overstays his or her visa. Travel agencies pass these liabilities on to tourists, requiring a deposit ranging from 50,000 to 200,000 yuan (about US$6,000–$25,000) for tours to the West or Japan (Qin 2006).

Foreign governments began allowing individuals to apply for tourist visas after experiments by Hong Kong and Macau, gradually introduced between 2003 and 2005, proved enormously lucrative. Singapore quickly began a similar experiment, at first limited to residents of Peking, Shanghai, and Canton. A handful of Southeast Asian countries—most importantly, Thailand and Indonesia—began issuing visas on arrival, effectively enabling large numbers of Chinese citizens to travel freely for the first time.

International travel has been picking up rapidly in recent years. According to official statistics, 41 million PRC citizens traveled abroad in 2007, eight times more than in 1997. While this figure is still low compared to the size of China's population, it is already several times higher than the number of overseas travelers from Japan. Going abroad is no longer limited to the upper crust: schoolteachers and lower ranking rural officials can also afford the occasional *Xin-Ma-Tai* (Singapore, Malaysia, Thailand) trip. In Vietnam, the number of Chinese tourists exceeds those from any other country by a large margin, so that at Halong Bay—the country's best-known scenic attraction—most hotel personnel speak some Chinese and shops take Chinese currency. In Cambodia, the number of Chinese tourists grew by 57 percent between January 2005 and June 2006 (Mengin 2007:22). The pace of growth is such that the number of Chinese tourists abroad is likely to exceed 100 million, becoming the highest of any country well before the year 2020 when the World Tourist Organization (WTO) predicted it would.

Foreign governments are scrambling to catch a slice of this market. According to Zhang Guangrui, a senior Chinese tourism researcher, the Indonesian government has gone as far as adjusting the official time in Bali in order to be aligned with Peking and Hong Kong and has been encouraging locals to learn Mandarin. Even the tourism office of tiny Malta created a Chinese-language Web site (Zhang Guangrui 2003b:85-86). According to its authors, *The Shopping Behaviour of Chinese Travellers* is used by "airports, transportation companies, retailers, tourism companies and organizations from over 28 countries . . . for adapting their services according to the needs of their Chinese consumers" (Chinese Outbound Tourism blog 2007). Hotels in Paris offer congee for breakfast, and the department store Galeries Lafayette has fifteen Chinese-speaking employees (Steinberger 2007). At Angkor Wat, the Sino-Khmer entrepreneur who has a concession for the sale of tickets to the temple complex set up a Cambodian Cultural Village, which

assembles all the miniatures of famous historical buildings and structures, local customs and practices of all races. There are 11 unique villages, which represent different culture heritages and characteristics of 19 multi races [sic]. At each village, the tourists will be able to enjoy the excellent wood houses, carving, soft skill in stone [and] traditional performances in the different style.[8]

This theme-parklike exhibition of "races" seems to be inspired by Chinese models and appears to cater mostly to Chinese tour groups.

The lucrative business of organizing Chinese tourists' activities abroad is run almost exclusively by local Chinese travel agents and tour guides. This could be due to Western travel agents' cultural and linguistic difficulties in servicing Chinese tourists, but is more likely a consequence of their disadvantaged position in communicating and building up contacts with outbound agencies in China and the state bureaus that supervise them. The Chinese government has been very cautious in letting the reins of outbound tourism loose. The motto of tourism development for many years has been "energetically develop inbound tourism; actively develop domestic tourism; appropriately develop outbound tourism" (*dali fazhan rujing lüyou, jiji fazhan guonei lüyou, shidu fazhan chujing lüyou*). The principal reason for this caution appears to be economic. Article 6 of the Regulations for the outbound tourism of Chinese citizens,[9] published in 2002, stipulates that each province receives its yearly quotas on the number of outbound tourists from the State Council and distributes them among licensed outbound travel agencies. Article 3 specifies that only those travel agencies that show outstanding achievements in inbound tourism can be licensed as outbound agents—apparently following the logic that any growth in tourists' spending abroad must be offset by foreign currency earnings from inbound tourism. Yet Zhang Guangrui writes that the government has "put political considerations before economic ones and emphasized control over liberalization" (2003b:88). These political considerations were related more to the need to assuage foreign countries' continuing fears of Chinese immigration than an inherent intention to limit travel (Li, Jin, and Zhuang 2003:27). In any case, the logic behind the ADS system is that the international mobility of Chinese citizens is a matter between two governments, to be regulated according to their mutual interests, rather than between an individual and a foreign government. In 2006, Zhang Jiangzhong, director of the Policy and Regulation Department of the National Tourism Administration, said that the government would stop controlling the number of outbound tourists, but would still regulate

> enterprise behavior which sometimes contributes to a negative image of China in the world and does not tackle the problem of overstays enough, and . . . the tourists' behavior . . . to promote the good image of a country with 5,000 years of history by being courteous and by respecting local customs and laws.[10]

By the mid-2000s, after barely a decade, domestic and foreign tourism have become an accepted part of the lifestyle not only of the entrepreneurial-managerial elite but also of the diverse middle classes, from upwardly mobile students to mid- and low-level government and corpo-rate employees. The widespread nature of this lifestyle change is illus-trated by three acquaintances with whom I spoke about their recent trips and plans in 2005–6.

I talked to Yang in April 2006. She was pursuing a doctoral degree in overseas Chinese studies, was married to a businessman, and worked at a museum in the prosperous coastal city of Xiamen. The couple had just returned from a weekend pilgrimage-cum-tour of the island of Putuo, famous for its temples, and was preparing to visit the "old towns" of southern Anhul and northern Jiangsu over the Labor Day "golden week." Feifei was an unmarried secretary at the Shanghai offices of Philips, with a vocational college education. In the few months before our conversa-tion, she had made weekend trips with a group of friends to Peking and Hong Kong and stayed at five-star hotels. In Peking, she visited well-known scenic spots, such as the Forbidden City and the Badaling section of the Great Wall; while in Hong Kong, she spent most of her time shop-ping. She was not planning a trip over the upcoming golden week, but was looking forward to the "team-building trips" her company was orga-nizing in the coming months to Putuo (to burn incense, she explained), Lijiang, and Mt. Meili (Khabad Karpo), popular ethnic/nature tourist sites in Yunnan Province.

Hongyan graduated from a vocational college. Divorced, with a teen-age daughter, she designs clothes inspired by traditional folk styles. She owns two small shops in central Peking, where she sells her designs, as well as other clothes and accessories she brings from Vietnam and Nepal. Because of her flexible work schedule, she is able to reserve several months a year for traveling, mostly with her daughter. In addition to lon-ger trips to Vietnam and Nepal, she goes on backpacking tours of various parts of China. She does not visit scenic spots: "I plan to go to scenic spots after I've turned fifty and I can't move around like I can now."

The three women's travel experiences reflect not just the growing den-sity and accessibility of tourist activities in China but also their increas-ing diversification. While rapid sightseeing trips are expected to remain the norm for some time, what the industry refers to as *jiari lüyou* (holiday tourism) or *xiuxian lüyou* (leisure tourism) is spreading. Beach tourism, for example, is booming in the tropical island of Hainan, and ski resorts near Peking and in the northeastern Changbaishan mountains enjoy great popularity; neither form of leisure was widely known in China just ten years ago. And although agency-organized group tourism remains dominant, the number of individual, or "self-service" (*zizhu*), tourists is increasing, partly due to growing private car ownership and the rapid improvement of the road infrastructure (see Lim 2008). In just a few years, two online travel agencies, C-trip and e-Long, that specialize in hotel and ticket bookings for independent travelers have captured a significant share of the tourism market. The first Internet site dedicated to backpackers, www.lvye.org, came into being in 1998 (ibid.:295), and has been followed by numerous others. More recently, the increase in independent travel also caused a guidebook boom. In the late 1990s, guidebooks were an infrequent occurrence at bookstores and mostly read like travelogues. By the mid-2000s, they numbered in the hundreds, occupying the place of honor in many large bookshops, and catered to many special interests, from *Restaurants of Hong Kong Movie Stars* to *On Foot in Tibet* to *Old Towns of Europe*. Tourism periodicals have also multiplied and become more differentiated. Glossy lifestyle magazines like C-trip's *Xiecheng* (CTRIP Mag) or *Xin Lüxing* (Voyager) advertise clothes, watches, etc., and feature articles about romantic French castles and interviews with movie stars. *Shanye* (Mountains and Wilderness) and *Tanxian* (Exploration) focus on adventure and advertise outdoor gear, interview alpinists, and report on competitions. Finally, Chinese National Geographic (*Zhongguo Guojia Dili*, no relation to the original) focuses on ancient towns and exotic peoples in and outside China. Youth hostels are opening one after the other (Ji and Zhang 2002), and shops offering outdoor gear for campers, hikers, skiers, and mountaineers have spread since the late 1990s. One of the largest, Sanfo, opened in 1997 and had eight branches across the country by 2005. Various travel clubs, from jeep safari enthusiasts with names like Yueye Lianmeng (Cross-Wilderness Federation) and Yezhanpai (Wilderness Warriors) to Great Wall clubs, have sprung up across China's large cities, and scores of places around Peking offer horseback riding, rock climbing, and bungee jumping.

Yet the diversification and individualization of tourism—which seems to follow the development of Western tourist practices—has not dislodged the scenic spot with its determined meaning and staged performances from its central position in tourism. For one thing, group sightseeing is certain to remain in the mainstream of Chinese tourism for some time, because even as individual travel spreads among wealthier, more educated, and younger people, new cohorts of first-time tourists will be entering the scene and are more likely to prefer group travel for their first tourism experience. For another, ticket revenue from scenic spots is central to the value of tourism corporations, some of which are already listed on the stock exchange, and neither local governments nor private investors are likely to give it up. As one researcher wrote, "while other tourism-related prices (such as for shopping, restaurants, and transportation) decline, most scenic spot entry ticket prices are stable, going up but not down, so the scale and weight of scenic spot revenue will continue to increase" (Peng 2003:6).

Finally, although the Chinese backpacker discourse valorizes authentic experiences, it is not concerned with the "authenticity" of art or architecture in the same way as Western tourist discourse. Most backpacker Web sites and guidebooks can be described as "inspirational": strongly focused on the experiences and feelings of one particular author and on her or his personal itinerary. They provide little historical or political context or opinion on whether a place is worth going to or not, all crucial features of English-language backpacker guidebooks. And backpacking in China is typically a highly planned group activity with a leader, rather than the individual free drift that it is supposed to be in the West (Lim 2008).

More important, while Western backpacker discourse distinguishes itself from the mainstream tourist discourse by being down-to-earth and even cynical about tourist activities, the Chinese backpacker language is highly poetic, focused on experiencing the sublime, with no room for reflection on tourism or irony. It is true that certain groups of backpackers take care to distinguish themselves from "tourists," just as their Western counterparts do. As Zhang Ning (2006) writes about one such group,

They admitted, not without pride, that they have never traveled with a guided mass tour facilitated by any tourist establishment and will never do it in the future. When they speak of [tourists], they refer explicitly to those joining guided tours and regard such tourist experience as phony.

But the reason they regard it as "phony" is their disdain of the institutionalized and thus unfree experience of tourist sites rather than an explicit questioning of their authenticity or the credibility of their narratives. In one of the earliest popular backpacker guides, called *The Cowhide Book of Tibetan Lands*, the section about Langmusi (Dagtsanglhamo), a much-liked backpacker destination on the Sichuan-Gansu border, relates the tale of the town's name—derived from a Tibetan monastery—and suggests an idyllic atmosphere. It does not mention that the current monastery was built in 1980, or that the town is the site of very extensive construction (Yizhi 2002:416). Similarly, most of the place descriptions in *Zhongguo tubu chuanyue* (Traversing China on Foot [English title: *A Guide for Chinese Hikers*]) consist of folk legends and rituals, but do not mention whether the place is worth stopping at or not (Shaanxi 2003). Even though sites of mass tourism, with their development and crowds, seem to stand for everything the authors of these books want to avoid, they—and more surprisingly, participants of online backpacker discussions—do not criticize or satirize these sites and their practices the way their Western counterparts do. Most authors ignore them, even when a route they are describing passes right through one; some include them.

In other words, the Chinese backpacker discourse lacks the subversiveness that is a central element of its Western counterpart. On the contrary, it shares some of the modernizing earnestness of mainstream Chinese tourist discourse. Backpackers describe their lifestyle as a quintessentially modern one that derives the legitimacy of its pursuits from the imagery of Western modernity, together with North Face fleece jackets, Timberland boots, and backpacks. In her account of a trip to India in the popular Shanghai-based *Travel Times*, a female backpacker's joy over the sense of fraternity she experienced with backpackers of other nations led her to claim that "the backpacker tribe is best able to embody a nation's economic strength and its national quality. The fact that Japanese backpackers are found in every corner of the earth is inseparable from Japan's enormous economic strength" (Lin Sheng'r 2002a). She adds, "When American and Japanese backpackers understood that I was traveling alone and stared at me in admiration—I would not have exchanged that feeling of national pride for anything" (Lin Sheng'r 2002b).[11] The triumphalism of this narrative derives from the liberating experience of traveling abroad on equal terms with Westerners and Japanese, while most carriers of PRC passports continue to endure humiliation at the hands of immigration officers worldwide. Nonetheless, it is remarkable how much the language of this article echoes the hegemonic, official discourse of Chinese nationalism and modernity that pervades mass tourism.

4
The Usefulness of Mobility
PRODUCING MODERN CITIZENS

The preceding chapters have demonstrated the rise of different forms of population mobility in post-1978 China. This chapter examines how interpretations of this newfound mobility have changed in the light of prevalent Chinese views on modernization and development, issues at the heart of official, popular, public, and private concerns for the past three decades.[1] While the original "four modernizations" put forward by Deng Xiaoping in 1978 referred to the modernization of agriculture, industry, national defense, and science and technology, the idea that China had to modernize its people's thinking and way of life—popular with reformers since the late Qing—was quickly picked up by the Deng and post-Deng leadership and became a truism variously expressed in discourses about "population quality" and "spiritual civilization." As the deputy chairman of the Hebei Province People's Congress wrote in 2006,

Man is the most flexible of the factors of production, and man's quality has a major impact on the speed and quality of economic and social development. . . . In fact, economic and technological competition [between countries] is nothing but the competition of human resources (*rencai*). (Zhang Qunsheng 2006)

A number of authors have pointed out that the Chinese government's concern with population "quality" is tied to the state's drive to create modern consumer-citizens (Anagnost 1997; Yan Hairong 2003; Friedman 2004; Murphy 2004; Woronov 2004). Certainly, the ideal of the modern subject in contemporary China is linked to productiveness and consumption, but the discourse of "quality" is both broader and more complex (Kipnis 2006). To pick a random quote from a 1999 conference on "leisure culture":

Our country's socialist modernization should include man's modernization. The modern man must have a modern mentality (*sixiang yishi*), modern way of thinking, modern morals and self-cultivation, and in addition, he must have modernized scientific knowledge and technological skills; furthermore, he must live a civilized, healthy, scientific lifestyle. (Sun and Lei 1999:123)

The imperatives for modernizing people charted in Shen Pinghua's *Remaking the Chinese* (1996) are broader still. They include implementing stricter eugenic policies to prevent racial degeneration—current population planning policies, he feels, provide "too much scope for those of lower quality to reproduce"—a tighter control over culture to defend it from "feudal and foreign vulgarities" (Sun and Lei 1999), and an insistence on the morality of struggle (Song and Sigley 2000:60). For Peking University leisure studies professor Sun Xiaoli, the modern personality possesses attributes like openness, orientation toward the future, respect for science and friendliness, environmental consciousness, and a respect for time and planning. According to Sun, such a personality is achieved through both eugenics—a long-standing concern of the Chinese state (Dikötter 2005)—and a "scientific view of consumption" (as opposed to "Mammon worship and hedonism") (Sun Xiaoli 2004). In the words of yet another scholar, "modernization of the person requires the modernization of lifestyle, of behavior and habits, as well as of thought and ideas"

(Fu Tengxiao 2003:64). As we will see below, various forms of mobility are linked not only to economic modernization but also to developing the attributes of the modern person.

Peasants into Chinese

In *Flexible Citizenship* (1999), Aihwa Ong argues that international mobility, the juggling of locations in which to make money, educate one's children, and take advantage of the benefits of a retired life, is a component of the modern self-image of the peripatetic Hong Kong business elite. She traces this imaginary of the "globally modern Asian" back to the "Rimspeak" of Western business schools and authors fascinated by the rise of tiger economies, to the political exigencies of Hong Kong's colonial history, and to the neoliberal American model of the ideal, productive citizen in late capitalism. A number of authors, including Rachel Murphy (2002, 2004) and Yan Hairong (2003), have pointed out how this same logic of flexible capitalism has resulted in the valorization of domestic migration in China as an activity that turns, to use a variation on Eugene Weber's (1976) phrase, "peasants into citizens," making them more productive and better attuned to the needs of a modern market economy, and therefore more aligned with the expectations of the modernizing state.[2]

The State Council, the highest executive body of the Chinese state, affirmed in a 2003 document that "the migration of surplus rural labour to nonagricultural production and to towns is a necessary tendency of industrialization and modernization."[3] In addition to direct economic benefits of satisfying demand for cheap and flexible labor, migration "is said to instill a 'commodity consciousness,' a good work ethic, and an appreciation of the value of time" (Murphy 2002:45). Foreign advisors on China's economic development are also supportive of migration. At a conference on China's rural development, a senior analyst at the OECD remarked that "the only way to increase productivity is to be mobile, to be flexible. . . . Migration is an extremely positive factor."[4]

This public endorsement of mobility as an attribute of modernity signals a major turnaround. As Murphy (2002) and Jacka (2006) discuss, in the first half of the 1980s, the tone of public discourse on internal migration was a stern one, stressing the need for continued control. In 1983, letters to the *People's Daily* expressed outrage at the laxity of officials in giving city *hukou* to their own relatives in Anxiang County, Hunan (*Renmin Ribao* 1983). Ten years later, the newspapers were writing about the *hukou* regime as an obstacle to urbanization, which was now seen—in the words of an official from Shaanxi Province—as "an indicator of whether the economy, culture and technology of a country or region is developed or not" (Zheng Deyi 1994). The official concluded that "allowing some peasants to enter the cities and become 'city dwellers' is the only effective way of transferring labour." As the Party secretary of Huaihua City in Hunan entitled his article, *hukou* reform was now "the springboard of urbanization" (Fang Xinqi 1994). Freeing up the mobility of peasants was seen as a precondition for helping China "follow the path of European and American countries" and move from a "small peasant civilization" to an "industrial civilization." It was also considered necessary in order to free up China's savings and accomplish the government's goal of stimulating consumption. One author in *Reform and Management* criticized the *hukou* regime for discouraging peasants from developing more diversified consumption—by migrating to the cities—and from investing in productive activities, encouraging them to channel their money into building ever more elaborate tombs instead (Pan Yiyong 1993). Elaborating on this point, Zha and Zeng (2000) wrote that the current *hukou* policy kept internal migrants in an unstable position and prevented them from spending more money on their homes, such as buying appliances, either in the village or in the city. A year later, demographer Wang Guixin was even more emphatic:

Population movement promotes the development of modernization. Looking forward to the twenty-first century, an even more active, spontaneous and market-oriented population movement will necessarily become a powerful "engine" of accelerating modernization in our country. (Wang Guixin 2001:33)

The idea that modernization can be expressed as a set of numerical indicators translated into specific target figures for urbanization. As Li Qiang, a senior Peking University sociologist, wrote, "When the proportion of a country's urban population exceeds 50%, it is an important sign that that country has entered the process of modernization" (Li Qiang

1998). Subsequently, regions developed specific urbanization targets: for example, the Ningbo region in Jiangsu is supposed to achieve 42 percent by 2020 (He Wei 2001). These targets were often set in comparison to Western indicators and could not be reached without freeing up migration: "The experience of developed Western countries shows that there is no successful development without population movement" (Lu Jing 2002:15).

But mobility was clearly more than just a means to accelerate economic modernization; it also helped the rural population develop "qualities compatible with the principles of market economy, such as competitiveness" (Barabantseva 2005, chap. 4; cf. Jacka 2006:52). Rachel Murphy quotes Chinese authors that suggest "out-migration and return as development strategies by using migrant experience as an inexpensive substitute for education" (Murphy 2002:45; see also Jacka 2006:49–50). The Civilizing Handbook for Outside Working Youth in Pudong New Area[5] states that "authorities must ensure that the quality of . . . sojourners is improved through urban exposure" (quoted in Murphy 2002:45). Or as Ye Nanke writes,

> Peasant workers (*nongmingong*) are regarded as the pioneers of China's modernization. . . . Among the various strata of villagers, their quality is higher, which is not only manifested in their higher thought quality—protecting reform and opening, adapting to the development of the market economy . . . but also embodied in their higher cultural quality and professional skills compared to other groups of villagers. . . . They have begun to realize that if they want to get rich themselves and raise up their families, they have to speed up the collective development of their communities and enterprises, and that means serving the group, obeying the laws. . . . For the thinking and views of peasants . . . this has undoubtedly been a huge leap. (Ye 1995:10)

As Murphy (2002:124–43) points out, the Chinese state envisages a role for returned migrants in diffusing an awareness of civilized manners, hygiene, law, and modern culture throughout the countryside. This view is eloquently supported by Wang and Li in an article published in the Communist Party's *Fortnightly Forum*. The article praises migrant women from Anhui working as maids in Peking for having "bravely left the closed-up world of farm and field."

[They] have been baptized in civilization (*shoudao wenming de xili*)[6] and increased their abilities. They have awakened their thousands of brothers and sisters in the countryside and led them toward the great classroom of the city to be tempered and trained by the market economy. They have brought important benefits to their home county by dealing a blow to their fellow villagers' traditional concepts and ways of thought, and at the same time they have trained a production army. . . . To transform your poverty-stricken, backward home you must rely on yourself, blaze a path for yourself, and fight.[7] (Wang and Li 1996:24; quoted in Jacka 2006:51)

Article 27 of Shanghai's Regulations on the Management of the Shanghai Outside Transient Population states that local migrant management bodies are responsible for carrying out patriotic education among migrants,[8] and Article 33 says that employers are to train migrant workers in "legal knowledge, technical skills, work safety, and social morality" (translated in Human Rights in China 2002a:66). Accordingly, the Yudu Labor Export Company in Shanghai runs "spiritual civilization" classes for migrants; activities include praise meetings and sweeping the Martyrs' Shrine during the Qingming Festival. These pedagogic projects also warn migrants against urban vices (e.g., gambling and prostitution) and remind them of their moral obligations to the rural household (Murphy 2002:45). The State Council's 2003 Notice on Gooddoing the Management and Service Work of Peasants Entering Cities for Work and Employment calls on each local government to "organize trainings to raise the quality of peasant workers." Pilot projects have been started in sending areas providing legal and vocational training under the so-called Sunshine Project, which is supposed to become nationwide by 2010 (Tan Shen 2006). Various localities have reportedly organized "loving my second hometown and building my second hometown" and "how to be a civilized citizen" activities (Zhu Li 2006:148), and the labor and commerce office of a Shanghai district organized migrant traders at a particular market to collectively read newspapers every day, while a shipyard set up an "Outside Personnel Spiritual Civilization Fund" (Xu Deming 2003:159, 164). Some Chinese scholars supportive of migrants have also urged local governments to recognize that "enrich[ing] the pastimes of the migrant peasants is a piece of 'virgin soil' in community management that needs to be tapped"; otherwise, "the lack of colorful pastimes will make the energetic youngsters wander around and try things like gambling and whoring, thus leading to dangers" to public safety (Zhu Li 2006:148).

Shanghai has probably been most active in implementing "outside population thought work." An entire publication has been devoted to the task (Xu Deming 2003). The *Guide to Entering Shanghai: For Brothers and Sisters Who Come to Shanghai to Work*, published by the Shanghai Transient Outside Population Management Leading Group in 1995, is an eloquent example of the civilizing project directed at migrants. After an introductory chapter that starts with the heading "Do Not Blindly Come to Shanghai to Work" (3), the book consists of chapters entitled "Work and Business," "Respecting Rules and Abiding by Laws," "Morality and Self-Cultivation," and finally "Life and Health." It is structured like a catechism, with short educational epistles, or questions and answers. Part of the book contains practical information that ranges from "How Can Outsider Communist Youth League Members Who Come to Shanghai to Work Get in Touch with a Shanghai League Branch?" (108) to "What Regulations Should the Transient Population Follow When Giving Birth in Shanghai?" (139), and "How Is AIDS Transmitted?" (133) to "What Fees Should Private Entrepreneurs in Shanghai Pay?" (48). But a significant part of the handbook is taken up by a variety of guidelines on leading a more hygienic, polite, and civilized life that befits urbanites.

The chapter "Work and Business" provides advice on workplace safety (29–44, 137) and on whom to contact in case of a labor conflict (28). "Respecting Rules and Abiding by Laws" offers information on obtaining various types of documents, fire safety regulations, and where to report crime, and then goes on to list the punishments for offences ranging from battery and theft to forgery, prostitution, gambling, the use of drugs, and the selling of pornography, and to explain "What Is Disturbing Public Order?" and "What Is Obstructing Public Business?" (75–76). The chapter "Morality and Self-Cultivation" covers diverse aspects of good manners, a "modern" world view and social morality, ranging from "Cultivate the Traditional Virtue of Respecting the Old and Loving the Young, Mutual Help and Mutual Love" (94) to "Promote the Scientific Spirit, Extirpate Ignorance and Undesirable Customs" (105). Finally, the "Life and Health" chapter's headings include "Absolutely Avoid Gluttony" (117), "Do Not Spit, Urinate and Defecate Indiscriminately" (119), "Wash Your Hands Before Eating and After Defecation" (120), and "Wash, Comb, Air Your Bedding

Diligently" (121). Clearly, the book aspires to bring about a comprehensive reform of rural migrants' bodily practices, social behaviors, and beliefs in order to align them with the ideal of the productive, competitive, healthy, law-abiding, well-mannered and forward-looking modern citizen.

Finally, commentators state that migration expands the gene pool of particular localities, creating a unique historical opportunity for improving the physical and intellectual quality of the Chinese race. As a law journal article argued, the *hukou* system "gravely impeded the improvement of the Chinese people's physiological quality and the raising of its scientific and cultural quality" (Dong Shaoping 2003; cf. Jacka 2006:49). Educational projects for migrants have been implemented to take advantage of that opportunity. For example, migrants attend obligatory classes on family planning and eugenics at the Pudong Migrant Floating Population Management Offices in Shanghai (Murphy 2002:46).

The view of migration as a development tool was particularly clearly voiced in the discussion of China's Great Western Development project, announced by Chairman Jiang Zemin in 1999. The rural population was encouraged to acquire new skills and a more modern mentality by migrating to cities. Regions with low rates of rural-urban migration announced plans to expand it. Thus, in 2007, the Xinjiang Uyghur Autonomous Region's Labor and Social Security Bureau declared a target of 330,000 rural laborers migrating to cities. In addition, factories on the eastern seaboard recruited young rural men and women from the western regions with promises of free transportation and wages of 800 yuan, with the ultimate aim of relocating those factories to lower-wage Xinjiang (D.T. 2007:100).

In China's West, two additional aspects of migration were strongly promoted. The first was the planned resettlement of agriculturalists (villagers and nomads) whose areas (and/or modes) of cultivation or grazing were deemed unsustainable or were earmarked for dam construction or nature conservation projects. The largest resettlement in Chinese history, the plan encompassed 7 million people, of which 2.5 million were reportedly resettled by 2005 (Du Ping 2005). Significantly, the term used for such resettlement in Chinese is *yimin*, which also means voluntary domestic or international migration (with the addition of the recently introduced and modern-sounding adjective "ecological," *shengtai*). Like labor migration, resettlement was expected to help meet urbanization goals.

The second aspect of migration unique to China's West was the promotion of migration from the more economically developed eastern sea-board to newly developed areas of the West as a harbinger of investment and "advanced ways of life" (Ma Ping 2001; quoted in Barabantseva 2005, chap. 6). The settlement of cadres and technicians from the East in western minority areas goes back to the Maoist years, when it was called *zhibian* (supporting the frontier). In her ethnography of Han migrants in two ethnic minority areas in Yunnan Province, Mette Halskov Hansen (2005:7) writes that "there is, among post-revolution Han settlers in eth-nic minority areas, a high degree of shared identification as civilizers" who have brought "indisputable advantages" to the conditions of minori-ties. Across social classes, Han settlers in both locations identified two particular areas in which the local ethnic groups needed help: adapting to the conditions of the market economy and developing a national con-sciousness (ibid.:218).

In the minority areas even Han peasants who in some contexts were criti-cized for their low educational level and poor moral qualities were put forward as being at least more advanced, more educated than the local ethnic minorities, and they were therefore seen as bringing "moderniza-tion" to the minority areas. . . . "Modern," to most, implied better living standards, Chinese education as opposed to local religious training, and developed trade that ensured an abundance of different goods and hous-ing facilities and public buildings of a standard approaching what was seen as the standard in the large Chinese cities and symbolizing prosper-ity and global outlook, possibly with a touch of local tradition. (Halskov Hansen 2005:177)

In 2003, the Communist Youth League started a program recruiting university graduates to volunteer in education, health care, agriculture, and "cultural development" in the western provinces. A State Council cir-cular issued in 2005 promised these volunteers preferential policies in civil service tests and graduate school entrance exams. In four years, the program recruited over 50,000 volunteers (Li Mu 2007).

In discussing east-west migration in China, a number of authors draw parallels with the migration of Americans to the western United States (see Halskov Hansen 2005:65). Tim Oakes (2007) argues that the paral-lel between the two frontier myths goes beyond the lure of fortunes to be made and heathens to be civilized: they also share a fascination with exploration, adventure, and ruggedness as a special kind of psychological experience. Recently, some Chinese authors have developed a second comparison with the American West, invoking the human-rights rhetoric of freedom of movement. Liu Wujun, for example, writes that Americans' migration to the West has played an important role in the creation of "the American spirit," and goes on to state:

> Freedom of movement helps in establishing the ideal of the "free citizen" endowed with independent human dignity and autonomy, and thereby benefits the improvement of the overall quality of a nation and the establishment of a modern civil society based on human dignity and autonomy. (Liu Wujun 2001:100)

This argument is aligned with a new trend, which emerged in the 2000s, to portray rural-urban migrants both as victims of injustice and prejudice and as heroes of development (Jacka 2006:47). As migration became associated with modernization, it was suddenly something to boast about in the competition of cities and regions. Several authors from Shenzhen, a city created and populated by outside migrants, described Cantonese culture as a "culture of migration" (Liu Zhishan 2003; Fu Tengxiao 2003). These writers link the migrant Hakka population and the seafaring merchants of the Tang and Ming with the overseas workers of the nineteenth and early twentieth centuries and the skilled and unskilled internal migrants that have flocked to the province—especially to Shenzhen—since the 1980s. This historic "culture of migration," they argue, advances Shenzhen's modernization because it carries a pioneering, innovative, and creative spirit. According to Liu Zhishan, it has five distinguishing characteristics: a strong entrepreneurial mentality, an innovative and competitive spirit, respect for time and efficiency, creativity and a pursuit of pleasure and happiness, and independence (Liu Zhishan 2003:266–69). It is easy to see that these qualities, which are supposed to set the Shenzhen person positively apart from people in other regions, are the very qualities of the "modern person" discussed earlier. But, more than other sources, Liu links attributes such as the liberation and freedom of the self and the pursuit of pleasure to the ideal of the modern person (ibid.:300–304). This positive spin on individualism and on the creation of a civil society (ibid.:305–7) suggests that while the picture Liu draws is undoubtedly that of the ideal neoliberal subject, his vision includes some elements of political liberalism and draws inspiration from the "creative class" and "bourgeois bohemians" policy fads. Read against the background of southern regionalism in China, these arguments for a mobility-centered, outward-looking view of Chinese history, in which China is the active center and not the passive periphery, also rewrite the history of the South and Guangdong in particular in a way that brings them closer to the West.

Do rural migrants themselves feel modern? Most scholarly accounts, from Solinger (1991) to Jacka (2006), focus on how they are seen and treated as the embodiment of "low quality" and backwardness in cities. But the higher status, better economic position, official celebration, and sometimes cooptation of migrants who returned to their home villages (X. Liu 1997; Murphy 2002) makes them likely to identify with their "modern" designation to some extent. Yan Hairong (2006:227) writes about migrant maids in Peking who self-consciously discuss their need and desire for self-development, manifested, for example, in the realization that the petty embezzlement of shopping money that they used to practice is morally wrong. In a number of other studies, migrant women responding to questions about their motivations to come to the city directly reproduce the state's discourse of civilization in asserting the improvement of their "quality":

Beijing is China's cultural center, its political heart, so coming out is a way of experiencing that [and] gaining knowledge. (Gaetano 2004:70).

Migrant work increases our exposure, so that we talk more politely and we become wiser. (Fan 2004: 197).

[To migrant maids,] the differences between city and countryside in terms of civilization and ignorance, and the differences among people in terms of beauty and ugliness, are all fully exposed. . . . Peasants who've been locked away for thousands of years at long last have the opportunity to go to the outside world. Through struggle and hard work they are changing their lives. (Mian Xiaohong 2004:293)

My spare time is rich and colourful. . . . I clip the important articles [from newspapers], copy all the elegant phrases, and write them in my diary. . . .

I like learning English . . . watching the national news every day is a must for me. . . . On my days off, I like to take a camera to Beijing's tourist sites and go sightseeing.[9] (Wang Xiangfen 2004:296)

As Pun Ngai (1999:16) writes, popular fiction and reportage depict young rural women who go to the cities not only as trailblazers of modernity but also as the "modern young working woman who challenges traditional sexual relations and takes on an active role." The soap opera *Nannies for Foreigners* (2001) makes the same point (Lee 2006). In it, rural migrant women and laid-off urban women become cosmopolitans at middle age, with access to new opportunities for entrepreneurship and travel when they work as maids for expatriates and learn about modernity. The series turns "three unemployed and seemingly unemployable women into the Cinderellas of China's millennial capitalism" (Lee 2006:511). Employment in the households of foreigners represents, in addition to the real mobility of the migrant maid, a vicarious mobility resembling studying or working abroad. It "doubles as a kind of apprenticeship that grants more direct access to the essence of being global than does employment in a foreign firm or joint venture" (ibid.:516).

Some women migrants, like the bar hostesses studied by Tiantian Zheng (2004), actively cast themselves as modern and ridicule the "backward" urbanites who look down on them: "Who is better in this society? . . . Let's see who can earn more money and be more modern! Look at those urban laid-off workers, so pathetic and poor. We are much better than them" (T. Zheng 2004:80). While most female migrants continue to be constrained by traditional gender roles, and few become the successful entrepreneurs touted in the press, there is a consensus among researchers (see Gaetano and Jacka 2004; Jacka 2006) that they do generally see the city as "a classroom . . . that teaches about modern life" (Gaetano 2004:68) and, though its lessons are often bitter, makes them superior to their backward and feudal nonmigrant village peers (Fan 2004:197).

Tourists into Citizens

The above comment by migrant maid Wang Xiangfen places photographing scenic sites as a civilizing activity next to reading newspapers and watching the news. The dictum that "tourism synthesizes material civilization and spiritual civilization" first appeared in the State Council's 1981 resolution on developing tourism (*Renmin Ribao* 1981). "Constructing a socialist spiritual civilization" has been the government's framework for achieving a desirable citizenry since the early years of reform and has undergone some modifications in the process. The government body currently in charge of constructing spiritual civilization, the Spiritual Civilization Construction Guiding Committee (established in 1997 and led by the head of the Propaganda Department of the CCP Central Committee) has three main tasks: (1) constructing minors' moral thinking (*weichengnianren sixiang daode jianshe*); (2) managing patriotic education; and (3) strengthening and improving the thought and political education of university students.[10] But references to spiritual civilization entail a much broader range of sometimes contradictory, "socialist," traditional, and "modern" elements and rhetoric. Mixed together are political desiderata such as love of the Fatherland and the Party; "traditional" virtues such as industry, frugality, filiality, respect for elders, and so on; and a modern, scientific, open-minded, and entrepreneurial outlook. Spiritual civilization is supposed to be manifested in "healthy" activities and preferences, such as pursuit of education, "culture," and sports, and the forswearing of superstition, gambling, promiscuity, and heresy.[11] Spiritual civilization is achieved primarily through eugenics and education, but particular forms of consumption can stimulate the formation of a productive and modern subject—one endowed with "qualities compatible with the principles of market economy, such as competitiveness, and adaptability to the requirements" of a neoliberal economy rather than a wanton and wasteful one (Barabantseva 2005, chaps. 4 and 6).

In the 1980s, tourism's inclusion in discussions of spiritual civilization was in the context of underlining the importance of being hospitable to foreign tourists while displaying the superiority of socialist civilization (Li Jinghua 1982). As late as the mid-1990s, when incoming tourism was being intensively developed, public commentary on whether domestic tourism was a good or bad thing was still divergent:

One opinion holds that domestic tourism helps foster patriotism and can effectively help people broaden their horizons; another opinion holds that tourism at public expense, which accounts for most of domestic tourism, is a grave manifestation of impropriety (*bu zheng zhi feng*) and has to be suppressed. This was the main reason for the "three don'ts" (don't support, don't promote, don't oppose) policy towards domestic tourism in the early eighties. (Long and Ding 1994:35)

Zhang Guangrui, an influential researcher of tourism, belonged to the first group. Tourism "is an important element of spiritual civilization construction" that "helps raise the quality of the people and the quality of life," he wrote (1992). The journalist who praised peasants for "galloping into the great wave of tourism" was also in this group:

> This generation of young peasants has some cultural knowledge; in their mentality, there is more enterprising spirit and more readiness to go out and get things done. By touring other places, they increase their knowledge; along the touring route, they learn from experiences of getting rich and can also get to know the conditions of the market. (Zeng 1995)

In other words, by being tourists—like migrating to cities for work—peasants can become subjects better suited for the new ideals of the market. More generally, a 1995 article in the journal *Tourism Culture* argued that domestic tourism was beneficial in that it helped economic development, created jobs, helped "guide people toward correct consumption," and developed their patriotic fervor (Hong Jun 1995).

Once the government decided to promote domestic tourism, its advocates were legitimized. It was now official orthodoxy that—as Wei Xiaoan (2001:271), head of the Planning Department of the National Tourism Administration, wrote—"the culture of tourism . . . aids society's development and change." First of all, it fostered a modern consumer mentality:

> Since reform and opening . . . traditional, backward consumer mentality (i.e., high savings, low consumption) has been greatly challenged; new, modern consumer mentality has gradually gained acceptance. But the roots of traditional consumer mentality run deep. . . . The fact that holiday travel has become a growth area of the economy has . . . accelerated the transformation of consumer mentality. (Liu Zhaoping 2001:182)

Second, tourism was central to the development of "leisure culture," a concept whose discussion had begun somewhat earlier, in 1995, when China moved to a five-day work week. At that point, the government financed a number of research projects and publications extolling the "social and cultural value" of leisure as an "important stage in the social evolution of mankind" (Ma Huidi 2004b:4–5).[12] For example, Zhang Hong-yan, a professor of urban studies at Nanjing University, declared that leisure culture was a sign of "civilizational evolution" (*wenhua jinhua*; Chen Linhui 1995).

Economist He Wei justified the efforts devoted to studying leisure in this way:

> When we talk about leisure we are not advocating eating, drinking, and making merry, but rather achieving in this way a healthy, civilized life and cultivating the "highly civilized person" (Marx). In the course of leisure activities, people can . . . increase their knowledge and thus get patriotic education, improve their cultural quality, and assist the construction of spiritual civilization. (Quoted in Sun Yinglan 1996)

Liu Fei, a researcher of tourism, wrote:

> Currently, we have two main ways of improving national quality: one is improving the nation's physical quality and moral rectitude through economic development, the other is improving the nation's knowledge base and cultural quality through . . . education. The development of domestic tourism benefits the improvement of national quality. (Liu Fei 1998:62)

Tourism both "improves the physical quality of tourists" and "lets tourists experience dynamic learning of scientific and technological knowledge and exchange of information. . . . [It] provides them with more new ideas, which is the foundation of improving national quality (ibid.:62).

According to Zhu, Zhu, and Wu (2004), tourism "improves the quality of labor" by letting people "enjoy natural landscapes and immerse themselves in historic culture and modern civilization." As the English abstract of their article states, "the execution of Tour Golden Policy [i.e., the introduction of three Golden Weeks] and the development of holiday economy developed socialistic productivity, enforced the total capability of [the state] and improved our living standard" (ibid, 2004:72). This combination of the socialist idea of mass-bettering tourism with the ideology of modernization through consumption is an idiosyncrasy that is perhaps typical of contemporary China, where "the social revolution called for by the 'Internationale' is reoriented toward self-development" (Yan 2006:236).[13]

The final volume of *Zhongguo Xueren Xiuxian Yanjiu Zhongshu* (Leisure research by Chinese scholars) calls on the state to "make leisure education part of the construction of spiritual civilization" (Ma Huidi 2004b:265) so that "the broad masses learn to use leisure intelligently and create scientific, healthy and civilized leisure lifestyles with the aim of jointly creating a happy life and a beautiful future" (Ma Huidi 2004a:4). This phrasing echoes goals formulated by several Chinese officials at the first national academic conference on leisure in 2002 concerning the suppression of "unhealthy lifestyles." They called for the "propagation of correct notions of leisure" in order to "lead the masses to plan their leisure and cultural lives in a scientific, healthy, and reasonable manner" (Ma 2004b:218–19). This was the subject of a State Council resolution back in 2000, when it proposed that the Central Television and Radio run special programs to "correctly guide (*zhengque yindao*) tourist behaviour."[14]

As for overseas tourism, it is often perceived less as a tool of education than as a manifestation of "China's growing overall national strength" (Wei Xiaoan n.d.). Tourists themselves are unlikely to be directly influenced by this discourse, but, as elsewhere, they perceive travel as a quintessentially modern experience—whether as mainstream group tourists or as backpackers. In chapter 2, we have seen how backpackers explicitly reflect on the modern nature of their pursuit even as they eschew scenic spots. As for group tourists who visit scenic spots and theme parks, their expectation for the site/sight to have been "developed" (*kaifa*) is rather more explicit than that of Western tourists, who tend to value "authenticity" and would prefer to forget the hardware that goes into "staging" it for their benefit (MacCannell 1976; see Nyíri 2006a). The experience of the modern—accommodation, infrastructure, or entertainment—appears as an explicitly articulated central desire in mainstream Chinese tourism, reflected in the popularity of theme parks, the bounded and performative nature of sites that are based on nature or tradition, and the preference for glass-and-marble hotels. Even the experience of "eco-tourism" has to do with modernity, rather than just the protection of nature. As Wei Xiaoan (2003b:398) notes, tourists are willing to obey no-littering and no-smoking rules in "green" scenic spots, which they would consider a nuisance in other areas, because "they feel like they have also improved their own quality in the process." The refurbishment of Songpan (see chapter 3), involving the widening and repaving of public spaces in the urban style, the rebuilding of the town wall, and the erection of patriotic statuary and neon lighting, succeeded in attracting more Chinese tourist groups even though the town is marketed as "old."

Conversely, Chinese tourists in Europe, which they visit in pursuit of cultural tradition but also capitalist modernity, invariably express their frustration at the lack of the latter (see survey by Schwandner and Gu 2005). In a conversation in 2001, Zhao, a Chinese tour guide in Berlin, said that most of her Chinese customers are "a bit disappointed" at the lack of skyscrapers and broad avenues and find Berlin "backward" compared to Shanghai or even Hangzhou. Meng, a Chinese lecturer at a Berlin university, concurred: "Here the people are so proud of the KaDeWe, the big department store. But in China, a big restaurant can be larger than that." Speaking to a friend on the phone after returning to Peking from Sydney, another tourist commented: "Still, our capital looks more like a real capital. Sydney is just like a big village." In places where tourists are not expecting to find modernity, their reactions may be self-satisfied rather than disappointed. A young woman who went to Vietnam with the Hefei City Theoretical Studies Youth Group posted her impressions on a blog: "After arriving in Hanoi, my first impression was that it was crowded and messy, lacking the grandeur and luxury of our capital Peking. There are very few tall buildings in Hanoi." She added that while her native Hefei, a provincial capital, is full of supermarkets, the shops in Hanoi "are all just like the mom-and-pop groceries that line the streets of an average county town back home" (Wanshui Yifang 2006).[15] Antonella Diana describes her trip to Muang Sing in Laos with a young ethnic Dai woman from the village of Mengman, across the border in China. Despite the fact that she belonged to the same ethnic group as people in Muang Sing, and that her parents had friends and relatives in Muang Sing, the young woman's reaction was very similar to that of her Hefei peers:

"This place looks so underdeveloped (Ch. *Luohou*) and poor (Ch. *Qiong*). There is nothing here! . . . In Mengman, the houses of us Dai are much bigger and look nicer." . . . In her conceptualization China was associated with cultivated, urbanized and highly humanized/civilized values, whereas Laos was connoted as uncultivated, rural and savage. Yi Oi's remarks on Laos' lack of development were projected into a general criticism of Lao people's laziness, backwardness, and of the Lao government's inability to carry out good policies for its citizens. She came to the conclusion that Lao people need to *kaifa* (develop) their land to improve their lives. And the Chinese could assist them in this necessary endeavour.[16] (Diana forthcoming)

Moreover, Yi Oi felt that the ecotourism project promoted in Muang Sing for Western tourists was inferior to the minority theme parks she was familiar with in China. This observation was based on the fact that, although in this situation Yi Oi was a tourist, she was familiar with tourism development from being on the receiving side of ethnic tourism in China. If tourism's impact on tourists was initially the subject of some debate, then, as noted early on by Oakes (1998), its effect on rural recipients has been regarded as beneficial since the early days. Authors pointed out early on that beyond the economic growth tourism can bring, it also "promotes social progress, enriches culture, raises the quality of life, [and] heightens the people's patriotic enthusiasm" (Hu Shanfeng 1996). Similar to the effects of rural-urban migration, "through imitation and learning [from tourists], the residents of scenic areas can improve and elevate their manners and politeness, speech and bearing, habits of hygiene, thinking and outlook" (Jin Hua 1994).

Sipsongpanna in Yunnan Province is one of the earliest-developed tourist areas of China's minority-inhabited western regions. An author from the prefectural Party School, writing in 1997, credits tourism with the fact that "the masses of many minorities have given up old ways and hoary customs, 'jumped into the sea' to engage in trade, opened song-and-dance restaurants with ethnic flavour, sell ethnic crafts and so on" (Chen Ailing 1997:26). Among the negative impacts of tourism, Chen mentions tourists who fell prey to unscrupulous entrepreneurs, but nothing related to the lives of the locals.

In the 2000s, an increasing number of authors have warned against "excessive modernization" and the possible "collapse and dissolution of local culture, constituting a serious loss to the precious cultural wealth of the Chinese nation" (Li Zhushun 2003:50). They include not only anthropologists but also high priests of tourism development such as Wei Xiaoan. In the mid-2000s, a number of voices began calling for stronger protection of monuments in the name of authenticity. Indicating that these calls have reached the center of power, *Guangming Ribao*, the

Party's ideological mouthpiece, called for greater protection not only of monuments but also of their environments. True to its roots, *Guangming* used the former residences of Mao Zedong and Zhou Enlai as examples: "though the surroundings have been beautified," it observed, "there is nothing left of the environment in which the arduous struggle of those days took place" (*Guangming Ribao* 2007).[17]

Moreover, some recent provincial tourism plans have sections about controlling the social impact of tourism. For example, the Hubei Province Tourism Development Master Plan deals extensively with the negative impacts of tourism on villages, pointing out that it can lead to a "weakening of social and family cohesion" and "traditional social mores," as well as to resentment and crime among locals exposed to the high-spending lifestyles of tourists (Hubei and Sun Yat-sen 2003:158). Yet the same plan's chapter on the Enshi Tujia Autonomous Prefecture, which has a poverty-alleviation-through-tourism project, states categorically that tourism "has changed . . . some outdated, backward beliefs" in the area, "because in an exchange between cultures, the new and advanced culture will always replace the old and backward" (ibid.:778). Most authors continue to maintain that "the penetration of scientific management knowledge and modern concepts will have an immeasurable impact on local culture" and "the development of the tourism industry helps raise the civilization level (*wenming de chengdu*) of poor regions" (Li Zhushun 2003:49). As Wei Xiaoan comments,

In a way, rich people and foreigners want to see places as Nature-made zoos: don't touch your environment, don't touch your culture; leave it for us to go and look at at our leisure. If so, are we still to have local development? . . . If development is the ultimate point,[18] then in the end, all the different views and opinions [on tourism] must come together on the point of development. (Wei Xiaoan 2003a)

Elsewhere, Wei cautions against an "infatuation" with and "wholesale acceptance" of local cultural tradition, lest it "feed feudal superstition" and "impede renewal" (ibid.:423).

To what extent is this view of tourism internalized by tourees? Recent research at locations that are in the early stages of the tourism boom confirms Oakes's earlier finding that locals, especially the younger and more urbane ones, positively view the spatial and cultural changes brought by tourism (Hillman 2003; Kang 2005; Nyíri 2006a). For example, an ethnic Bai manager of a hotel in Dali remarked: "Tourism development will ameliorate Dali's backward face . . . and change traditional backward perspectives" (Notar 2006:115). Writing about rural Tibetans in the Songpan area, Toni Huber noted:

> As far as decline or loss of religious tradition goes, I found nobody in Shar khog [i.e., the Songpan area] who expressed the slightest regret about this fact, although they did express regret about a lot of other things that happened as a result of recent Chinese rule. . . . [M]any Shar ba [local Tibetans] were happy to derive extra income from various forms of tourism related service industries, which are by no means monopolized by Han [ethnic Chinese] or Hui [Muslims].[19] (Huber 2006:19–21)

Similarly, a Tibetan hotel owner supported changing the name of Zhongdian to Shangrila because of the tourist boom that it ignited (Kolås 2007:112–13). Like the majority of local Tibetans, he did not appear in the least concerned that the new name, drawn from an American novel, was erasing the cultural identity of the place.[20] In fact, I encountered the most dissatisfaction in places, such as Hongcun in Anhui, where the local government or tourism contractor forced residents (in this case, because of the World Cultural Heritage designation) to keep to "traditional" building materials and styles, preventing them from building "modern" new houses. Chen Wei (2006) and Antonella Diana (personal communication) encountered similar grievances, respectively, in the Danxia Mountains Scenic Area of Guangdong and in the Dai Nationality Park in Sipsongpanna.

Positive opinions about tourism development prevail even where there are grievances about the division of income that result from it, such as complaints against scenic site managers or tour guides who prevent or discourage tourists from patronizing local villagers (Chen Wei 2006), or against the local government for expropriating farmers' land plots without adequate compensation (Notar 2006). In localities that went through the tourism boom earlier and now have declining income growth, such as Sipsongpanna Prefecture, the local opinions of tourism are mixed (e.g., Duan and Yang 2001). Yet even here, young ethnic Dai women, who had worked as guides at a minority theme park and a Chinese-run casino across the border in Burma, talked enthusiastically about their jobs, seeing themselves not only as part as a modern and developed nation, but also as contributors to the developing process. . . . For Yi Keao, working at the "minority park" was a way to bring development (Ch. *fazhan*), to the impoverished border areas of the country. As she put it: "the village where I worked was quite poor before the park was established. There was nothing. After we started promoting tourism, the area became increasingly developed and local people enjoyed better lives.". . . [T]he two girls were reaching a multifold [sic] goal at once: improving their *suzhi* by separating themselves from low farming status, relieving their own homeland from poverty, and contributing to construct a modern nation (Diana forthcoming).

The young Dai informants, like the Tibetan ones, expressed no regret at the loss of religious tradition; on the contrary, one of them refused to engage in the customary circumambulation of a pilgrimage site "as she was worried that her Chinese companions might interpret it as an expression of superstition (Ch. *mixin*)," associated with "low-quality" rural people (ibid.).

Similarly, when talking about the benefits of tourism, respondents in Songpan emphasized to me not the increased prosperity it brought but how it had improved the "quality" (*suzhi*) of the people. Even a businesswoman who had earlier criticized the government's plans now pointed out that in the evenings people gathered in the new square in front of the government building to listen to music or dance. This, she said, showed that the changes had "improved their bodily and spiritual health." Like Hillman's (2003:185) respondents in Zhongdian/Shangrila, she was also proud of the dances and songs "minorities" performed at a tourist festival and felt that, as a result, locals appreciate their culture more. This may be the case even where locals regard the dances performed for tourists as inauthentic and sometimes make fun of them (Kolås (2007:124).

Migrants into Patriots

Since 1978, Chinese leaders have repeatedly reaffirmed that they see overseas Chinese as an important force of China's "socialist modernization" and in "developing international friendships"[21] (see Deng 1990; Jiang Zemin1999; Hu 2004, quoted in Cheng 2005:19); in other words, as sources or conduits of investment, technological innovation, and behind-the-scenes diplomacy. As is well known, overseas Chinese capital has been successfully mobilized to invest in China through economic opportunities and incentives as well as through the government's efforts cultivating and honoring overseas Chinese entrepreneurs, although to what extent such investments are based on economic rationality rather than patriotic philanthropy has been the subject of debates (see, e.g., Young and Shih 2004). In 2006, Fuqing Municipality in Fujian Province, an important sending area both historically and today, honored 162 "overseas worthies" for contributing more than one million yuan to public amenities (such as education and infrastructure). In addition to the government decoration, the "worthies" received eulogies such as this in the local press:

> Overall, overseas Fuqing folk, carrying on the outstanding tradition of the sons and grandsons of the Yellow Emperor and the Emperor Yan, through their extraordinary wisdom and amazing willpower, fighting to the bitter end with thrift and hard work, struggling tenaciously and continuously developing ever higher, have become a crack force in today's globalised economy and an important force enjoying great prestige in the overseas Chinese world. (*Shijie Rongyin* 2006)

Such hyperbole is by no means unusual. Six years earlier, another commentary in the local paper, *Fuqing Shibao*, insisted that Fuqing had become a famous *qiaoxiang* not just because it had numerous migrants but because they were all patriotic. Fuqingers were "industrious, frugal, and rich in the pioneering, fighting spirit" (*qinlao, pushi qie fu yu kaishi pinbo jingshen*); their determination and vitality had left "courageous traces" around the globe; despite their outstanding achievements wherever they were, they wanted to repay the homeland. "This indeed is the untiring national spirit of the descendants of the Yellow Emperor and Emperor Yan; this indeed is the old adage that Fuqing compatriots sojourning abroad steadfastly cling to: 'May a tree grow a thousand feet tall, it still will not forget its root!'" (*Shijie Rongyin* 2000b). Fuqingers abroad wanted to make their homeland "march in pace with the times; join the mainstream of the world" (*Shijie Rongyin* 2000b).

Donations and investment from overseas Chinese have been instrumental in two of the most important current public projects in Fuqing: the construction of the Jiangyin deep sea port, which the government hopes will revitalize the local economy, and the Min River regulation project. For the latter, Fuqing home-county associations in Indonesia alone raised 200 million yuan in the first stage of the project (*Shijie Rongyin* 2000a). The donation drive for the former was spearheaded by an elderly Indonesian tycoon, Lin Wenjing, who announced that he was "devoting the energies of his lifetime to the economic development of the homeland and the construction of the port" (Chen Renjie 2006). Altogether, overseas Chinese are reported to have donated over 1.4 billion yuan, invested in around 900 businesses, and brought more than $4 billion in foreign investment to Fuqing (Lin Qiuming 2006).

But overseas Chinese—or their parents or grandparents—left China before the Communists came to power, and thus their choice to emigrate could be put down to the corrupt and exploitative nature of the "old regime." "Since the people in the old China could hardly earn a living, some of them were compelled to cross the seas and work as coolies abroad" (*Peking Review* 3 [1978]:14–16). Those who chose to leave "socialist" China were initially regarded in a more ambiguous fashion. In the 1980s, students who did not return from their studies overseas were sometimes criticized as unpatriotic, and their host countries as brain plunderers (Zhuang Guotu 2000:51n.21). After the Tiananmen massacre, the portrayal of what the Chinese press had dubbed emigration fever was particularly ambivalent. Hu and Zhang (1988), still largely following the conventions of the so-called scar literature that emerged after the Cultural Revolution, write about those deciding to study abroad as making painful decisions in the context of their and their parents' bitter experiences during the Cultural Revolution and portray them as suffering from a perpetual longing for their homes and families. They write that "those who did not return after completing their terms are not necessarily unpatriotic," but claim that the number of those who plan to stay for the long term and obtain "green cards" is "very small" (Hu and Zhang 1988:32). At the same time, in an article about "migration fever," Zhang Zhiye (1990) uses the parable of a Mongolian horse that would rather die than live in a foreign land. According to Zhang Zhiye (1990:8), the students abroad have "brought back to the old country . . . civilization and riches that make people envious, but [also] stories that make people sad." Bai Yun and Hong Xiao (1989) write with disapproval of those students who go abroad to make money or "be free" rather than to seek knowledge, and describe in lurid detail the vicissitudes of Chinese students in Japan who "trade their dignity for riches" by becoming hostesses, collecting rubbish, or, worse, "selling out" to foreign intelligence agencies. Salacious stories focusing on female students "selling their bodies for a green card," and later about new migrants who squandered their hard-earned money in brothels and casinos, such as Li Zhongqiang's *Tearful Danube: Chinese in Hungary* (1993), continued coming out into the 1990s.

Nonetheless, after the government's announcement of its new "support study abroad, promote return, [uphold] freedom of movement" policy in 1992, accounts of students and former students abroad became more positive, emphasizing the contributions they can make to China by being abroad and downplaying the problem of brain drain (see Zweig and Chung 2004). Scholar-officials writing on the subject, like Cheng Xi (of the Qiaolian's Institute of Overseas Chinese History) and Zhu Huiling (head of division at the national Qiaoban), emphasize the contributions graduates can make to China being abroad and either evade the problem of brain drain (Zhu Huiling 1995), or judge that its negative effects are outweighed by the positive sides (Cheng Xi 1999). Cheng, for example, argues that a graduate who now works at a Paris bank and has signed over one hundred deals with China would not have been able to make such an impact had he returned to China. Counting Chinese graduates who are professors at American, Japanese, and Australian universities or executives of successful Internet companies is part of the media discourse about the rise of China. Zhuang Guotu, one of China's most respected academic specialists of overseas Chinese studies, writes: "It is well-known in China that perhaps 25-30% of first-level [i.e., top] American scientists are Chinese" (Zhuang 2000:46).

Around the same time, stories praising Chinese contract workers abroad also began to appear. Cao Peng (1992) wrote that Chinese laborers abroad "made a good name for themselves in the international labor market through their uniquely Chinese industry, hardiness, kindness, respect for the law and morality." He called for the further liberalization of labor export rules and wrote that the "great army of Chinese labor is moving from here toward the world, creating an even better tomorrow with their own two hands." More recently, the Party's central newspaper, *People's Daily*, praised peasants from Changxing County, Zhejiang Province, for going to Japan, the United States, and Singapore on work contracts. "In addition to bringing back more than 10 million US dollars in foreign currency," the paper wrote, they "brought back advanced technology and foreign investors" (Fang and Kong 2003). Similar phrasing was used in a report on villagers from Hebei Province working in the United States, Japan, Korea, and Israel: "Transnational work has not only brought in abundant revenue; it has also brought in advanced thinking and management methods" (Wang and Liu 2003).

In the late 1990s, when the focus on overseas Chinese work shifted to recent migrants who were seen as more educated and more committed to ties with China, the government constructed a new discourse on new migrants as pioneers of modernization both at home and abroad. The State Council's 1996 Opinion on Stepping up New Migrant Work declared that "new migrants . . . will become a backbone of forces friendly to us in America and some other developed Western countries." Therefore,

strengthening new migrant work has important realistic meaning and deep-going, far-reaching significance for promoting our country's modernizing construction, implementing the unification of the motherland, expanding our country's influence and developing our country's relations with the countries of residence. (Shanghai New Migrants Research Project Team 1997)

Much of the focus in "new migrant work" has been on current and former students who are seen as capable of bringing advanced technology and research to China (see Zweig and Chung 2004). Thus, in North America and Australia, it is high-tech entrepreneurs that the press usually singles out for portrayal as successful new migrants. For example, a Chinese-language magazine published in Budapest describes Howard Li, a New York–based businessman, in this way:

The new century is the century of the knowledge economy. Howard Li has included the Web in his vision. . . . The backbone of a worldwide Web-based goods exchange with hubs in New York and Hong Kong has already been formed. . . . By now, his joint and exclusive ventures in China extend over more than 30 provinces, cities, and regions. He has helped Chinese goods conquer (*jinjun*) the American market. . . . He has injected funds from abroad into China in order to promote the economic construction of the motherland. . . . He is also Chairman of the Asian-American Entrepreneurs Association, Honorary General Advisor of the New York Federation of Chinese Associations, and holder of forty or fifty other honours.[22]

At the same time, the government spares no effort in cultivating relations with migrant entrepreneurs, often from rural backgrounds and with modest education. Stories about new migrants in Latin America and Europe emphasize the rapid rise of their social status—often in stark contrast with stories in the European media, which tend to depict Chinese migrants as criminals or victims. One article characterizes Fujianese migrants in Argentina in three ways: "Entrepreneurial pioneers who accumulated capital to raise up their families from labour to supermarket ownership; path breakers of international business; harbingers of the Chinese race's culture."[23] Another article is entitled "Private Chinese businessmen on Africa gold rush: struggling to set up business, daring to think, daring to act."[24] A third article quotes Shi Yuegen, the Chinese consul in France, as dismissing negative French media reports about Chinese shopkeepers by saying that they have made "an enormous contribution to the local economy through their untiring labour and have also contributed to Chinese-French friendship—this is recognized by both countries' governments and the local people" (China News Agency 2007). The statement reveals considerable disregard for the negative reporting to which Shi was supposedly responding. A fourth credits Zhang Xianzhang, a former pig farmer who migrated to Czechoslovakia in 1992, with the improbable feat of introducing the idea of pig farming there. He eventually moved his business to the United States because of the cold Czech climate, and as a result "the Czechs still have to eat imported pork" while Zhang's pig business prospers in the United States (Fu Xiaobo 1995). The reports relish depicting migrants as cosmopolitan globetrotters who juggle their businesses in various countries at a breakneck speed. An interview with Wang Jiazhu, an entrepreneur from Wenzhou whose latest venture was the founding of a wholesale center called "Nordic Chinatown" in Finland, noted that during the hour he was talking to the journalist, Wang received "17 phone calls: one from North Korea, three from the Ukraine, four from Hungary, four from Finland, five from Russia" (He Yifan 2007).

Local governments with few economic resources that have experienced a surge of migration, such as rural Mingxi in the mountainous interior of Fujian Province, made it clear that they considered emigration a desirable tool of development before it became fashionable in Western development discourse:

> The Mingxi county party committee and government attach great importance to the work on labor export and the new migrants. They express a clear-cut stand of developing the ideology and strategic aim of "increasing the pace of labour export to construct a rising overseas Chinese area (*qiaoxiang*) in the interior of Fujian." Every year, the county calls several meetings . . . sparing no effort to support and promote in all possible ways the export of labour. To solve worries of domestic attachment among people leaving the county, the county has decided to let peasants keep their leased land. . . . [Upon their return, they and their dependants] are treated as returned overseas Chinese (*guiqiao*) and overseas Chinese dependants, and receive political privileges, support in production, care in life, and emotional encouragement. Every year at Chinese New Year, the government intensifies the contact with migrants, promotes amiable feelings between migrants and fellow villagers and stimulates the sentiment of migrants to love the fatherland and local community by paying family visits . . . and other methods. Simultaneously, the government vigorously adopts a range of preferential policies to accommodate, guide and assist returned migrant investors. (*Fujian Qiaobao*, 5 November 1999, 1; quoted in Pieke et al. 2004)

The government has organized an "exit service center" providing peasants with a visa application service, information on job opportunities, legal issues, and assistance with purchasing airline tickets. Vocational training classes are offered on matters relevant to would-be migrants such as sewing, cooking, computer skills, and trading; legal and cultural knowledge about foreign countries; and the Russian and English languages. Finally, the local government has relaxed its policies under which state-owned commercial banks and village credit cooperatives may provide mortgage loans or other types of loans to would-be migrants.[25]

All of this shows that the authorities in Mingxi are self-consciously engaged in creating their own "overseas Chinese resources" (*qiaowu ziyuan*) modeled on more prosperous old overseas Chinese areas such as Fuqing. In this, they are supported by the prefectural authorities of Sanming, which internally coined the slogan "creating emigrants" (*chuang-*

zao yimin).[26] Newspaper articles describe migrants from rural Mingxi County as playing "an important role in the construction of the homeland" (Zhang Zhongbin 1997). Villages honor them in symbolic acts such as a plaque that names 156 migrants as examples of patriotic citizens, and the ceremonial gate (described in greater detail in chapter 1), with the inscription "Opening the door to [ac]quire wealth in Europe by migrating and establishing business there; building the road to create glory in [the] native place by highlighting patriotism and solidarity here" (Li Minghuan 2005). The local political embrace of migration was experienced by 53 of 65 migrant families we surveyed in a Mingxi County village in 2000: local or county officials dropped by, sent flowers, helped migrant dependants solve problems, and even invited them to attend seminars (Pieke et al. 2004).[27] An article written by police officials of Sanming Prefecture, to which Mingxi belongs, proudly declares that migrants from Mingxi, thanks to "the highlander spirit of enduring hardship and working hard, [have] broken the paradigm that restricted the Chinese in Europe to the catering trade; many of them opened factories and companies, becoming the bosses of foreigners, some even turned into transnational entrepreneurs" (Wu and Ge 2000:70). They sympathetically describe rural migration brokers, known as snakeheads, as providing an indispensable service that even official agencies sometimes require. Instead of treating recruitment as the first step of smuggling or trafficking as their Western counterparts tend to do, their choice of words is that many villagers in Mingxi "go abroad to seek development with the encouragement [of] 'snakeheads.'"[28] Just like Wang and Li's article (1996) celebrating the achievements of migrant maids from Anhui in Peking (Jacka 2006:51), the article by Wu and Ge does not mention that these migrants, as small-scale traders in Hungary or workers in garment workshops in Italy where most arrive illegally, live near the bottom of the social hierarchies and often have difficulties making ends meet.

Faced with pressure from the West after highly publicized deaths of illegal Chinese migrants—notably the wrecking of the *Golden Venture* in New York Harbor in 1993 and the discovery of fifty-eight dead bodies in a container shipped to Dover in 2000—the central government has criticized some local leading cadres for thinking that "no matter by what means, the more people go abroad the better, since they see going abroad as a way for local people to leave poverty behind," and threatened to put in place a system of personal responsibility for cadres on whose territory large-scale illegal emigration occurs.[29] Yet at the same time, China has a policy of helping those illegal emigrants abroad who have a chance to regularize their status by replacing their passports.[30]

Overall, in just over two decades after 1978, the official view of migrants turned from treacherous to tolerated but ideologically suspect to useful and patriotic. The transition has been linked to government policy, but was also aided by an explosion of popular-culture accounts of migrants, both in press and on screen. The Qiaoban's injunction to promote migrants' image in the media would not have achieved the success it did if not for the popularity that the new migrant topic has enjoyed following the bestselling *The Chinese Woman of Manhattan (Manhadun de Zhongguo nüren)*, published in 1991, and the soap opera *Pekingers in New York* that is based on it. *Pekingers in New York* was so successful that it generated a new popular genre of "new migrant literature" and a number of copycat television serials. One example of that literature, *Studying in America* by Qian Ning, the son of then Foreign Minister Qian Qichen, reportedly sold over 300,000 copies after its publication in 1996 (Qian 2002:viii).

In stories that are set in the West, Chinese migrants appear in locations that were once beacons of modernity but have now run out of steam and, in order to take the next step, need to be infused with the flexibility, industry, and vision of the global Chinese. For China today, global cities of the West have come to signify migrant success in a plethora of films, television dramas, and fiction. In turn, migrants in these accounts play the roles of both scouts and voyeurs for the nation, providing a continuous peep show accompanied by a commentary on foreign localities as backdrops for evolving ways of Chinese life (Sun 2002:67–111). In these books and films, Tokyo, Paris, Sydney, and New York are sites of an unfolding global Chinese modernity. This function shapes the visual presentation of the cities through "fetishistic uses of clichéd icons of speed, such as cars gliding noiselessly (and seemingly pollution-free) along the surface of highways; power-imposing bottom-up shots of city skylines; and energy, suggested by sweeping shots of multilevel highways" (ibid.:77).

The heroes of these stories, typically young and resourceful men, usually engage in struggles with local adversaries and, after being steeled through a series of humiliations as kitchen hands or street artists, eventually earn their esteem. Thus, in *Zouru Ouzhou* (Into Europe), a soap opera directed by Chen Kemin for Southeast Fujian Television in 1999, the male protagonist arrives in Paris in a torn T-shirt and without a penny. After a few months of rapid entrepreneurial success aided by prominent local overseas Chinese, he develops an ambitious construction project. "Ladies and gentlemen!" he announces to his French audience, pointing to the drawing of a building complex with pagoda-style roofs. "What will be different on the new map of Paris two years from now? The beautiful banks of the Seine will be full of Oriental splendor: the Chinatown Investment and Trade Centre!" The audience breaks into applause.

The significance of the "new Chinese" showing Paris—the symbolic center of Europe—the road to the next level of modernity is obvious to any Chinese viewer brought up on narratives of how imperialist Europe has both humiliated China and forced it to modernize. The Chinese state looms large in the narrative of the film, produced and aired by state broadcasters: the Chinese embassy provides support for the protagonist's project, while funding for it is secured from China.

Another type of narrative found in both reportage and soap operas is that of illegal migrants who fall victim to snakeheads and end up in slave-like labor or prostitution, or are murdered by gangsters. This narrative closely parallels the Western discourse of human trafficking, which became particularly popular in the mid-2000s and in which the victims of trafficking are often Asian. Indeed, the Chinese government has cooperated with United Nations agencies in combating human trafficking and received funding for several radio soap operas on the dangers of placing one's fate in the hands of smugglers.[31] The serial on the sorry plight of illegal Chinese migrants in Thailand, *Mori de tiantang* (Apocalypse in heaven) was aired around the world on the popular Phoenix satellite channel in 2007. It ends with the protagonists returning to happy lives in China. Yet this body of cultural production does not provide an alternative view to the narrative of migrants as pioneers of development. Rather, just as reporting on migrant criminality and migrant victimhood within China "lend[s] legitimacy to the role of the state in maintaining social order" (Jacka 2006:54), reporting on similar situations abroad legitimizes the state's management of overseas migration and its continued role in the lives of overseas Chinese communities.

Meanwhile, the image of the successful migrant remains highly popular. A random perusal of recent arrivals at the National Library in Peking in early 2005 yielded titles such as *Love at Harvard*[32] (Wang Zhengjun 2004), *An Ordinary Family's Path to Sending Their Child to Study Abroad*

(Song Zhida 2004), *Let Your Friend Be Truth: My Harvard Experience* (Yue Xiaodong 2004) and *My Family's Race to Cambridge* (Zhang and Du 2001), mentioned earlier in this book. The protagonists of these books are held up as models of successful education. In his preface to *My Harvard Experience*, psychologist Yue Xiaodong (2004:1) states that his book reflects on "how a person can grasp opportunities and create chances through individual efforts." The introduction to *My Family's Race to Cambridge*, by the chairman of the Chinese UNESCO Society, emphasizes that the story of Zhang Chi, who got his PhD from Cambridge at twenty-two, is the triumph of parental attention to education rather than of genius. The photo insert of the book shows Zhang as an "ordinary child, like any other." *An Ordinary Family's Path* is the most practically oriented of these books: it is a collection of e-mail exchanges and Web chats between a Chinese student at the University of Wales and his father in China, arranged by sections dealing with getting a job, finding friends, dealing with money, and so on. But among parents who want to know how to raise a successful child, Harvard has a unique status in the Chinese mythology of success, and every now and then a Chinese Harvard student achieves true stardom in the press. At the end of 2004, it was nineteen-year-old Tang Meijie who was thus profiled in a series of articles with titles like "What Does Her Success Tell Us?" and "Meijie Knocked at the Door of Harvard. Do You Want to Copy?" (Hulbert 2007). She was also asked by companies to advertise their products, approached by publishers to write her life story, and invited by a private school to join its board.

Another subgenre of stories, originating from *Pekingers in New York*, shows the male protagonist gradually losing his integrity and becoming a cynic as he is forced to employ immoral and even illegal means to stand his ground. Yet there is a sense that these steps are ultimately caused by the environment and sanctified by the fact that the desire for success is ultimately an altruistic one, driven by a sense of responsibility for family and homeland. The nationalistic tenor of the films and novels earns them official kudos for their patriotism even as they attract audiences with their lurid descriptions of sex, gambling, and crime. In 1992, the Chinese Writers' Association commended "new migrant literature" for possessing a "patriotic spirit" (*aiguo qinghuai*) (Barmé 1999:456–57n.116). Indeed, Geremie Barmé titled his description of the ways in which sex with foreigners has been fit into lowbrow production of patriotism "To Screw Foreigners Is Patriotic" (ibid.: 255–80). The author of a *Why Did We*

Go Abroad? published in 1997, intended his book to be overseas students' answer to the well-known nationalistic tract, *China Can Say No* (Yangge 1997, front flap).[33]

In stories from the developmental periphery (e.g., Eastern Europe, Africa, and Southeast Asia), Chinese migrants are cast in the more unambiguous role of harbingers of development. An article by two Chinese public security officials claims that the Burmese border town of Möng Yawng, "just a few years back [was] hardly more than a small village with a few straw huts," has become the "model zone for northern Burma's economic prosperity" thanks to tourism from China, the influx of Chinese trade, and the planting of fruit orchards and other cash crops by Chinese farmers to replace opium (Zhang and Zhang 2002). According to the official *Overseas Chinese Economic Yearbook*, "thanks to the efforts of the Chinese, Serbia experienced unprecedented economic prosperity" due to the increase in Chinese immigration under Milošević (*Huaren Jingji Nianjian* 2000–2001:360). An article in Paris-based *Ouzhou Shibao* (2004), entitled "Chinese migrants in Russia: Billionaires through hard toil, they hire majors as bodyguards," claims that "girls compete to marry Chinese migrants; authorities welcome Chinese investment."[34] The hero, Zhao, migrated to Russia in the early 1990s, and now owns sixteen lumber yards and thirteen trading companies, employs five hundred people, and has assets worth nearly 100 million yuan. Beyond these successes, the article praises him as a capitalist with a caring heart; his farm has "solved the local people's difficulties with vegetables, so they no longer completely rely on importing vegetables from China." His Russian wife, Nadia, has a high opinion of the Chinese; not only are they hardworking and sober but they are also "courteous: every time they meet someone they say hello."[35]

Numerous articles and television programs have also profiled Liu Jianjun, a former city official from Baoding, Hebei, who claims to have founded a network of "Baoding villages" of Chinese farmers in Africa. Liu describes Africa as a promised land of fertile soil and high profits for farmers that Africans have not cared to exploit (e.g., CCTV 2007). A report in *Global Times*, the *People's Daily*'s popular offshoot, claims that people in the Sudan address Chinese as *habibi* (dear) and that every Chinese farmer in Africa is seen as a foreign expert. A driver in South Africa asked the reporter if "you Chinese are the richest people in the world." The author comments that the driver's "views are representative of the respect a very large number of lower-class South African blacks have for success. Because of this respect they want to learn from the Chinese" (Huang, Shao, and Zhou 2006). In these stories, locals morph from equal adversaries into a hapless supporting cast dependent on crafty Chinese entrepreneurs: female assistants having affairs with their Chinese bosses, interpreters falling in love with female Chinese traders, loyal waiters, or wicked middlemen.

As one proceeds to the east and the south, not only do judgments about "backwardness" become increasingly harsh but also the "quality" of Chinese migrants is cast in a more favourable light compared to that of locals. Chinese interviewees and media in Hungary broadly agreed that while Hungarians might be lazy, unambitious, and willing to live in backward circumstances, their "quality" was higher than that of people in China. This manifested itself in such things as education levels, politeness, well-behaved children, and what they perceived to be harmonious family life—attributes linked to low population density and ones that people in China are supposed to lack (see Anagnost 1997:117–37). As an article in a Chinese-language Budapest newspaper characteristically put it,

> at the bottom of their hearts, Hungarians are pure, kind and peaceful, like the benign old man who greets you good morning at daybreak, the innocent youth who patiently explains how to find your way, or the burly fellow who feeds pigeons at the roadside. . . . When will the homeland [i.e., China] have such carefree pigeons? When will China have such peaceful evenings? . . . When will our elders have such graceful smiles? (Xiangnan 1994:3)

Thus, while the degree of economic modernity in Hungary or Argentina may be disappointing, their peoples, being white and having low reproduction rates, at least share the "Western" attributes of high quality. But that view does not hold for others, such as Gypsies in Eastern Europe, Southeast Asians, or Africans, who are often described as *both* backward and uncivilized. [36] Interestingly, recent reports by Chinese living in Africa challenge these views, pointing out, for example, that African industrial law and quality standards are often more sophisticated than China's.

The roles of migrants in "Eastern" and "Western" stories differ; but their image as contributors to modernization runs through both portrayals. It is important to note that their contribution is shown as being twofold: not only to the homeland but also to the country of residence. While the stories reserve pride of place to educated "knowledge entrepreneurs," rural migrants receive praise not just for generating income but also for "improving their quality." Indeed, an official in Yanbian Prefecture asserted that the first goal of labor export was not to earn money but to learn new skills and expand horizons (Luova 2007:187). Thus, contract workers from Changxing County are commended for learning Japanese (Fang and Kong 2003), and traders from Mingxi for developing a stronger "taxpayer consciousness" by getting used to paying taxes in Europe (Li Minghuan 2005). An article entitled "Going out bravely" in *People's Daily* sings the praise of overseas work in this way:

> Working abroad benefits both the country and the individual. For the country, it alleviates contradictions between supply and demand in the labour market. For the individual, it is another pathway to employment, and offers opportunities to study foreign languages, advanced technologies and management experience, to train one's willpower and open up one's horizon, to improve one's labour quality and skills. (Wang Jun 2003:2)

In an article entitled "Overseas laborers are the everyday heroes of our time," *Guangming Daily*, regarded as the ideological mouthpiece of the Party, similarly praised migrants for "not huddling up idly in China but bravely going overseas to open up new frontiers."[37] The language of these reports seems kneaded together from the Party's rhetoric of struggle and selfless sacrifice—struggle being, of course, a term with strong positive connotations, used to describe the victorious history of the Communist Party and the laboring people[38]—and neoliberal ideals of flexibility, productivity and speed.

By the mid-2000s, the celebration of migrants has thus become trenchant. At the same time, unwillingness to migrate has come to be seen as stubbornness, a sign of backwardness, reluctance to move with the times, and low "quality." Officials in provinces that lagged behind in migration were expressing their frustration. In Suining, Sichuan, Saudi and Jordanian companies did not receive enough applicants when they were recruiting nurses and seamstresses. The director of the City Labour Export Department, Yang Xingming, commented that "although economic difficulties (paying for the visa and ticket) have stood in the way of some people's going abroad to work, the biggest obstacle currently is backward mentality." He expressed the hope that returning workers from abroad would serve as models and persuade people to leave (Wang Huan 2004). Similarly, the low rate of overseas employment in nearby Chongqing was blamed on the purported closed-mindedness of the locals, in addition to their lack of means to pay for the arrangement, The director of the city's Centre for Employment Abroad blamed people's "overly conservative thinking" and urged the city government to promote overseas employment more strongly (Guo Jing 2001).

The willingness to migrate is now described not only as a praiseworthy individual characteristic but also as part of an "outstanding Chinese cultural tradition." Chinese narratives about voluntary forms of late-nineteenth and early-twentieth-century migration portray migrants as active contributors to modernization. Thus, the official *Encyclopedia of Chinese Overseas* (published under the auspices of the All-China Federation of Overseas Chinese) writes that, in the early twentieth century, people in the Russian Far East

> lived in Chinese-built houses, used simple implements made in Chinese workshops, drank Chinese tea, ate flour and vegetables produced by Chinese, purchased all of their daily necessities in Chinese-run shops. . . . In the eyes of the Russians, the Chinese were geniuses of commerce: industrious, honest, clever, capable, and endowed with an indomitable competitive spirit. (Li and Lin 1999:94)

Western colonial narratives of the time likewise stress the diligence and usefulness of "middleman minorities" such as Chinese, Indians, and Syrians, but interpret them as self-serving and opportunistic, and thus as evidence of slyness and disloyalty. Though they help colonial modernization, they are by no means its conscious agents. By contrast, the Chinese narratives make them into pioneers of a more humane globalization. Furthermore, with the elevation of the early fifteenth-century admiral Zheng He, who reached Africa, Southeast Asia, and possibly Australia and America, to national hero status in the 2000s, the Chinese state threw its weight behind the view that China could have become the world's colonizer and bringer of civilization much earlier than Europe.[39] If, as China's *Yellow Paper on World Socialism* claims, "capitalist globalization led by the United

States" will eventually be replaced by a "socialist globalization led by China" (Chinese Academy of Social Sciences 2006), China will simply be claiming its long overdue status.

In this process, overseas Chinese and migrants old and new have become revalorized. After a period when overseas Chinese were considered marginal to the self-definition of China, migration was suddenly seen as an essential part of Chinese culture (as it has, indeed, long been regarded in the West).[40] Suddenly, it is worth competing for the regional custodianship of this tradition. Hence the recent emphasis in Cantonese cultural regionalism on a "culture of migration" as a way to incorporate domestic immigrants, overseas emigrants, and their descendants into an imaginary in which tolerance and cosmopolitanism is a central element of cultural distinctiveness (Fu Tengxiao 2003).[41]

For migrants themselves, the portrayal carries an important moral: regardless of their education, social background, and way of migration, they have the chance to prove themselves good citizens by being "successful" abroad. By providing recognition, the government promotes a discourse of success whose measures (whether investment, consumption, social status, or official honors) are tied to the sending area. Recognition of success comes, however, with the expectation that they will share the fruits of their success with the homeland in the form of remittances, donations, and investments, all of which receive wide publicity and generate more recognition.

To what extent do migrants identify with the image of modernizing pioneers? For those migrants who receive no public recognition from the societies they live in, such portrayal can be particularly gratifying. In his study of an earlier generation of Chinese migrants to Sarawak, Borneo, Souchou Yao found that they similarly stressed the industry, perseverance, and solidarity of "the Chinese spirit" in a terrain characterized by physical danger and hostile natives. Without the additional element of superiority coming from modernity and speed,[42] this discourse, Yao writes, was perceived as

an inexhaustible truth of the Chinese everywhere, a story evoking the unbroken theme of hard work and sacrifice wherever Chinese find themselves. The feeling that the story has been told and will be told again impresses the listener, and turns each story into a cycle of a common theme. (Yao 2002:54)

This older discourse served to elevate the successes of overseas Chinese merchants, of often humble social origins, into a moral triumph in front of an imagined or real pan-Chinese audience, heartened those still struggling through a promise of eventual success, and countered hostility from the majority population through a claim of moral superiority. Similarly, the recent story of pioneering modernity helps new migrants assert their superiority vis-à-vis the majority society and established overseas Chinese, who typically regard them with suspicion. In an interview in *Shijie Rongyin* (a Hong Kong–based magazine catering to migrants from Fuqing), the president of the Melbourne Fuqing Association said:

> In Australia, Chinese immigrants are divided into new and old immigrants. . . . It is impossible to talk about old immigrants and new immigrants at the same breath. . . . Twenty years ago, Chinese were considered the most backward ethnic group in Australia. [By contrast,] new migrants have all received higher education; they have a strong ability to live here and develop quickly. (*Shijie Rongyin* 2001)

These statements are consonant with the mainstream discourse on new migrants in China, but at odds with dominant views in Australia, where Chinese who have received public recognition, such as the mayor of Melbourne, tend to be earlier immigrants from Hong Kong or Southeast Asia. By contrast, new migrants from the PRC that began arriving in the 1990s were "convenient objects of mirth among their Hong Kong and Taiwanese compatriots, but also stigmatized by the broader Australian community as potential 'dole [welfare] cheats'" (Ip 2007:127).

In places where new Chinese migrants are in fact eyed with suspicions of illegality and associated with crime (much as rural migrants are in China's cities), the triumphalist image of the new migrant constructed by Chinese media had a powerful impact on the way migrants saw themselves and their various environments, in their relationship to China and the countries they resided in and in the way they justify their choices and actions (Nyíri 2002a, 2005a). Although Chinese migrants I interviewed in Europe in the 1990s and early 2000s did not share the social status of a Howard Li, and indeed were acutely conscious of the discrimination and bullying they suffered, they shared a strong sense of their contribution to local society. When describing their impressions of Eastern Europe, they often used the term "backward" (*luohou*). "What's good about Europe is that it's quiet and there are few people. For the rest of it, Shanghai is better. It's more developed," said Sun, a twenty-eight-year-old from Shanghai who worked as a waitress in Budapest. Similarly, the owner of a shipping and customs clearance company recalled her arrival in Hungary in 1990:

> I found out that Hungary was actually an agricultural country with a very backward industry; having only just embarked on reform and opening, goods were very scarce . . . there were no industrial goods at all, all of them had to be "imported"; so I went home, organised suppliers, and started importing. (*Shichang* 2003:11)

Another businessman, Wang Jiazhu, likewise recalls that "inexpensive Chinese small goods came like a timely shot in the arm for goods-impoverished Hungary," not to mention neighboring Ukraine. Sometimes, Ukrainian businessmen coming over to Budapest "found that there wasn't enough merchandise; those hefty fellows were so upset that they prostrated themselves in front of Wang Jiazhu and cried" (He Yifan 2007). Later, Wang moved to Finland, where he claimed to have obtained an "immigration quota" for one hundred Chinese families in recognition of his investment in a wholesale center called Nordic China-town. His counterpart, Michael Song, the mastermind behind the Asia Center in Budapest—heralded at its 2002 opening as the largest shopping center in Europe—claimed that it would not only raise Hungary's international profile but actually contribute to Hungary's Olympic bid, a hyperbole that echoed Chinese officials' language when talking about the state's engagement in infrastructure projects overseas. A marble stele in front of the Asia Center bears the following English inscription (reproduced verbatim):

> Great Asia center fuse fengshui theory from the East with material culture from the West, extending traditional Chinese culture, as well as enriching modern western material technology. The palatial Asiacenter is a rare creature in the world, its name will spread to each corner of the world.

Chinese in South Africa have similar memories as those in Hungary. For example, in 1990, the Chinese entrepreneur and association leader Wang Jianxu found that the South African "economy was still in its initial stage. . . . It is a third-world country, still not very developed in terms of light industry and others" (*Nanfang Ribao* 2002). Another business-man and association leader in South Africa, Li Xinzhu, described how he found a scarcity of goods when he first arrived in the 1990s, and how, through "arduous toil" (*gan pin jia qinfen*), he proceeded to open a chain of twenty shops, then a shoe factory, and, "employing 150 local blacks, has made a contribution to solving the employment problem and develop-ing the economy" (*Fujian Qiaobao* 2004b).

Practically the same story is recounted by a fellow Fuqing native of Li's in Argentina (*Fujian Qiaobao* 2004b). Chen Daming started out in 1994, "barely making ends meet on a minuscule wage working at a grocery, sometimes even sleeping in the street in exhaustion and hardship." But, "thanks to the 'Fuqing spirit' of thrift and perseverance, endurance and industry," he eventually opened his own shop and now owns a chain of ten, and is a leader in four different Chinese organizations. The article stresses that Chen has been received by Argentine president Néstor Kirch-ner, who praised Chinese merchants (principally small-scale grocers) for making an "untiring, outstanding contribution to the prosperity of the economy and the development of trade" (Chen Guohong 2006).

A senior manager at a Chinese rubber company in Laos draws an explicit and unflattering comparison between the impact of Western aid and the activities of companies like his own: "Westerners have been here for so long, building one bridge, one hospital, one school . . . villagers are still poor, still living the way they did ten, twenty, fifty years ago. What we bring is real development, real modernity" (Shi 2008:72). A migrant from Chongqing in central China who runs a deserted-looking restau-rant at the bus station of Udomxay in northern Laos points disdainfully to passengers storming the local noodle stalls: "Everything those stalls sell, the meat and the vegetables, comes from this restaurant. The veg-etables all come from China."[43] In the capital, Vientiane, the president of the Lao-Chinese Chamber of Commerce adds: "If today this city has a bit of a city look, it's thanks to the Chinese companies."[44] Many of the compa-nies are backed by concessional loans from China's policy banks, and in 2008, a group of Chinese specialists released a development master plan for northern Laos commissioned by the Yunnan Province Development and Reform Commission, the province's top body in charge of ensuring economic growth. The plan does not hesitate in prescribing the Chinese recipe of improving population quality. It states that "the mentalities of most people are still . . . unsuitable for development of market economy. . . . Their awareness of development, competition, openness and hard working [*sic*] still need to be improved" (Northern Laos 2008:15).

In Cambodia, skilled blue- and white-collar workers from China are employed not only in projects financed by the Chinese state, but also as foremen, accountants, and quality controllers in the booming garment industry that is principally owned by Taiwanese, Hong Kong, Malaysian, and Cambodian Chinese investors. Across the Cambodian business sphere, migrants from China are increasingly identified with particular skills, rather than just with commerce. A former editor of a Chinese newspaper in Cambodia, who migrated there from Shanghai in 1992, told me that strikes at garment factories occurred because the managers, mostly ethnic Chinese from Taiwan, Malaysia, or China, were not prepared "to deal with people whose quality was lower than in their own societies," and who could not take too much work (*jieshou nengli di*) or cope with hardship (*bu neng chiku*). But, gradually, the workers saw that strikes did them no good and learned that "if I have my $40 a month I can still buy a necklace, I can still give my family a couple thousand riel; if the factory closes I won't even have this." The editor believed that because they were very simple, Cambodians had not understood this earlier; they needed to be taught/guided (*jiaodao*), but under the guidance of Chinese owners, managers, and shift supervisors, they were becoming more productive individuals, better suited to the iron logic of market competition.[45]

This oft-repeated account echoes comments by early-twentieth-century American industrialists like Henry Ford about immigrant workers needing to learn capitalist discipline. In some versions, the constructive role played by Chinese managers is contrasted with what is seen as the irresponsible agitation of Western-backed NGOs that talk to workers about labor conditions in Sweden at a time when the country should be using the advantage of low labor costs to attract investment (Xing 2008:158–60). Some of the lower-ranking Chinese workers, who work on construction or mining contracts, also see themselves in the role of harbingers of a superior path to development. At a Chinese-owned gold mine in Preah Vihear Province in northern Cambodia, a miner from Henan, one of China's poor provinces, pointed to a Cambodian colleague and exclaimed: "Look! It's 2 o'clock but that Cambodian guy is lying down! And look at how many children he has, and his wife is pregnant again! This country has rich soil, it has minerals, but this is why it's so poor. I have only one child!"[46] The lament that locals are lazy is, as we have seen, very common from Eastern Europe to Africa, but in this particular comment an intriguing connection is made between the Chinese state's population control policy, the industry and rationality of the Chinese people, and China's superior level of development.[47]

Another interesting discursive situation in which assertions of modernity emerge is the narratives of female entrepreneurs, in which they justify behavior that would, in rural China and the traditional Chinese diaspora, be seen as transgressive of gendered norms of behavior. In their *Research Report on Overseas Chinese and Ethnic Chinese Women in Europe: Social Status, Family Roles, and Children's Chinese-Language Education*, Yang Yijia, the chairwoman of the Hungarian Chinese Women's Association, and Wang Zhenyu, a senior researcher at the Sociology Institute of the Chinese Academy of Social Sciences, describe women who came to Europe from China in the 1990s in this way:

They have a clear advantage in knowledge, are resourceful and pioneers by nature. Unlike the old generation, they are not content with gradual accumulation over a long time; instead, they hope to use their advantages to achieve rapid development. They have higher expectations toward the quality of life. Most of them had a fairly good economic base and professional background in China. What made them come to Europe is not the need for a living but the drive to broaden their horizons, to seek even further development. . . . In Eastern Europe, the majority of Chinese females reside there as persons involved in commercial affairs; moreover, most are independent operators: this particularity is an extremely prominent one among Chinese females in Europe. (Yang and Wang 1998:10)

Yang Yijia is a former teacher of fashion design in China who has since died. With a predilection for leather clothing and quoted as saying that one of the best things about Hungary was that it was all right to kiss in public, even at middle age, she was unusual among Chinese organization leaders overseas. Yet, no maverick feminist, she was a frequent invitee to conventions sponsored by the PRC government, from National Day parades in Peking on October 1 to the 2001 World Chinese Conference for the Promotion of Peaceful Reunification Across the Taiwan Strait in August in Berlin. Yang and Wang's research suggested that in Eastern Europe, the fact that Chinese women migrants were often involved in the same activities as men meant they were more independent and "modern," which justified the acceptance of extramarital partnerships. They wrote:

> Because it is lonely to be abroad on one's own and because of business management needs, some people have temporary life partners in Europe; moreover, such relationships are commonly accepted by people around them, because they labour together, start enterprises together, and live together, so that it is like a *de facto* marriage. (Yang and Wang 1998:12)

Mu, the author of an autobiographical story that appeared in a Budapest newspaper, echoes them:

> At the time of starting our businesses . . . to compete alone with those who had their families in Hungary was, of course, difficult. . . . For the sake of adapting to life, many lonely men and women established temporary families. . . . I'd rather leave it up to sociologists and psychologists to discuss the truths and lies of this special product of society; as to my own situation, my two years' cohabitation with Old Huang certainly was for expediency and lack of alternatives. After two years, the situation gradually improved, and I calmly separated from Old Huang. And then I arranged for my husband, Song Guoguang, who was still in China at the time, to come to Budapest. (Mu 2001)

Li Zhongqiang's *Tearful Danube: Chinese in Hungary* (Zhongguo Wuzi Chubanshe; 1993), a book of pulp reportage, devotes a whole section to extramarital cohabitations:

> It is not a relationship between illicit lovers; it has nothing to do with affairs that are mysterious to outsiders; . . . it is usually the product of mutual consent. Those Chinese women who are working hard without relying on anyone in many countries around the world are certainly no easy prey. Almost all of them are clever, capable, determined, real women heroes. How could they be taken in by sweet talk?

Thus, both Chinese reportage and Yang Yijia's research on new migrants in Eastern Europe stress, often luridly, entrepreneurial and sexual freedom in general and of women in particular. This picture is much like those depictions of *dagongmei*, migrant working girls inside China, that glorify the success of a few workers-turned-entrepreneurs while ignoring the low social status and precarious working conditions of countless others (Jacka 2006:56–87).[48] Jacka (2006) finds that this image of success bears little resemblance to the experiences of the migrant women she interviewed in Peking. As wage laborers at the margins of urban society, they typically remain trapped by gender constraints.

In Hungary, the fact that most women are entrepreneurs permits a closer identification with media images of the sexually and professionally independent woman. Indeed, a number of my female informants there invoked arguments about economic development to justify their sexual behavior. Thus, Chen, a college-educated woman in her early thirties who had come to Budapest in 1999, told me about her ambitions to

> do some bigger business. For example I could get to know a customs officer. There are all those fake brands that they confiscate from Chinese. If I could get these shipments released I could make a lot of money. Or I could import stuff on my own and sell it directly to the big Hungarian department stores, as some people are doing.

But for the time being, Chen had no money. So she accepted the attentions of

> a rich shoe merchant who always waited for me at the clinic and took me out to dinner. That guy was an ignorant fool, a real traditional Chinese, maybe even illiterate. A bachelor looking for a wife. I told him I didn't like him and I wouldn't marry him, but he just kept going after me. When I went to Madagascar to visit a Chinese friend of mine he went with me and paid for the tickets. When I went to the casino he would just sit behind my back and hand me the money.

This kind of talk is certainly a transgression of gender constraints on sexual, social, and economic practices typical of earlier Chinese migration, where women migrants usually followed men, and their role was limited to the family and helping out in restaurants (see, e.g., Ong 1999). My argument (Nyíri 2002a) is that, apart from the loosening of social restrictions on sexual behavior in Chinese cities, manipulation of the special place awarded to overseas migration in the national obsession with modernity—and the link between migration and sexuality in popular cultural production—has enabled women to evade regimes of discipline.

Private enterprise and the commodification of social capital in the 1990s opened an opportunity for upwardly mobile women to break gender boundaries while creating or recreating new ones in education and employment, and particularly for subaltern groups such as rural female labor migrants. By the second half of the decade, taboos on sexual and social behavior were increasingly transcended. The process was further aided by physical mobility, which removed women from the gaze of their families and neighbors. At the same time, the removal of taboos and wider economic and social maneuvering space for women has facilitated the expectation that while women may pursue the same money-making strategies as men, they will deploy specifically feminine and sexual forms of social capital in the process.

In Eastern Europe, the acceptance of cohabitations is rationalized in terms of flexible accumulation. But the breaking of taboos associated with a regime of truth that twenty years ago could not be openly challenged, and the kind of cynical utilitarianism with which women like Chen describe it, is also a way of distancing oneself from older generations of overseas Chinese. Yang and Wang (1998:19) comment that the high incidence of sharing household chores between men and women, practiced by 37 percent of their respondents, is "an important characteristic of modern society." These distinctions are assertions of modernity, as indeed sex with foreigners or having a foreign-looking child can be. When Shi, twenty-seven, a hotel clerk in a small city in Zhejiang, moved to Belarus in 2000 with her boyfriend, she suggested that he have a child with a local girl so they can adopt it because "mixed children are so beautiful." She explained that she expected the girl to agree to that in exchange for money, as she had heard that it was common for Belarusian girls to sell their children to local Chinese. In Shi's narrative, the modernizing of the self is achieved through the colonialist exploitation of the former masters, the whites, as objects of aesthetic pleasure that have lost their agency. The process of colonization involves feminization and sexualization, but both Chinese women and Chinese men play the active, masculine part in this imaginary.

Just as media stories and official accounts of migrant women inside China often suggest promiscuity, fecundity, and uncontrolled, dangerous sexuality, "new migrant literature" is also replete with sexual adventures and reversals of gender hierarchies, bordellos and female managers. Some of the women in these stories are "female strongmen" (*nüqiangren*). Describing a cohabiting couple in *Tearful Danube*, Li Zhongqiang (1993) stresses the mutual dependence of a man and a woman, both of whom have spouses and children in China:

> "I still love my wife and children very much. My only wish is to scrape together some money and go home as soon as possible, to be with them. . . . But now, I could not bear it without Miss Wei. If we separated, I would again be a zombie like I used to be."

The protagonist of the novel *Holy River*, Pan, sees a more dramatic reversal of age and gender hierarchies (Chen and Chen 1997). On the plane to Budapest, Pan meets a snakehead leading a group of peasants from Fujian who had paid him to get them into Hungary. Upon arrival, the snakehead disappears, and the deceived Fujianese hold Pan responsible, believing he is an accomplice. Pan is saved by eighteen-year-old Shanshan, the daughter of Boss Lin, who came to the airport to meet him. Shanshan drives a Mercedes-Benz SL and manages Lin's restaurant. Pan confidently suggests that they look for the snakehead and get the peasants' money back by force. But Shanshan looks at him derisively.

> "I am asking you what you are planning to do now?" the lass said angrily. "We don't need you to fight!"
> Pan Hua stared at her helplessly. . . .
> "A dumb kid we got there . . . ," the lass muttered. Pan Hua realised that she meant him and became red in the face. (26)

Although Shanshan's portrait is drawn with some irony, the fact that Pan's first encounter with Chinese society abroad is in the form of a bossy teenage girl nonetheless delivers a clear message; in the new generation of successful, modern, dynamic, and thoroughly global Chinese, the gender hierarchies he is used to are no longer valid.

An even more unequivocal reversal of gender hierarchies is in Mu Yunkai's story "Budapest, I Hate You Forever" (2001), published in a Chinese newspaper in Hungary. Here, however, it is shown as an undesirable result of the clash between moral values and the pursuit of modernity. The protagonist hates Budapest as the city that broke her family apart.

She had come to Budapest ahead of her husband and child, and opened a stall at the market with the help of a cohabiting partner. Then she separated from her partner and arranged for her husband to come to Budapest. Her husband refused to help her with the business, and she put up with it because of the guilt she felt about the "shadow of *bangjian* [cohabitation] over me." Eventually, the heroine goes to the United States, while her husband sells the market stalls she had acquired, then loses the money gambling. In the story, she returns from New York to Budapest to rescue her former husband.

> He used to be quite manly, but by now he had lost all semblance to a human. I took six thousand dollars out of my handbag, put them on the chair next to the bed, and said coldly: "This money is to pay your bills; otherwise, your life'd be over. I am giving you another five hundred dollars; buy a plane ticket and go back to Jinan. . . . And this is the last time I helped you." (Mu 2001)

Other authors reserve the roles of business movers to men, but portray women's agency in mobility and sex. The message is a mixed one of sinfulness and modernity, with the underlying logic that modernization requires the sacrificing of values. A frequent utterance is, "This is just what things are like overseas." In *Into Europe*, director Chen Kemin shows a clash between the rules of family-managed migration from a traditional sending area (modeled on Qingtian, Zhejiang) with the individualism of the modern migrant, and his sympathies are on the side of the latter. An overseas Chinese family agrees that their cousin's China-born daughter should come to Italy to marry their Italian-born son. After a clash with the host family, the girl elopes, not with her original paramour who migrated to Italy with her, but with the repentant snakehead who had stolen her passport. Although the object of her passion has changed, the film portrays her as the moral winner.

In the twenty-episode soap opera *Duonao hepan de huang taiyang* (Yellow Sun on the Danube), written and produced in 1996 for a Chinese TV station by Chinese in Hungary, three men and three women meet on the trans-Siberian train to Budapest. The thirty-year-old protagonist, Lin Yifan, moves in with twenty-five-year-old Zhang Ning, a music student. But he has a rival, Yan Gang, whose wife left him in China for an American. In order to split Zhang from Lin, Yan arranges for Lin's wife and daughter to come to Hungary. Zhang moves out, but his wife later catches her *in flagranti* with her husband. Lin "agonises between his emotions for his wife and lover." Meanwhile, Shi Shangwei leaves her Hungarian boss with whom she had been living, "because of the difference between Eastern and Western cultures." She soon meets and falls in love with Yan Gang and becomes a partner in his company. But Yan still pursues Zhang Ning. Zhang eventually gives up her love for Lin and decides to go to Austria to study music. After she gets her visa, she has a few drinks with Yan and finds herself in bed with him. She becomes pregnant and decides to have an abortion, but she dies on the operating table. Condemned by his friends, Yan Gang shoots himself.

In these stories—widely watched by audiences in China and by migrants, and thus involved in shaping the expectations applied to migrant women—women are shown as active agents who, like men, manage a complex web of business relations to optimize their strategies of economic accumulation. They manipulate the discourse of modernity and the imaginaries of migration and gender linked to it in order to evade the social and entrepreneurial constraints imposed by what Ong (1999) refers to as "the regime of the Chinese family" (as a value discourse, not as an actual entity). In other words, they balance the admiration the status of a successful modern woman may bring against the expectations of their families and peer groups toward a woman of their particular social status. Migration, domestic or international, increases individuals' ability to manipulate cultural constructs of distant places in order to gain the privilege of different behavior.

Mobility and the "Civilizing Project"

We have seen that in reform China, especially since the 1990s, various kinds of mobility have come to be associated with modernity.[49] In part, this new discourse sees mobility as serving a market economy. In this framework, internal migration (seen as the redistribution of surplus rural labor) advances economic growth by increasing, rationalizing, and reducing the cost of production; international migration generates foreign currency and attracts investment; and tourism contributes to domestic consumption, reducing overly high saving rates.

In equal measure, however, mobility also serves a function of embour-

geoisement. As in nineteenth- and twentieth-century European national-
isms, tourism—including the proto-tourist activity of visiting theme parks
and the viewing of statuary and performative enactments of the national
narrative at tourist sites—is an instrument of getting to know one's nation
and situating oneself within it as a citizen. At the same time, and more
particularly in the contemporary Chinese case, learning proper forms of
consumption (or "healthy forms of leisure," *jiankang de xiuxian fangshi*),
experiencing modern infrastructure, witnessing "advanced ways of life"
(*xianjin de shenghuo fangshi*), and learning "modern methods of entrepreneurship" are also seen as contributing to the improvement of "population quality." Both the migrant and the tourist spread "civilization,"
particularly to the "backward" countryside, which is characterized by
an anemic "small peasant consciousness" (*xiaonong yishi*) and "feudal
superstition" (*fengjian mixin*). The former does so primarily by becoming
a better producer and the latter by demonstrating better ways of consumption. At the same time, mobile individuals are inevitably interpellated by
the state, whether as targets of "overseas Chinese work," applicants for
temporary residence permits, or consumers of tourist performances. For
many of them, especially if they have lived in rural areas, this is their first
intense encounter with the state.

In addition to contributing to China's modernization, there is also an
emerging narrative that frames Chinese migrants as pioneers of modernization abroad. In the context of China's emergence as an international
investor, which the government often pitches as help offered to developing countries, Chinese entrepreneurs and workers abroad are seen as
contributing (*gongxian*) to the development of their countries of settlement or work.[50] Once again, this contribution is not seen as purely economic; the accounts, as we have seen, also carry civilizational overtones.
As a result, the civilizing mission is exported across the borders simultaneously and contiguously with the domestic civilizing project (see Nyíri
2006b).[51] But while the cultural production that emerges around new
migrants depicts them as globally mobile harbingers of modernity, it also
puts them into an ambivalent relationship with foreigners that is framed
by the imperatives of the civilisatory discourse of development.[52] In this
competitive relationship, where it is assumed that both parties follow
the goals of entrepreneurial modernity, the migrants are alerted to the
"quality" of their hosts and—like rural migrants in Chinese cities (Jacka
2006:52)—simultaneously reminded of their own task to "improve their

quality." Thus, Zhao Shengyu (2003) identifies the low quality of Chinese workers, manifested in their poor skills and lack of labor discipline, as one of the three difficulties of labor export. He quotes managers of labor export companies in Jiangsu as complaining that workers

> violate their contracts, wantonly leave their employers and engage in illegal work, and even violate the laws of the country or region they are in. But as soon as a conflict arises, some workers immediately begin kicking up a fuss (*nao*) at the embassy or consulate, gravely affecting the image of workers overseas and harming the development of overseas markets. (Zhao Shengyu 2003)

Sun and Yang (2001) compare the low share of China in labor export to that of Pakistan and the Philippines and the low wages of Chinese workers compared to Filipinos, and attribute these to their "low quality": "Why are hotels in Singapore bent on choosing Filipinas, who are both ugly and short, instead of pretty Chinese girls as hostesses? Because . . . those (Filipinas) going abroad are all fluent in English" (Sun and Yang 2001). Mothers who take their five-year-old children to Australia so they can undergo their education in English do not simply want them to be more competitive in global markets; they also want them to acquire the putative "quality" (manners, bodily discipline, and so on) of Westerners, just as rural migrants' children are supposed to do in China's cities.

There is a dialectic between contributing to the modernization of foreign countries and overcoming "China's internalized sense of lack" (Anagnost 1997:123) that manifests itself in the population quality discourse. Ann Anagnost (ibid.:88–93) has analyzed a 1983 newspaper story about a model household in Hebei Province, which converted from gambling to entrepreneurship and became a contributor to local civilizing projects. Like the heroes of this story, successful migrants, often of lowly origins, become model individuals who persuade others (Chinese and foreigners) of the wisdom of the state's modernizing policies and either put them on the path to modernity for the first time or helped them overcome Western anomie. Unlike Western coloni(ali)sts, they do not go about educating or reforming natives, but rather show them an example of success. As Megan Ferry (2007) notes, though Chinese migrants are portrayed as technically superior to natives, they are not always portrayed as *morally* superior. But it is precisely this *lack* of a moral agenda that underlies the claims of altruism Chinese officials use to subtly indicate the moral superiority of China's economic contributions to the more socially interventionist aid schemes of the West. This is the central theme of the 2000 soap opera *Forever Africa (Yongyuan de Feizhou)*, which centers on a team of Chinese doctors in a fictitious African country. Steadfastly striving to improve the hygiene of superstitious (and cannibalistic) Africans, the Chinese team is trusted and accepted and praised by the country's president. This is in contrast to the Frenchman, Dr. Louis, who has to coax locals into allowing him to treat them. The difference in their reception is due to the Chinese team's dedication to improving people's lives while the Frenchman pursues research on communicable diseases in a quest for the Nobel Prize. Catharsis comes when the natives capture Dr. Louis and are about to sacrifice him to their tribal god. A Chinese doctor successfully intervenes and saves his life, declaring that "he is less concerned about having another competitor for the Nobel Prize than he is about having one less doctor around." The hero of the series, Dr. Zou, not only helps Africans improve their lives; he returns to China with "a greater sense of national mission . . . as a model of [the] renewed cosmopolitan citizen" (ibid.).

The positive, developmentalist view of Chinese migration contrasts with the dominant Western view, which is shaped by wider fears of Chinese expansion (fears that share their Malthusian concerns with China's population quality discourse) as well as by the kind of economic, political, and cultural concerns that are now ingrained in the discourse of sustainable development used by international development agencies (and increasingly in China as well). Chinese narratives see Chinese migration to Indochina and Burma (and Han Chinese migration to Tibet and Xinjiang [East Turkestan]) as inherently positive; as one that brings development to the locals. By contrast, Western narratives see it as inherently detrimental, causing economic and cultural damage, and do not regard it in the frame of development at all (e.g., Lintner 2002; Mengin 2007).

Lewis Henry Morgan's and Herbert Spencer's social evolutionary theories (often referred to as social Darwinism) maintain a pervasive influence in today's China. This influence has been described to some extent by Harrell (1995) and especially by Dikötter (2005), but is still insufficiently analyzed in the state's subject-making ideology or in the quotidian processes of subject formation. That races and nations[53] are biological entities endowed with different capacities and that they compete for economic resources and hence political dominance is as evident for ordinary Chinese citizens today as that they as individuals are endowed with different faculties and must compete—as they are told every day by a media that recites the success mantra of the "socialist market economy." It is in these terms that the competition between China and the United States is explained and understood in Internet chatrooms, and that the endless discussions of "overall national strength" (*zonghe guoli*) and government pronouncements and media reports on the "arduous struggle" (*jianku fendou*) and eventual success of "yellow-skinned, black-haired descendants of the Yellow Emperor" abroad are read. A literally millenarian (cf. "Pacific century") sense emerges from this discourse; *it is the turn of the Chinese*, with their unique endowments of flexibility and efficiency, now backed by a strong modernizing state, to lead the world to a new, improved version of modernity and capitalism (Ong 1999). This view is underscored by the twelve-part documentary *Rise of the Great Powers*, which was made following a Politburo decision in 2003, began airing on China Central Television in 2006, and was later turned into a series of nine bestselling books. The film describes the rise of great powers from Portugal through Germany to the United States in a far more positive way than the customary focus on imperialism and exploitation (Kahn 2006). In the part on Germany, the heroes are Bismarck and Friedrich List, the economist who proposed the customs union of the German lands, rather than Marx (Siemons 2006). A sequel to the series, entitled *China's Road*, is in preparation (Callahan 2007). The fantasy of the Chinese following in the footsteps of the great globalizers of the past is, of course, shared by many Western commentators; indeed, Ong (2002) argues that the "globally modern Asian" is the new ideal American subject in the era of flexible capitalism. And as the inevitable flipside of the same coin, in the West, and increasingly in Africa,

China is more and more seen as the new imperialist threat. . . . China is no longer seen as an alternative to Western neo-colonialism, but as the proponent of a new colonialism that comes with the same inferiority as the old one. . . . More and more, talking about Chinese becomes a new idiom for expressing concerns about social change in general. (Dobler 2008)

In other words, China is coming to be associated with the fears of globalization—a role previously reserved for the United States.

The view that global modernity now rests upon the shoulders of Chinese migrants reverberates in official speeches, but its circulation goes far beyond state-endorsed narratives. In the rapidly growing global Chinese evangelical movement—which enjoys the sympathy of the government in China as long as it accepts subordination—there is, in the words of Reverand Edward Wei of the British-based Chinese Overseas Christian Mission (COCM), a "worldwide sentiment that the responsibility for or instrument of mission has moved over to the Chinese" (Nyíri 2002b:291). COCM's 2000 International Mission Conference was entitled "The Light of Ten Thousand Countries: God's Grace Chose Overseas Chinese Compatriots to Spread the Gospel All Over Europe." As Mr. Qiu, a Chinese Christian convert in Hungary, told me:

> Since I believe in God, I think the reason so many Chinese leave China is that they too are the seed of Abraham, as it is said in the Bible, and it is now their turn to spread the gospel on Earth, as the British and Americans formerly did, because there are many Chinese and they are everywhere. We did not leave China by chance; God summoned us out of China so we get to know Him. We will not be here long, because God will need us in other countries, especially China. Christian countries are generally more civilised, more democratic, and more developed. Therefore China, too, needs Christianity. Many people used to think that science or democracy could save China, but actually, only God can save it. (Nyíri 2002b:292)

Mr. Qiu's reasoning makes explicit the links between ethnic belonging, modernity, migration, and Christian mission. Those who, like him, have taken upon themselves the full weight of the "yellow man's burden" are, of course, a minority.[54] But the sentiment that the Chinese people must tomorrow take over the mission of modernizing and civilizing the world, carried by Americans since World War II and by the British before them, is a widespread element of Chinese nationalism. In official ideology, it is disguised by the united-front rhetoric of opposing hegemony and solidarity with developing countries. Yet, ultimately, it is not nationalism but the obsession with the culture-unspecific yardstick of modernization—tied to a genuine faith in development that is now considerably stronger than in the West—that makes Chinese anti-colonialism and anti-Americanism so different from similar ideologies elsewhere. In this view, global intervention and hegemony in the name of development and civilization is *not* in itself illegitimate; indeed, it is understandable if not necessary. Read carefully, the emphasis on cultural difference in the orientalistic tales of Burmese or Hungarian natives is really a foil for competing claims of superiority in hierarchies of modernity and capitalism—just as it is in many Western development projects. The difference is that Chinese subjects themselves feel handicapped and continuously pressured to strive upwards in those hierarchies.

5
The Dangers of Mobility
DISCIPLINING THE TRAVELER

The economic benefits of human mobility within a market logic have been at odds with the Chinese state's continued desire to exercise fairly close control over its population. As people begin to move, they slip out of the grip of traditional systems of administrative control based on household registration and work units. They also, as Murphy (2004) argues, increase what Appadurai, drawing on Amartya Sen, calls their "capacity to aspire," that is, to imagine a range of life-goals—even unattainable ones—beyond the previously unquestioned ideas of the good life dictated by the family, the village, or the nation. This happens through individuals' exposure to different lifestyles, as well as through learning to access and use new sources of information. Fishermen from Fujian and nannies from Anhui go to Internet cafés in Budapest or Peking to chat to their friends over Webcams. Tourists from Shanghai are exposed to the lifestyles, and potentially to the worldviews, of Tibetan herders and Australian surfers. In some cases, as we have seen, public discourse in China constructs such exposure as explicitly desirable, since it contributes to modernization, assists "building spiritual civilization," and enhances patriotism. This is typically the case with peasants' migration to cities or with travel to canonical sites of Chinese culture. At the same time, the government actively works to control and shape tourists' experiences.

In an early speech on developing border tourism, the then vice-director (later director) of the National Tourism Authority praised its contribution to the construction of spiritual civilization in border areas through the exposure of tour groups from these areas to "positive phenomena in Russia and North Korea such as clean cities, orderly traffic, civilized and courteous residents" (He Guangwei 1992). In the same speech, however, He also emphasized the need to "strengthen propaganda and education of tour participants, make them clearly understand the significance of border tourism, respect the rules of the tour group and obtain healthy and correct benefits from participating in the tour" (ibid.:14). Accordingly, early participants in Russian border tourism were required to undergo training on "foreign affairs regulations and the protection of (state) secrets."[1] Every tour group had to have a leader and a deputy leader, who had to report back to the organizer (travel agency) upon return.[2] Concern about the potentially corrupting influence of cross-border tourism was stronger in the southwest, which borders on relatively freewheeling Thailand, drug-producing Burma, and Laos and Vietnam, where casinos target Chinese visitors. As a fairly typical article put it:

Since reform and opening, the influx of culture from abroad has brought both the wheat and the chaff to the educationally rather backward area inside the border. . . . Border-area tourism and cross-border tourism in Yunnan has . . . enabled tourists to see and appreciate natural sights of foreign regions as well as special sights such as border rivers, border markers, border bridges and border gates. Tourism authorities will have to collect and prepare historical documents related to these special markers for tour guides to distribute them to tourists, as well as add on-the-ground commentary in order to attain the goal of increasing knowledge . . . [and] cultivating patriotic enthusiasm. (Zhao Ling 1998:34)

In addition to concern about the ideas tourists might be exposed to across the border, authorities were also worried about what ideas about China they might project to the locals. For the government, tourists, like everybody else going abroad, were representatives of the nation because their behavior reflected on China. Back in 1986, the selection criteria for state-sponsored study overseas, issued by the State Education Commission, began with "love of the Fatherland and socialism, goodthinkfulness,[3] good character, and manners (*sixiang pinde xiuyang youliang*)."[4] Before going abroad, students are supposed to undergo a training covering China's foreign policy, the rules on study abroad, the rules of diplomacy (*waishi jilü*), and the situation of the country they are going to (*Huaqiao Huaren Baike Quanshu* 2000:124).

Similar but stricter criteria were issued in the early 1990s for those going abroad on official business. The Regulations on Approving Personnel Going Abroad on Official Business state that individuals must be "politically reliable, with a clear history, love the socialist Fatherland, of a healthy mentality and upright character."[5] Specifically, the regulations prohibit anyone who disagrees with the Party line, supported the "Lin Biao-Jiang Qing clique" during the Cultural Revolution, was implicated in the 1989 "riots," supports bourgeois liberalization, or "is highly individualistic, dissipated, prodigal (*fuhua duoluo*) and immoral" from traveling abroad on official business. Although the criteria remain in place today, with the increased number of people going abroad it is unlikely that they are taken very seriously.

Quaint as these regulations may seem in the 2000s, there are nonetheless continuing attempts to enforce them. Thus, before a delegation of county-level officials from Yunnan Province left for an "inspection" tour of Australia and New Zealand in 2006, they were summoned to Peking and given a two-day training on Threerepresents Importantthought, a key doctrine of the Communist Party. They were told to apply it to everything they saw and experienced, and write a report on it upon their return. The participants quietly ignored this mandate; as one of them told anthropologist Zhang Juan, he did not know what to write because "China lags far behind Australia, so what can Threerepresents represent?"[6]

At least on paper, similar training and monitoring regulations exist for workers going abroad on contracts. A handbook on labor export defines the goals of pre-departure training in the following way:

Provide education in patriotism, ardent love for the Party, ardent love for socialism, capability to consciously resist the rotten ideology and [life] style of the capitalist classes and . . . to maintain the true qualities of a citizen of a socialist country, and to gain glory for the socialist homeland (Zhang Guoyu 1993:123, quoted in Luova 2007:177).

The handbook further stated that the state should not leave it to the workers to organize their own lives abroad, but should closely oversee them, because "if their life and work are not organized properly, they very easily feel lonely which creates a feeling of uneasiness and swing[s] in emotions, which harm work" (ibid.:125; quoted in Luova 2007:181). It laid down ten rules governing the behavior of Chinese workers abroad, which included not joining foreign organizations, not drinking excessively, not spending their money extravagantly, and not saying or doing anything that could harm China (Zhang Guoyu 1993:126–27, 130–43; cited in Luova 2007:182).

When Luova conducted her research in Jilin Province in 2004, workers going abroad were required to take classes that, in addition to information about their destination country and basic language skills, included "political and ideological education" and training in "the proper codes of conduct" (Luova 2007:176). Additional classes were provided for migrants' family members. In some areas, local authorities sent an official along with the migrant workers. In other places, two workers in the outbound party were chosen to routinely report on the group's performance and living conditions (ibid.:182). These individuals were also charged with conducting ideological work in the group. Luova reports that, at the time of her research, Yanbian Prefecture was planning to implement a system of collective responsibility that would make household members in China responsible for the conduct of their relatives abroad. This system appears to have been modeled on attempts to reduce illegal emigration in places such as Fuqing (Chin 2003).

Regulations concerning the behavior of Chinese citizens going abroad display great concern with the bodily and mental temptations individuals may be subject to abroad. Article 12 of the Temporary Regulations on Punishments for Communist Party Members Who Violate Discipline and Party Rules While Dealing with Foreigners, state that Party members who patronize prostitutes while abroad are to be expelled; those who seek entertainment at lewd and low-class (*yinhui xialiu*) venues, have inappropriate relations with foreigners of the opposite sex, or gamble are to be relieved of their Party positions; and those who repeatedly watch or peruse lewd films, books, or pictures must be reprimanded.[7]

Similar concerns are reflected in how-to manuals published for citizens going abroad. The appearance of such books is unsurprising in a society where foreign travel is suddenly becoming accessible and popular. Such books were published in Hungary in the late 1980s after the lifting of travel restrictions. Intended for tourists, they included travel tips and passport and visa information (e.g., Erdös and Léderer 1988). In contrast, the Chinese publications mostly contain information for people going abroad to study, settle, work, marry, or inherit property. To meet the needs of this diverse group of travelers, Chinese manuals include information on the official procedures one has to follow in each of these cases, etiquette ("how to talk with foreigners in public places"; "ways of drinking beer, coffee and tea" [State Statistics Bureau 2002:25–27]), and sketches on "customs and taboos" in different countries (ibid.).

Some of the books also reflect the Chinese government's concern about foreign travel. They portray "abroad" as dangerous terrain, where "foreign intelligence agencies and other enemy forces" wage a "battle for hearts and minds" by engaging in "reactionary propaganda to topple the leaders of the Chinese Communist Party and our country's socialist system and to split the Fatherland" (Zhang and Guo 2002:154). These books include sections on how to avoid disclosing state secrets or voicing inappropriate opinions in interactions with foreigners who, it is claimed, would attempt to obtain internal documents or research. The authors warn travelers against splitting off from the group they are traveling with and advise them to exercise caution when dealing with foreigners. "In public places . . . do not discuss problems of the country you are in or of third countries." When encountering demonstrations and protests, "generally, try to achieve the 'three no's: don't carelessly ask about its subject and reasons; don't blindly voice opinions or participate in discussions; don't carelessly join such activities" (ibid.:147, 150). Similarly, travelers should accept invitations to meetings, banquets, and celebrations only after having discerned their nature and participants. More generally, travelers are advised not to "actively bring up or directly promote our political views; do not enter into discussions of political issues of your host country" in private conversations, although it is acceptable to "do some explaining work." By contrast, if an "attack" on China takes place at a public venue, travelers should protest vocally and, if necessary, leave the event. Any opinions expressed about China must not be "subjective" but should "follow the line of the Centre's foreign propaganda." Finally, when interviewed by a journalist, travelers are advised to "answer in a simple way; avoid the truth and stress the empty" (ibid.:151, 160). There is also extensive advice regarding religious activities. Only "religious personnel" should accept religious publications as gifts; but they should not disseminate them, and they should not accept them at all if they are "reactionary or pornographic" (ibid.:153). If, despite all these measures, they encounter "reactionary propaganda," they must conscientiously "not look, listen, believe, or disseminate" it.

This hysterical language sounds more like the 1950s than the year of publication, 2002, when foreign travel was becoming relatively common. Yet, considering the authoritative tone of the book, it is unlikely that the authors came up with this guidance on their own. It is much more likely that they had consulted with "relevant authorities."

When tourism to the three Southeast Asian countries started in 1990, tour groups were similarly supposed to undergo "education in patriotism, internationalism and diplomatic protocol . . . in order to avoid international incidents."[8] But the authorities soon developed different concerns. After Chinese tour groups were allowed to visit Western destinations, the National Tourism Administration (CNTA) took measures to counter what it perceived to be an unflattering impression left by the tourists. In 2003, the government enlisted the cooperation of travel agencies such as China International Travel Service (CITS), which introduced special courses on the "habits and customs" of destination countries (*People's Daily Online* 2003). CITS also asked guides to remind tourists about proper behavior during the trip. In addition to educating tourists about etiquette, the government was especially concerned that "some Chinese look down on our poor neighbors like Vietnam, which offends local people," according to Liu Xiaoping, manager of Beihai Youth International Service (ibid.).

Three years later, the Spiritual Civilization Commission and the National Tourism Administration released an "Action Plan to Raise the Civilizational Quality of Chinese Tourists" ("Tisheng Zhongguo gongmin lüyou wenming suzhi xingdong jihua"). According to the text, "The civilizational quality of our citizens has not caught up with the rapid development of the tourism industry; it does not match the international stature of our country" and "has gravely harmed the image of China as the 'land of propriety' (li yi zhi bang)." In order to remedy the situation, the plan called for regulating tourists' norms of behavior through the media. One way it proposed to do so was by circulating the "Ten major uncivilized behaviours of Chinese tourists" and the "Ten major recommendations for improving the civilizational quality of Chinese tourists." In addition, the plan called for publishing a Guide to Chinese Tourists' Civilized Behaviour Abroad and a Civilized Behaviour Convention of Chinese Domestic Tourists. These were to be circulated widely at airports, bus stations, tourist attractions, and institutions of adult education. They were also supposed to serve as a basis for quizzes and competitions, as well as trainings for public employees, delegations, and personnel abroad. The plan also recommended monitoring travel agencies to ensure they carry out "civilization education work" among tourists; making tour guides personally responsible; publicly censuring those who failed to do so; and awarding titles such as Civilized Tourism Image Ambassador (wenming lüyou xingxiang dashi), Civilized Tour Guide, Civilized Travel Agency, as well as Civilized Tourist (at domestic scenic spots) to the best. Chinese citizens traveling abroad were to be subjected to monitoring (ducu) by the organizers.[9] Reportedly, participants in tour groups traveling to Europe now receive leaflets explaining the rules of proper behavior (Steinberger 2007).

Soon after the release of the action plan, the Spiritual Civilization Commission and the National Tourism Administration published the Guide to Chinese Tourists' Civilized Behaviour Abroad and the Civilized Behaviour Convention of Chinese Domestic Tourists. The former outlined the manners to be observed by Chinese citizens traveling abroad (for example, "respect time," "queue up in an orderly way," "ladies first," "eat in silence," and "reject gambling and salacious activities") in an eight-line nursery rhyme.[10] More or less the same commandments are contained in the eight articles of the Civilized Behaviour Convention of Chinese Domestic Tourists.[11]

This concern with the need to order and control citizens' exposure to areas beyond the border is akin to the emphasis on "civilizing" migrant workers in the cities or contract workers going abroad.[12] But because tourism, more than other forms of mobility, almost invariably involves some self-conscious form of cultural consumption, it is particularly rich in examples of cultural control. As we have seen, Chinese tourist practices have been shaped essentially by domestic experiences because income levels, government restrictions, and the visa policies of destination countries have severely constrained the opportunities of Chinese tourists to travel abroad until very recently. This made it easier for tourism developers to control tourists' interpretation of what they see. Back in 1988, the *Pocket Tourism Encyclopedia* admonished tourists-to-be to adopt "the attitude of the healthy and optimistic observer; photographing the backward, unsanitary, or impoverished should be resolutely avoided" (Shandong 1988:494). We have seen that even as direct state intervention in the details of tourism development was mainly economically motivated, the process ensured the proliferation of a discursive regime in which scenic spots and their state-endorsed hierarchy became tools of patriotic education and modernization. The state remained the ultimate authority to determine the meaning of landscape, regardless of the investor.

Tourism as "Indoctritainment"

Chinese authors have interpreted the spatial transformation of touristified villages and towns as a result of the intrusion of the global market whose inexorable force locals are unable or unwilling to resist (e.g., Duan and Yang 2001). No doubt, commercial developers or local governments bound touristic spaces and erect ritualized markers such as gates and walls because they believe these correspond to tourists' expectations, will improve their experience by directing them to the "nice" parts of the place, and thus will attract more visitors. But although the exigencies of the market are often cited as a catch-all rationale for the changes, they provide only part of the explanation. True, the social and spatial engineering that places like Songpan or Zhongdian were subjected to was intended to generate income, and it would be easy to cynically dismiss the government's civilizing rhetoric as so much eyewash to cover up the plainly economic motives. Underestimating the disconnect between ideology and everyday life has been a common mistake made by researchers of state socialism.

Yet the effects of "civilizing" these places beyond market-induced change are real, precisely *because* they have been linked to the inducements of the market. Town spaces have been nationalized and their inhabitants civilized to become suitable for tourism. The old town of

Songpan, for example, was bounded by a wall in 2004, and the border between mundane and touristic space ritualized through gates and pedestals. It has several wide ceremonial spaces, a miniature Tiananmen Square with a flag platform, which every third-form student learns to see as "majestic and grand" (Woronov 2004:303), and a standard monument that explicitly identifies the town with the Chinese nation and is used for the "healthy" activities of photo-taking and dancing. In addition, the tourist street is lined with "soft monuments," such as traditional-looking lanterns and fake flower beds familiar from the Wangfujing pedestrian street in Peking (Wu Hung 2005). (The latter was constructed between 1992 and 1999 following Western models to create a more modern image for the city. It was subsequently imitated in numerous cities; see Zhang Fa 2006.) In Zhongdian, similar plans were drawn up for a new main street and a Mandala Square, to be completed by 2020. Kolås (2008:109) quotes a local Tibetan as commenting that "in Beijing they have the Tiananmen Square and this is probably meant to be something similar; a place where people will get together when some kind of public event takes place." In Lhasa, the capital of Tibet, a Potala Square, complete with a flag platform modeled on the one in Tiananmen, was erected for the 1995 celebrations of the thirtieth anniversary of the Tibetan Autonomous Region (Woeser 2007:46). Where the nationalization of space has not yet occurred, official commentators urge tourism developers to undertake it. For example, Anhui Province's central official daily urged the managers of Mount Jingting ("Jiangnan's mountain of poems") to "erect a forest of steles with famed poems . . . (*mingshi pailin*) in order quickly to turn round the current situation in which . . . the beautiful myths have no [corresponding] sights" (*"Jiangnan shishan" wu shipai, meili chuanshuo wu jingguan*) (Wang Shizhong 2000).

Soviet officials liked to describe the culture they promoted as "national (ethnic) in form, socialist in content." In a perhaps unconscious variation on this phrase, Wei Xiaoan (2001:139) describes the "tourism culture" he promotes as having "ethnic form [but] modernized content." With the intention of emphasizing ethnic form for the development of tourism, the public spaces of Songpan, which escaped the great spatial standardization of early Communist times (Wu Hung 2005) because of its poverty, have belatedly acquired "socialist content." The logic behind these developments is not antagonistic but synergistic. From the government's standpoint, the relationship between tourism and civilization is evidenced by the simultaneous appearance of slogans about party members' education and the town's new appearance. That the project actually works is reflected not only by the tourists taking photos at the monument, but also in the endorsement of the changes and purchase of the state discourse of "quality" by locals.

Advocating greater state attention to "leisure culture," Chinese researcher Ma Huidi wrote that "the state's governance and control (of society; *zhili yu tiaokong*) requires not only economic, administrative, scientific, technological, and legal means; even more, it requires the workings of cultural guidance" (*wenhua yindao*; Ma 2004b:170). She was no doubt attuned to the interest the new leadership of Chairman Hu Jintao was taking in engineering a "cultural turn" in governance by focusing on "community building" (*shequ jianshe*), a slogan that refers to the creation of local communities of citizens actively engaged in mutual education and surveillance in order to attain a "harmonious society" (*hexie shehui*), which is healthy, morally correct, well-mannered, educated, and politically loyal.[13]

Travel and displacement heighten people's susceptibility to new ideas and interpretations of the world and relax the boundaries of what is socially acceptable. Therefore, movement often serves as a laboratory for creating new social practices. Mobility in China, simultaneously encouraged and limited by the state, is an arena where the shift to cultural forms of control is both, from the state's standpoint, necessary—in order to counteract the loosening of administrative control and to control how new impressions are interpreted—and promising, because travelers are sensitized and exposed to cultural representations (in the form of performances, displays, and explanations). Tourism is an arena with the potential to both civilize "tourees" (Oakes 1998) and respond to official calls for the "propagation of correct notions of leisure." At the same time, the Chinese state, like others over the course of history, sees correctly framed consumption of places as an instrument to strengthen the national consciousness. Songpan's transformation into a scenic spot has necessarily entailed the conversion of spontaneously evolving local ways of consuming space into national spaces of civilization. As Zhang Gu 2000:121), deputy director of the Sichuan Tourism Bureau, declared,

> The construction of scenic spots and scenic areas must both fully reflect modern material civilization and fully display the positive and advanc-

ing spiritual civilization of the Chinese race (*Zhonghua minzu*). Indeed, this is what distinguishes the socialist tourism industry with Chinese characteristics from the Western capitalist tourism industry.

What has enabled the Chinese state to carry through this agenda more successfully than some other states is that even where tourism development is undertaken by private investors it is channeled through the organizational and discursive spaces of government bureaucracy. This process affects not only the economics of tourism, but more importantly, its cultural grammar by enforcing a kind of narrative uniformity, forcing it into a hegemonic discourse and ensuring that the affective and sensual experiences of the places as well as their narratives of history and geography conform to the state-endorsed "structure of feeling" (Williams 1961). This mechanism, which functions in much of Chinese public culture from the development of urban space to filmmaking, further amplifies the homogeneity of tourism development projects, which in any case are often copycat developments by entrepreneurs and municipalities desirous of rapid profits from the tourism boom.

Nowhere is the state's desire to control the perception of tourist sites clearer than in the effort to regulate the commentary produced by tour guides. This is because group tourism is prevalent in China and, as a result, the vast majority of tourists will be accompanied by guides, while the popularity of guidebooks is limited. An article on the CNTA Web site warns:

> In introducing scenic spots, [guides] must display their love for the homeland, the nation, the people, and the native place. . . . While [talking about] a natural landscape, they should take care to introduce China's long and outstanding history, the nation's ancient and outstanding culture; to introduce the Chinese people's fine tradition of hard work and frugality, national unity and harmony.[14]

CNTA's guidelines for the licensing of tour guides stipulate that they must "love socialism and the Fatherland." The *Guidelines of Tourism Management of the Tibet Autonomous Region*, published in 2003, provide further detail. They specify that tour guides must be "patriotic, with an unwavering political stance, protective of the fatherland's unity, opposed to splittism, caring for the socialist system," and must "talk according to unified standards" (Articles 26–28).[15] In 2002, Hu Jintao, soon to become the Party's Secretary-General, mentioned the necessity of including the training of tour guides in the national program of aid for Tibet. In 2005, the National Tourism Administration's Party committee explained that this was a political task designed to "contribute to the stability of Tibet and the unity of the peoples[;] ... to promote Tibet's economic prosperity and social progress; to resolutely implement a scientific view of development" (National Tourism Administration 2005). Kolås (2006:229) explains that, in the late 1980s and early 1990s, the Chinese government welcomed Tibetans who had fled to India and Nepal and their descendants to come back to China. Many who returned knew English and became tour guides but later were found politically untrustworthy and lost their jobs.

In many places, guides are required to undergo training administered by the local Tourism Bureau. In Shangrila County, guides "are trained and tested about the essential characteristics of ethnic minorities," as well as

what is considered politically appropriate behaviour on the part of the guides. If, for example, they are asked about the importance of the Dalai Lama to Tibetans, they are instructed to answer that they do not know about such things. The Shangri-la Guide's Handbook, an internal (*neibu*) foreign affairs and tourist bureau publication, has plenty of information about ethnic dress, food and song, but nothing about the independent history, culture or patterns of social communication of these groups outside the boundaries of the Chinese state (Hillman 2003:187).

The Hubei Province Tourism Development Master Plan (2003:135) also envisages the standardization (*guifan*) of guides' explanations and signs (*lüyou jieshuo*) and the unification (*tongyi*) of guides' talks in the main scenic areas. In Xiamen, back in the late 1990s, guides had to learn explanations published by the city Tourism Bureau as part of their training.[16]

As noted earlier, watching "folk" performances that adhere to a more or less standard choreography and narrative mirroring that of the national Spring Festival Gala, is an integral part of visiting scenic spots. In the early nineties, Chinese tourism authorities and developers laid great emphasis by organizing performance teams. To overcome a shortage of performers, part-time amateur players were recruited from tourism employees. The CNTA's 1993 yearbook proudly reported that at a hotel on the top of Mt. Wutai in Shanxi, the general manager and the party secretary personally joined the troupe to "offer a show with a distinctive local flavour in accordance with guests' demands" (Wang Qun 1993).

Abroad, the state's ability to channel travelers' experiences and influence their interpretations is much more limited, but still significant. As I have shown in chapter 1, many Chinese abroad, whether long-term migrants or short-term travelers, are exposed only to Chinese-language media, an increasingly large segment of which is contiguous with the media in mainland China in terms of both content and style. Many expectations of Chinese travelers are shaped by these media, particularly by the stories about Chinese lives abroad. In addition, many travelers encounter foreign countries exclusively through the eyes of local Chinese. This is particularly so in the case of group tourists.

In 1997, the director of CNTA explained that outbound tourism should be developed in an "organized, planned, and controlled" way (He Guangwei 1997). The authorities see the Chinese tour guides accompanying the group (called group leaders) as representatives of the state in charge of ensuring that members of the group behave with dignity and that they do not visit places they should not (such as casinos or brothels).[17] Moreover, CNTA officials have pressured local Chinese tour guides in Europe, who accompany groups from China but who possess local licenses, to undergo training in China.[18] This would bring revenue to CNTA and enable the Chinese government to expand its influence on what sites Chinese tourists see and what commentary they hear. The fact that nearly all travel agents and guides who work with Chinese tourists abroad are themselves Chinese—many of them, especially in Europe, are recent migrants—makes them much more amenable to CNTA's demands. Besides, as these migrant travel professionals compile Chinese tourists' itineraries and comment on sights, they share their clients' expectations toward the tourist experience: the desire to experience modernity on the one hand and, on the other, the expectation to consume scenic spots with unambiguous stories.

How Tourists Respond

Several authors, beginning with Oakes (1998), have observed that Chinese tourists realize they are being shown staged performances and yet appreciate, even expect, them. Unlike the post-tourist of Western literature—who has stopped pursuing the authentic because he has realized that everything is fake anyway and that he might as well have a good time—Chinese tourists seem to "play along" because they consider participating in performances of the nation serious business. Schoolchildren are supposed to visit forty patriotic education sites before they graduate from secondary school (Guo 2004:26), and, as Woronov (2004:306) reminds us, appropriate behavior at tourist sites is part of the instruction. School visits to national historic sites are occasions not simply of edification but of rehearsing exemplary discipline and solemnity. "Children are supposed to see and then appreciate China's history and aesthetics in specific ways . . . the attempt always exists on the part of all pedagogues (parents, teachers, state textbook writers) to make the experience 'right' by appreciating the site." (ibid.:307). An article by Ding Guang'en on CNTA's website formulates the same goal for tourists: "Scenic spots are a front of propaganda for thought work. Sites of patriotic education . . . may not be turned into places of leisure and entertainment."[19] Another article argues that in addition to organizing festivals, the government's leadership in defining the image of a tourist destination should include inventing slogans, unifying signage, and "limiting and regulating social behavior at the destination" (*xianzhi yu guifan mudidi shehui xingwei*) so as to satisfy tourist expectations (Shu and Yuan 2003).

Ku Ming-chun's (2006) ethnography of tourists at historical sites in Western China, demonstrates the success of such state-led pedagogy among participants of tour groups. One of the richest sites of Buddhist art in China, the Mogao Caves at Dunhuang, is included in UNESCO's World Cultural Heritage. The caves acquired their renown in the early years of the twentieth century, after an expedition by the Hungarian Orientalist in British service, Sir Aurel Stein. Since many of the statues and frescoes of the cave were taken to London, Paris, and St Petersburg by Stein and others who came after him, Dunhuang is a perfect site to represent not only the splendors of China's cultural history but also the depredations perpetrated by foreign powers in a China that, before the Communists took power, was weak and humiliated. Accordingly, Dunhuang is not only a popular tourist site—marketed with the World Heritage brand—but also a key patriotic education site.

"Nationalist terminology—for example, 'national treasures stolen by foreigners' . . . constantly surfaced in my interviews with other domestic tourists in Dunhuang," writes Ku (2006). Even as the tour guide focused on Dunhuang as World Heritage, visitors, all too aware of Dunhuang's significance in the broader national discourse of history,

> would constantly issue . . . comments that reached beyond the framework of the introduction. For example, a domestic tourist may broach the topic of how foreigners stole the treasure of the Mogao Caves, and immediately the other tourists would add their own comments to this topic until the staff-guides would ask everybody to move to the next caves because other groups were waiting in front of the cave in question. These stories of foreigners' smuggling of national treasure out of China, though widely disseminated in China's public readings and through people's lips, constituted one topic that staff-guides rarely covered in their introductions, which . . . focused on the value of relics as Buddhist art relative to World Heritage. In one of the Mandarin tours that I joined, the domestic tourists completely ignored the staff-guide and, instead, were very enthusiastic and articulate about the national shame that the Mogao Caves embody. The staff guide had no way to stop the tour group, which turned into something like a forum of patriotism and nationalism. She silently standing aside during the visitors' conversations, and finally had to reign in this out-of-control situation by declaring, "Sorry! Our time is up. Let me show you the way out." (Ku 2006)

Ku also reports on a dissenting voice, that of Mr. Xin, who joined the English-language tour because he felt that his fellow Chinese tourists were not interested in what he thought was important about Dunhuang, namely, the artistic and historical value of its art. Yet Mr. Xin's frame of reference, too, was determined by the dominant state-sponsored discourse of World Heritage, which positions a Chinese site in a competitive fashion among the treasures of world history.

> In his description of the value of this site, he used the Sistine Chapel in Italy as the referential counterpart. . . . The value of the relics in the Mogao Caves, in Mr. Xin's words, derived from their relation to relics in other civilizations around the world. (Ku 2006)

Another site Ku visited was Yan'an, the center of the Communist Party's legendary "liberated area" before it had taken national power in 1949.

Learning that Ku was from Taiwan, a fellow tourist undertook to tell her the story of Yan'an with a flair that

> made me wonder whether he had lived in Yan'an in the 1930s and the 1940s. The answer was no. He told me that he had familiarized himself with these stories by reading books, watching movies, and listening to the radio. He explained to me that one did not have to live in Yan'an through that period to know the Yan'an legend and added, "Yan'an symbolizes the legend of the Chinese Communist Party's contributions to the revolution. We've all known about these since we were kids. That's the way we learn about our country and our history. (Ku 2006)

Ku sees these various reactions as characteristic of three types of responses to sites by Chinese tourists. She describes the discourse embraced by the man at Yan'an as reflexive of a "nostalgic self"; that used by Mr. Xin as reflecting a "cosmopolitan self"; and that of nationalist visitors to Dunhuang as characteristic of a "contesting/learning self." But what is noteworthy from our perspective is that all of her respondents behaved in a way foreseen by dominant, state-endorsed or state-imposed interpretations of places. None of them displayed a truly subversive attitude toward what they saw, not even to the extent of ignoring the guide's explanations and wandering off with a beer or an ice cream. This, I suggest, has to do with the seriousness of Chinese tourists' "play." Just as tourist enclaves in China are not separated from but play an important role in the national body, and as consumption is not just play but an act of partaking in modernity, the experience of performances and participation in play at these sites is not an ironic postmodern distancing of the self from reality by acting out a fantasy; on the contrary, it is partaking in the rehearsal of a high modern hegemonic discourse (see Nyíri 2006a:83).

This chapter has focused on ways in which the Chinese state tries to limit uncontrollable encounters and interpretations that mobility can give rise to, and thereby keep its effects as aligned with the state's vision of creating a new national citizenry as possible. Such efforts are important, for, as in the cultural industries, at stake is the state's grip on representations of the nation, on which much of the Communist Party's legitimacy and power rests (Guo 2004). In the realm of tourism, they appear surprisingly successful, as they are aided both by the state's economic and discursive control over tourism development and by the revived tradition of Chinese literati travel. The dual effort to encourage but discipline tourism is likely to persist for some time to come, and group tourism that is its main object is bound to remain dominant as a large reserve of first-time tourists enters the market. At the same time, maintaining a hegemony of state-endorsed representations is bound to be an uphill battle, especially as individual travel abroad becomes common and gives rise to a range of alternative travel narratives that can spread on the Internet.

6
Conflicting Impulses
MOBILITY ENCOURAGED AND HINDERED

The association between movement and fecundity and the imagery of uncontrolled swarming that migration evokes in China (as it does elsewhere) are expressed in the following quote:

Apart from chungong (pornography) and chunyao (aphrodisiac), chun-yun (the mass movement of migrant workers around the Spring Festival) is probably the most exciting, the most unhealthy as well as the most disrespected compound with [the character] chun (spring) in the contemporary Chinese language. . . . Experts say that this demonstrates China's "rapid urbanization" . . . I don't know what the signs of the imminent tide of "urbanization" should be, but I believe they shouldn't include this "feast of mobility" that makes no one except the ticket touts excited. (Shen Hongfei 2003)

Chunyun, the spring migration, conjures up images of an unstoppable, formidable biological event, like the drift of ice down the rivers, the migration of fish, or the swarming of bees. The text, in the popular *Sanlian Life Weekly*, makes fun of the official equation of mobility with modernity by reminding readers of the feelings of nuisance, revulsion, and danger associated with *chunyun*. It also reflects the tension between the ideology that tells Chinese people to get moving for the sake of prosperity and the reality of obstacles, both official and mundane, that spring up on their way. In this chapter, I discuss how the emerging discourse that frames what Xiang Biao calls China's new mobility regime ("a constellation of policies, cultural norms and networks that condition migration" [Xiang 2007:73]) deals with that tension.

Most discussions on the future of the *hukou* regime, while nowadays emphasizing the importance of the freedom of movement, nonetheless stress that this freedom should be kept within limits. For example, Wang Taiyuan, an associate professor of *hukou* management studies (*huzhengxue*) at Public Security University, says:

> No matter how high a degree of freedom of movement we implement, it must still be carried out within the framework of appropriate national and local laws and regulations; only population that meets the requirements contained in these laws and regulations will be able to exercise its freedom of movement and residence as it wishes. (Shi Yaoxin 2000)

This sense that freedom of movement cannot be absolute stems from the conviction that an uncontrolled flow of migrants is bound to overburden urban services and infrastructure to the point of collapse. The term *liudong renkou*, which I have translated as "transient population" and which remains one of the most common terms for internal migrants, itself carries connotations of a wave or flood (*liu* means "to flow"), similes often used in reporting about rural migrants in cities.[1] The character *liu*, as Jacka (2006:44) points out, has additional negative connotations, as it is used in the terms *liumang* (hooligan) and *liulang* (to roam, to wander). Another pair of terms often applied to internal migrants is military-related: *jun* (army) and *dui* (troops). Although in Chinese newspaper language these terms can have positive connotations of victory and progress, they can also sound threatening, as in the heading "The Southwestern Railway Is Groaning: A Report on Seeing Off the 'Sichuan Army' This Spring Festival" (Gan and Deng 1993).

As Tamara Jacka (2006:31n1) points out, the view of rural migrants that conjures up images of chaos is broadly shared between official and popular discourse. She quotes sociologist Yu Depeng:

> Regardless of whether it is the conversation of ordinary urbanites or the opinions of important government officials that one is listening to, regardless of whether one is watching a popular film or television program or reading the work of an authoritative expert, one will be given more or less the same description of rural people who enter urban areas: that is, that they are, in the main, stupid, dirty, lacking in breeding, and without any sense of shame. You will be told that the country people pouring into the cities are, if not active, then latent, robbers and plunderers, prostitutes and pimps, "out of plan guerrillas" [i.e., violators of family planning] and carriers and transmitters of contagious diseases. (Ibid.:42)

Jacka points out further that articles on the floating population tend to conform to a standard structure (ibid.:46–47). In the 1980s and 1990s, they adopted what she calls a managerial perspective: having first established the division of urban society into city people (including the author and the readers) and rural migrants, they proceeded to lay out the benefits and then the dangers of migration and finally concluded that migration is necessary but that its overall control and management must be strengthened. In 1995, for example, an official of the Canton PSB wrote that, while the transient population was an indispensable component of constructing a modern international metropolis (*xiandaihua guoji da dushi*) as it contributed to economic prosperity, it was also responsible for deteriorating safety. In 1993, over 70 percent of those arrested in the city and 96 percent of prostitutes were transients. Also, because of their "low quality," migrants had the deplorable habit of "fighting over their rice bowl" (Zhang Shengchun 1995:10). In order for the benefits created by the transient population to exceed the harm it caused, it had to be managed well, because "only orderly population movement can contribute to social and economic development. . . . Disorderly population movement will damage social stability and affect normal life. . . . A modern international metropolis must be shipshape and orderly" (ibid.:11–12). Other authors argued that the patriarchal, feudal and discipline-averse mentality of peasants could have a negative psychological impact on the overall "civilization level" of the city.

Such accounts "help[ed] to generate a desire for strong central control, thus legitimating the role of the state" (Jacka 2006:47), even though the crime statistics that pointed the finger of blame at migrants were flawed. As Xin Frank He points out, they reflected detention rather than conviction figures (and outsiders were far more likely to be detained without a reason than locals), and people of unknown domicile were automatically added to the columns of outsiders (He 2003:178n4). In the 2000s, as we have seen, accounts of migrants became increasingly diversified and more sympathetic, with portrayals of heroes of development, advice for migrants, and sexual titillation and voyeurism becoming subgenres of their own (He 2003).

Articles written by Shanghai police officials in 1989, show that they considered immigration into their city as an inevitable but negative consequence of development, one that seriously threatened safety and overburdened public transportation and health care (Zhu, Li, and Fan 1989:70). While it has contributed to "relieving some contradictions" in the labor market, it has also posed a threat to the employment of Shanghainese (ibid.:71). In order to protect local workplaces, the authors proposed a system of fines (called city construction fees) to be imposed on the employers of migrant labor, as well as a system of discriminative rents to "make it difficult for low-level outside population to remain in the city in the long term" and thereby accomplish the task of "attracting high level, controlling middle-level, and limiting low level outside population" (ibid.:76). In a detailed report on the activities of various migrant "gangs," Zhou and Sheng (1989) reiterated that migrants' participation in serious crime "poses a great danger to public safety," that migrant ticket touts, con artists, counterfeiters, and prostitutes "seriously disturb public order," and even that the influx of cars from the countryside constitutes a threat to traffic safety (Zhou and Sheng 1989:78–80). Although they added that migrants made up 90 percent of scam victims and 70 percent of burglary victims (as compared to 30 percent of those detained on suspicion of committing crimes), they devoted only six lines to this fact and three pages to describing migrants' criminal activities. Furthermore, they wrote that the high rate of migrants falling victim to crime is related to the fact that they "usually walk around with huge sums of money" and have a "poor awareness of self-defense," suggesting that it is in part their own fault (ibid.:80–81).

Thirteen years later, in 2002, officials of the Shanghai Transient Outside Population Leading Group continued to call for the introduction of the city construction fee in order to "erect a 'fair, equitable and open' barrier to the torrent of low-quality peasant workers" (Xu Changle et al. 2002:14). A book published by the Shanghai City Thought and Politics Work Research Association described the goal as "controlling the population but not human resources" (*kongzhi renkou dan bu kongzhi rencai*) and reiterated that the policy should "reduce the settlement of low-quality personnel in Shanghai" (Xu Deming 2003:20). "The door should be open to the outside population, but the threshold must be high," the editor (the head of that association and a police official) wrote (ibid.:146). The strategy he proposed was called "three transformations" (*san ge zhuanbian*): "transform peasants into qualified (*hege*) workers; transform qualified workers into managers with some technological and scientific knowledge; transform outsiders into future burghers of Shanghai" (ibid.:23). He also called for "unearthing and promoting exemplary personalities and cases among the outside population" in the media (ibid.:26).

Overall, in the 2000s, articles by police officials give the benefits and risks of immigration more balanced coverage. They reiterate that "outsiders" are responsible for 50 percent of crimes, but they lay the blame specifically on the "three withouts," i.e., those without a fixed place of abode, without stable employment, and without a fixed income: "As a great number of 'three withouts' blind drifters enter Shanghai, they add to the city's burden and have an extreme impact on the stability of social order" (Le Weizhong 2000:255–56). Also, there is more emphasis on promoting the "integration of the outside transient population into the community" (Xu et al. 2000:14). But even so, the association of rural migrants with crime, filth, overcrowding, and immorality continues in both official statements and popular literature. As an article in a Canton periodical devoted to "spiritual civilization" put it, migrant enclaves in the city "have become hotbeds of lewdness, drugs, and gambling, and hiding places of [violators of family-planning policies]" (Ma Zhonggui 2000; quoted in Li Peilin 2003:55).

Many officials continue to explain this alleged prevalence of crime among migrants as a result of their irrational mindset and lack of moral standards, a reflection of their "low quality" that is both cause and effect of limited education. Zhao Weixiong (2000:76) of Shanghai's Xuhui District Public Security Bureau writes: "With low education levels, cultural cultivation is also low, so ability to adjust and control oneself is bad, the ability to distinguish right from wrong is lacking." On the other hand, lack of children's schooling is often blamed in part on the "quality" of their parents, who supposedly do not motivate them to study (He Nanying quoted in Human Rights in China [HRIC] 2002b:27).

This explanation recalls the "cultural distance" theory used to explain the low educational achievement of American Blacks in the 1960s, or the more recent assertions that the high dropout rate of Gypsy children in Eastern Europe is because their families lack a "culture of learning." Generally, accounts of rural migrants in China closely parallel accounts of foreign immigrants in Western, especially European countries: they are a necessary evil, a work force without which the cities can no longer function, but a culturally alien body that does not know "our" ways and is prone to crime and immorality. At its base, this view is informed by two assumptions: that migration is a deviation from the norm of sedentary life and therefore requires an explanation; and that the two-tiered society consisting of urbanites and peasants—though we may not like it—is a sociocultural fact, rather than a political construct. In most accounts, even in the more friendly ones, peasant workers appear as a generic, homogeneous category. Sociologist Cao Feilian, for example, sees them as trapped in a "culture of poverty" with such psychological traits as

> gregariousness, a high incidence of alcoholism, frequent resort to violence in the settlement of quarrels, use of physical violence in the training of children, wife beating . . . a high incidence of abandonment of mothers and children, a trend toward mother-centered families, and a strong predisposition toward authoritarianism. (Cao Feilian 2006)

Nonetheless, the 2000s brought an overall change of tone in the media in accordance with the new government line stressing migrants' contributions to society and the need to uphold their rights. Cities pioneering *hukou* reform (Shenzhen, Shijiazhuang) are praised; cities reneging on it (Zhengzhou) are criticized. Instead of overcrowding and accidents, reports on the *chunyun* (the mass homegoing of migrant workers before the Spring Festival), now commonly focus on how railway stations have made the wait comfortable. Lu Jing (2002:21) rejects arguments linking population movement to rising crime, saying this is a matter of management and is largely a result of unequal opportunities and exclusion. She proposes that the freedom of movement should be enshrined in both the constitution and a new *hukou* law. She warns, however, that freedom of movement should be limited by a clause stipulating that it cannot violate "the security of the state and the benefit of society," and that the basic function of the *hukou*, "identifying citizens and protecting social order," must be preserved. She attempts to reconcile mobilizing and immobilizing imperatives by advocating an "appropriate degree of freedom of movement" (ibid.:23–25). Similarly, Huang Renzong of Peking University, writing in the conservative-leftist *Qiushi*, argues that while the current *hukou* reform's ultimate aim is urbanization, it should instead be freedom of movement (Huang 2002).

The new discourse on migrants exemplified by Lu's writing and manifested in a plethora of new books and workshops is related to the recognition of migrant laborers as a large and disenfranchised segment of society outside the Party's control, an argument first sounded by noninstitutional researchers such as Victor Yuan (Yuan and Wang 2000) but now adopted by influential academics.

The movement of nonelite migrants into China's big cities continues to be treated in a conflicted way. Their movement is tolerated in practice and officially endorsed as contributing to modernization, but it is also controlled by administrative, economic and cultural levers pulled by the government, and occasionally by force. They are allowed varying degrees of economic participation, but are rarely granted full social rights and continue to live with the threat of crackdowns.

When going abroad, Chinese citizens encounter the same conflicting impulses to encourage and to hinder mobility, and not only on the part of the Chinese state. Although during the Cold War, the West condemned all Communist countries for not granting their citizens the freedom to leave, very soon after the liberalization of the passport regime in 1986, Chinese travelers found themselves being singled out for suspicion and distrust at airport immigration desks. Even the sympathy generated by the 1989 Tiananmen Massacre, after which tens of thousands of asylum applicants were granted refugee status in the United States, Australia, and elsewhere, was short-lived. "When I dutifully handed my official passport[2] to the Hong Kong immigration official, . . . although the face I saw before me was that of a yellow-skinned Chinese compatriot, that cold and disdainful look was hardly milder than that of the archetypal haughty

English gentleman familiar from foreign novels," a Chinese journalist wrote in 1990 (Zhang Zhiye 1990:7). "When the Chinese people opened the country's doors after thirty years of closure, they discovered that others were closing their gates just at that time" (ibid.:9). The author went on to describe his experience trying to get a visa to a third country while abroad. The consular official at first mistook him for a Japanese, and "a smile spread across his face," but when he saw the Chinese passport he politely told the journalist to go back to China to get his visa (ibid.:10).

A People's Republic of China passport is indeed among the worst to have when applying for a visa or arriving at a border. Even as states vie for the Chinese tourist, they are wary of his overstaying his visa. In 2005, soon after becoming an approved destination for Chinese tourists, Germany announced that if the visa application of any one member of a tour group arouses suspicions, the entire group will be denied visas. Many EU member states require travel agencies to turn in the boarding passes of all tour group members upon return to China to ascertain that there are no overstayers (Qin Lingnan 2006). The humiliation of being denied a visa, taken out of the queue, searched, verbally abused, and forced to pay bribes to border guards and customs officers is a recurrent topic in migrants' and tourists' conversations, although it is generally downplayed in the media. For example, the hero of the soap opera *Into Europe* arrives in France illegally, with the help of a smuggler. The film portrays this as testimony to his ingenuity and tenacity in the face of a challenge to his mobility.

Migrants acutely perceive the frustration of their movement as yet another attempt by an envious West to frustrate the modernization of China. This strikes a chord with the pugnacious nationalistic stories in mainland Chinese and migrant media that nurture past humiliations: the particularly rankling experience of being mistaken for a Japanese and treated with courtesy is a recurrent trope. A Chinese resident of Hungary, returning in a defiant mood from the U.S. Embassy in Budapest where she had applied for a tourist visa, said to me: "If they turn me down I won't go to New York until it has been bombed by China."

This comment is as much a product of the mobilizing discourse of Chinese modernity as of another global narrative, one that strips Chinese migrants of their enfranchisement and equates the cross-border movement of Chinese people and goods with illegality, exploitation, and crime. Headlines across the *Los Angeles Times, El Pais, Libération,* and *The Guardian* use similar language to call our attention to Chinese "traffickers" and "sweatshops." Moreover, there are slippages between imagery of demographic, economic, criminal and hygienic danger that recreate the classical Yellow Peril imaginary. In *The Art of War*, a Wesley Snipes action thriller from 2000, the discovery of corpses of illegal Asian immigrants in a container is linked to the assassination of the Chinese ambassador preparing to sign a treaty on China's accession to the United Nations trade charter, creating an implied connection between the threat of demographic and economic domination. The same trope resurfaces in two 2007 releases: the Italian-German TV drama *La Moglie cinese* (The Chinese wife), based loosely on Roberto Saviano's bestseller *Gomorra*, in which shiploads of Chinese migrants are brought to Italy by the Triads and sold into slavery to the Mafia; and in Jerry Allen Davis' *Shanghai Hotel*, which depicts the plight of Chinese women sold to brothels in the United States. This view, in a mirror image of the leisure culture campaigns in China, finds it hard to believe that Chinese at their borders could simply be tourists (the metaphor of the tourist being, after all, reserved for the modern Western subject [see Nyíri 2006a; Alneng 2002]); they are seen to be lying in wait, in the hundreds of thousands, for the opportunity to cross and remain illegally (see Nyíri 2002a:333–34).

Since the Wen Ho Lee case in 1999 (when a Taiwan-born American physicist was accused of stealing nuclear secrets on China's behalf; the charges were later dropped), mobile Chinese are periodically depicted as white-collar criminals, and high-profile stories associate them with military or industrial espionage. In 2007, *Der Spiegel*, Germany's most influential news magazine, published a cover story entitled "The Yellow Spies," with the accompanying photo showing a pair of "Oriental" eyes peering out from behind a slit in the Chinese flag. The article alleged that China marshaled a network of 800,000 informal spies and that "every student, every businessman who is allowed to go abroad is indebted to the Party," ominously adding, "of course, not every student, doctoral candidate or visiting professor is a spy—probably only a minority of them." But while media in China and those which cater to new migrants indignantly protest such accusations, they rarely engage with or dispute them; instead, they tend to repeat pronouncements to the effect that Chinese migrants are hard-working and good-natured and contribute to the economy of their host countries. (This is in contrast to traditional, local Chinese media, which, particularly in America, are well versed in the discourse of human rights and anti-discrimination, have their own investigative journalists, and actively engage with local media.)

The recent scandal triggered by a videotaped scene of a Malaysian policewoman stripping a female Chinese tourist naked signals that the association of Chinese travelers with smuggling, prostitution, and illegality is not limited to the West (Arnold 2005). Indeed, Dobler (2008) suggests that in Namibia—where the arrest of a Chinese businessman with US$530,000 in his suitcase at Windhoek airport made headlines in 2007—the "rather positive image of Chinese shop owners as energetic people who bring affordable goods to the poor has been supplanted by the negative image of greedy businesspeople profiting from selling worthless junk." Dobler found that sinister rumors of Chinese migrants are as rife in Africa as in the West: "one of the most persistent was that Chinese convicts could choose to serve time on Namibian construction sites. This rumor aptly combines wariness about unfair competition with human rights issues," two subjects that come up whenever China is discussed. "Wherever Chinese contractors are awarded public tenders, suspicions of favoritism or corruption come up, as well" (Dobler 2008). Clearly, this criminalizing narrative is the flipside of another, equally powerful one: that of the global Chinese businessman with family in constant motion between continents, who displays his wealth by snapping up real estate in Vancouver and creating prosperous but segregated "ethnoburbs" (W. Li 1998) around Los Angeles, as well as golf course-casinos in Laos and Burma. In fact, Ong (2006) suggests that the two narratives are united by a sort of dialectic, as the exploitation of illegal labor is naturalized in the same ethnocultural terms as the rapid accumulation of wealth.

In the 2000s, states worldwide have been simultaneously securitizing their borders in the name of fighting crime, terrorism, human trafficking, and illegal migration, and implementing skill-based migration schemes favoring the highly educated, previously known only in Canada, Australia, New Zealand, and the United States. In the emerging global regime of *selective mobilization*, mobility (of persons, goods, or ideas) is seen as useful and praiseworthy when it fits a particular model of capitalist rationality, and as threatening and illegal in other cases. Although internationally mobile Chinese are actually overrepresented in the latter category and underrepresented in the former, they embody Western fears of being overrun by overwhelming numbers of cultural aliens suspected of serving the expansionist ambitions of a single-party dictatorship. Yet the fact that, in reality, very few unskilled Chinese migrants are reaching Western shores—certainly compared to China's population—is in no small part due to the efforts of that very regime. The Chinese government sees the liberalization of the passport regime and the acceleration of cross-border flows on the one hand, and the more systematic blocking of cross-border movement by people deemed undesirable on the other, as two sides of the same modernization coin. It shares this view with most Western governments; what is unusual is its outspoken embrace of both sides. Indeed, in the 2000s, a number of articles by Entry and Exit Administration officials have enthusiastically advocated speeding up passport deliveries, construction and modernization of land border crossings, and creating a national database of "persons prohibited from entering and leaving" in the same breath (e.g., Zhang and Zhang 2002). As the head of the Shanghai Entry and Exit Office noted with satisfaction,

> the scale of the work of reporting, detecting and controlling persons prohibited to enter and exit has developed from manual detection and control based on a "blacklist" only a few dozen names long to a computerized information database of nearly 20 thousand, and after need-based passport delivery has been implemented this year, the database will expand to tens of thousands of persons. (Ma Zhengdong 2002:14)

The construction of the Yunnan-Thailand transport corridor will both facilitate traffic and upgrade surveillance. Speaking to *The New York Times*, the director of the expressway leading from Kunming, Yunnan's capital, to the Thai border, which opened in 2006, was equally proud of the 430 bridges and the 168 security cameras that allowed him to "zoom in on the faces of passengers as cars passed through toll booths" (Fuller 2008).

The conflicting imperatives of encouraging the cross-border movement of capital and goods and of controlling the flows of individuals sometimes results in elaborate farces that are invisible to uninitiated outsiders. During her research in Hekou, a county seat in Yunnan across the Red River from Vietnam, Zhang Juan found that while local residents could cross the border without visas, many preferred to cross the river informally, as it was cheaper. Local authorities seemed to close an eye to this and to informal, small-scale, cross-border trade and money exchanges.[3]

The contradictory incentives and barriers are perhaps most fully demonstrated in Yanbian Prefecture, Jilin. Local governments here provide loans to migrant workers to pay the security deposit designed to prevent them from absconding; but these loans are often guaranteed by the house in which the migrant's family lives (Luova 2007:181). The remittances sent by migrants, as well as the fact that emigration reduces rural unemployment and saves scarce education and health care funds, mean that local governments are generally favorably disposed toward migration, though areas with fewer opportunities for economic development—such as Mingxi County in Fujian or Yanbian Prefecture in Jilin—have been more likely to promote it openly. But the national and even provincial bureaucracies are divided: for the overseas Chinese affairs apparatus, whose effort to strengthen "new migrant work" is also a strategy to maintain its own relevance as earlier generations of overseas Chinese leaders and tycoons age, more migration means a greater constituency. But for the more powerful foreign affairs organs the hype about illegal Chinese migration in the West creates an embarrassment that is not worth whatever economic gains it may bring, and the Public Security apparatus gets more rewards for catching snakeheads than for making legal departures smoother. During a 1999 interview, the deputy director-general of the Foreign Affairs Office of Fuzhou, Fujian's capital, expressed his disapproval of lax passport issuing practices in Sanming Prefecture, which had declared creating migrants its goal. Once, he said, the Sanming Foreign Affairs Office's right to issue passports had been suspended as punishment for illegal migrants' use of them.[4] Hu Jieguo, the secretary-general of the West African Association for the Promotion of China's Peaceful Reunification, enjoys the support of the Party's United Front Department, but has complained that some embassy officials are less than enthusiastic about his recruitment activities (Mao and Zhou 2007). Similarly, the Vientiane Chinese Association in Laos has worked closely with the United Front Department of the CCP when organizing meetings to oppose Taiwanese independence, but only low-level embassy personnel attended them.[5]

It is not only on the Chinese side that the contradictory imperatives of migration management produce farces. In their research on migrants from northeastern China to Britain, Frank Pieke and Xiang Biao (2007:15) document how every time the British government turns the immigration screw, the thriving migration brokerage sector "manipulates and creates the relevant biographical evidence to fit the categories of the UK's immigration policy, turning 'illegal,' 'unskilled' and 'unwanted' individuals into 'legal,' 'skilled' and 'useful.'" For instance, a migration agency trains clients as slaughterers so that they can obtain visas as skilled workers in Britain, whether or not they actually intend to work in a slaughterhouse, and charges 110,000 yuan (around US$14,000) for the training.

> When we said that RMB 110,000 sounded high, the founder and legal representative of Liaoning Services, who also was an official of the local Overseas Chinese Affairs Office, stood up and said: "This is *completely* legal! . . . You can spend 30,000 on a business visa, but you will have to become illegal later. With us you don't need to worry at all." Legality clearly is manufactured in different degrees and kinds, all of which carry their own price tag. (Pieke and Xiang 2007:12)

Even in the context of Africa's seemingly far less regulated immigration regimes, Chinese migrants increasingly have to resort to similar strategies. As a Chinese businessman in Namibia told Dobler (2008), since the government tightened the issuance of work permits to Chinese traders, "we all invest in manufacturing." Factories are duly set up, but most "consist of second-hand machinery imported from China, awaiting repairs for most of the year. . . . Manufacturing plants' real output is not manufactured goods, but work permits for Chinese migrants who then work in shops."

There is a widely circulated remark attributed to Deng Xiaoping, dating from the aftermath of the Tiananmen Massacre. Irritated by Western demands to put an end to restrictions on Chinese citizens' leaving the country, he is supposed to have said that it would only take China to "relax things a bit along the coast" for the West to see hundreds of thousands of boat people coming ashore in neighboring countries. Even if this story is apocryphal, it is ironic that soon after Tiananmen, Western pressure was compelling the Chinese government to impose stricter punishments on illegal emigration, whose mechanisms had been instrumental in the flight of a number of student leaders three years before. A joint "Opinion on further preventing and stopping the illegal settlement of Chinese citizens abroad" was issued in 1992 by five government bodies.[6] In 1997, complying with further foreign pressure, China introduced the crime of human trafficking, punishable by a prison sentence of up to ten years, into its penal code, and have since been an enthusiastic supporter on cracking down on "traffickers" (including those who organize the departure of Chinese citizens as well as those who help North Korean refugees across the border into China). The coastal counties of Fuqing, Changle, and Lianjiang in Fujian Province, which have become the main sources of illegal Chinese immigrants in the United States and Europe, have been targeted in a high-profile campaign against illegal emigration by the central and provincial governments. This resulted in the implementation of a collective responsibility system, in which all township and county leaders are punished by loss of bonuses or even dismissal if illegal emigration occurs in their area. Some local governments reacted by grouping village households into units of ten and making every family in the unit responsible if a member of one household attempted illegal emigration (Chin 2003:60–65). In 2003, the Ministry of Trade issued another directive instructing citizens to refrain from "blindly going abroad" to work without having obtained a permit or business visa from the government (Yu Hai 2003). As China becomes a destination of migrants from North Korea, Vietnam, Burma, and elsewhere, the interests of the central government in curbing illegal migration are increasingly aligned with those of Western countries.

7
Conclusion
MOBILITY AND CULTURAL CONTROL

C hinatown, Manhattan, 7 March 2001. At the Yidong shopping center at 88 East Broadway, Fujianese vendors sell international telephone cards. One vendor stocks fifty-one kinds, many with Chinese text and distinctive design. On one card, called Great Wall, Deng Xiaoping extends his congratulations with the return of Hong Kong to the Motherland. Phone cards embody the way globalized communication technologies have created unexpected new markets for ethnicity and nationalism, and also the way the mobility of technologies is intertwined with human mobility. International calling is now a largely ethnic business that targets Mexicans, Chinese, or Ukrainians in migrant neighborhoods across the globe. In the United States, at least 40 percent of those working in the prepaid card industry are said to be immigrants (Sachs 2002). They target certain groups by offering special low rates to particular countries, and even provinces such as Fujian. For low-income migrants, calling family and friends is often the only nonessential spending, and the cards do not require registration that deters undocumented migrants from getting home phones.

This particular vendor, from Fuzhou, is a woman around twenty-five years old. She came to America five years ago, following her parents who had since gone back to China with her two children. Her situation is typical for the neighborhood. At the nearby American East Fuzhou Restaurant, the waitress comes from a township to the north of Fuzhou; she has a nine-year-old child back home. She came to the United States to join her husband, an illegal immigrant, but her brother-in-law, who had less money and could not afford passage to America, went to England instead. She phones him every week. Another phone card customer, who like the two women does not have legal residency papers, paid $40,000, an amount frequently mentioned in connection with illegal immigration from China, to come to the United States in 1994. He calls his friends in England once every two weeks. He tells them not to come to America, because "the weather is bad and life is bad"—he works twelve to thirteen hours every day—and if they were caught they would be sent back to China.

Around the corner on Elizabeth Street, the Houyu Overseas Chinese Association of America (Meiguo Houyu Huaqiao Lianyihui), one of around four dozen organizations in New York founded by migrants from Fujian in the last two decades, celebrates its sixteenth anniversary at Jing Fong Restaurant. Outside, the restaurant is inconspicuous, but inside it displays all the latest splendors of modernity one finds in Chinese cities: an escalator leads to two large halls with marble floors and gilt crystal chandeliers. In Chinese newspapers, Jing Fong advertises itself as the largest restaurant in Chinatown. Most of its business comes from Fujianese wedding parties, at which elaborately posed photos are taken and sent back home. Since the 1980s, hundreds of thousands of migrant workers have come to the United States from Fujian, mostly via New York and largely illegally (see Pieke et al. 2004).

Houyu ("Monkey Island"), in Changle Prefecture near Fuzhou, is one of the major sending areas of migrants to the United States. After listening first to the PRC and then the U.S. national anthems, the Chinese consul-general mounts the stage, decorated with huge American and Chinese flags, to thank the association for its contribution to homeland construction. The association's secretary-general responds that seeing the great

Fatherland ever more prosperous and strong is their common desire. Someone reports on the construction of a culture palace in Houyu, for which the association has raised $900,000. After the speeches, the evening continues with a show of nationalities' arts, including Han dancers performing flirtatious pop dances in Uighur costumes. (A major event in China may have the luxury of engaging dancers of various nationalities, but in this small troupe, the majority Han have to perform the roles of the minorities.) For my benefit, the chairman of the Fuzhou United Friendship Association of New York, a construction entrepreneur, points to the stage: "This is the art our Chinese ancestors left to us."

A vice president of the Fu Tsing American Assocation (representing migrants from Fuqing Prefecture) sits at one of the tables. A former teacher in his mid-thirties, he came to America illegally eleven years ago. "Do you think the bosses around this table all have papers? . . . In America, even millionaires can be without papers!" With officials from the consulate nearby, the vice president loudly and cheerfully explains that he "does immigration work" (*gao yimin*). This chiefly means handling applications for political asylum. Is there any conflict between doing this kind of work and entertaining official delegations from China? "None whatsoever. It's business. We do our business; they do theirs. Every year, $200 million is sent to China from the Bank of China in New York. And that's only one of ten banks. It goes into building houses, helping relatives, and investment. This is very important for China." Fuqing's main official paper, the *Fuqing Ribao*, reported in 2000 that the president has donated around a million yuan to his home area since the eighties, including a contribution to a village Party committee office building. The vice president says he came to America because here, unlike in the European welfare state system, if you have strength and brains you can get by. His sister lives in the Netherlands; his brother, in France.

Can the way illegal migrants from Fujian Province in Manhattan's Chinatown make sense of their experience of mobility, and the way that experience makes them relate to China, be understood in the same framework as the experience of a middle-class Chinese tourist at a popular scenic spot in China? Do these very different situations point to something common in terms of how newfound mobility is affecting subjectivity and its state conditioning in China?

I suggest that both kinds of individuals have to negotiate their positions as modern Chinese subjects as they cope with the contradiction between the expectation of mobility and barriers in front of it. While unifying and mobilizing images of Chinese modernity are transmitted to them through a range of media technologies from telephone cards to tourist brochures, they have to make their way through everyday situations and contradictory local discourses that stand in the way of movement and strip them of their enfranchisement.

I have argued in this book that dominant discourses valorize and encourage both migration and tourism, within and across borders, as ways of being modern Chinese citizens. They seek to unify migrants and tourists by placing their experiences within an interpretive framework of a national Chinese modernity, transmitted through a range of media technologies, not just print (Anderson 1983) and television or video (Yang 1997; Schein 2005), but also technologies and performances that are adapted to the lives of mobile individuals and therefore more effective, from DVDs to theme parks. Standardized participatory rituals of the nation, with "ethnic" songs and dances, "five-thousand-year-old traditional culture," and landscape clips can be reproduced in Jiuzhaigou, New York, a migrant workers' settlement, or, in the case of the Central Television's Spring Festival Gala, on satellite television.

This "indoctritainment" is clearly inspired by the state discourse celebrating the rebirth of China as a powerful, harmonious, multiethnic nation with a glorious history, but it is produced by quasi-capitalist market mechanisms and popularly consumed. This standardized textual and visual symbolism firmly places migrants within the officially endorsed interpretations of globally mobile Chineseness. The arches and dragon dances in Chinatowns, the displays of red banners and brass plaques from Chinese officials in the offices of Chinese organizations, the congratulatory telegrams from the same officials, patriotic pop songs performed at festive events, and the layout and language of new-migrant newspapers communicate, in the same way as tourist brochures and "nationality" shows, not just a homogeneous and timeless ethnic identity but, more specifically, continuity with the Chinese national project (Nyíri 2002b). These occasions rehearse the interpretation of movement as a modernizing mission by a global vanguard, a mission that is primarily for the Fatherland's benefit, but one that profits the rest of the world as well.

As more people begin to move, the state attempts to maintain its authority over the interpretation of their movement through a heavy transnational presence in the migrant public sphere, economic and administrative control of tourism, and a hegemonic televisual discourse that today's Chinese capitalists willingly mediate not just domestically but also in a burgeoning global media.

Domestic tourists are not such heroic figures, but they have much the same tasks of bearing witness to the modern nation through experience and performance. Where migrants are expected to affirm the ethnic aspect of an essential China, drawing together "the Chinese race" though they might no longer be citizens, tourists reinforce China's territorial aspect, often in minority regions. The locations onto which mobility is projected, be it global cities of the West or scenic spots, are devoid of agency; along with the locals, they become immobile backdrops to Chinese modernity. The orientalistic scene of dancing Hungarian waiters accompanying the dinner of the Chinese businessman in Chen Dian and Chen Mei's novel *Holy River*, like the "minority culture night" of a package tour of China's southwestern ethnic regions, tames the locals and provides them with a place in a nationalized Chinese cultural universe.

The discourses of the migrant and the tourist communicate that it is essential for the modern Chinese subject to be mobile. Mobility is something that distinguishes him from less modern foreigners or minorities. The tourist spreads civilization through consumption; the migrant, through production, though the two are, of course, intertwined. Rather than being the ironic behavior of "post-tourists," Chinese tourists' enjoyment of the performative—photographing the stone stele with the World Heritage inscription or joining in a minority tug-of-war—and their wariness of the "authentic" everyday life of toured places that Western tourists pursue seem to stem from the same root: impatience with the backward and stationary, and a desire to distance themselves from it. According to a manager from one of the largest travel agencies in Sichuan Province, "Chinese tourists don't want that [seeing authentic village life] because they know it already . . . because they lived like that when they were little, or if not they, then their parents or grandparents or great-grandparents." The persuasiveness of these hegemonic discourses is undermined by the fact that movement remains formidably difficult for Chinese citizens; sometimes more so than before. Those who have succeeded in moving abroad put on the brave face of mobile modernity when they visit home, but for the Fujianese kitchen hands or garment workers in New York or Tuscany, this is preceded by years of struggle against immobilization, first crossing borders, then averting deportation and hiding out in Chinatown basements. At home, the Chinese state, too, had long sought to immobilize its own threatening and illegal migrants, the so-called blind flow (*mangliu*) of rural-urban migration. Today, while encouraging them to move, the regime confines them to a legally disenfranchised urban underclass. These experiences of frustrated modernity produce a tension in which mobile Chinese subjects must live.

The Western discourse on Chinese migrants, like the Chinese one, suggests their exceptionality: the latter endowing them with a unique ability to contribute to global modernization and the former seeing them as a human flow of a potentially unparalleled scale and threatening cultural and political difference. Ultimately, both of these discourses derive migratory, economic, or criminal patterns from reified cultural traits (hard work, mutual help, and so on). In essence, the two discourses represent alternative visions of globalization, but, in the end, both use the language of culture as a foil for competing claims of superiority in hierarchies of modernity and capitalism. Both attempt to discipline mobility by asserting cultural authority over their representation.

For its part, the Chinese state does so through the massive imposition of interpretive authority in public spaces and the media both domestically and abroad. This succeeds for three principal reasons: the actors who control these spaces are linked to the Chinese state structurally and/ or by economic benefits; the discourse of pioneers elevates their status; and, finally, both mobile subjects and those sedentary populations that are exposed to the new mobility are emotionally invested in the discourse of modernization and national strength. They want to share the emotional and economic benefits of China's rising power and, for many, growing social wellbeing by adopting the discourse of modern national citizenship to distinguish themselves from the losers of the process. The rapid globalization of Chinese-language media infrastructure, the overwhelming weight within it of corporations either based or with business interests in mainland China, and recent migrants' often limited consumption of non-Chinese media contribute to the conservation or strengthening of the officially endorsed discourse of the nation.

Perhaps the most eloquent demonstration of this were the worldwide protests of April 2008. During the run-up to the Peking Olympics, Chinese students and other migrants took to the streets in numerous cities to protest Western media coverage of the recent unrest in Tibet and to protect the Olympic torch relay from Tibetan and other critics of the Olympics.

These demonstrations would probably not have gone ahead without the tacit approval of China's embassies, but the emotions of participants were clearly spontaneous and genuine. They were motivated by a genuine fury and a desire to defend the discourse of the harmonious, happy, forward-looking nation against those who challenged it. Rather than government kudos, their reward was being celebrated as national heroes across the Chinese Internet, from the Strong-Country Community (Qiangguo Shequ) of *People's Daily Online* to Chinese Students and Scholars bulletin boards in the United States. The tens (perhaps hundreds) of thousands of students and other migrants who turned out to demonstrate in London, San Francisco, Buenos Aires, Sydney, and numerous other cities and campuses with Chinese flags, chants of "One China forever—no separation" and slogans like "Protect the Fatherland's unity, wish the world peace," and the hundreds of thousands (millions?) of Internet users in and outside China who demonstrated their patriotism by adding a red heart icon and the word CHINA to their MSN Messenger screen names, were not doing the government's bidding; in fact, in conversations many emphasized that they were critical of the Party. But they were, to paraphrase James Scott, seeing and talking like the state, voluntarily and forcefully perpetuating the state's language and its view of history, and questioning the Chineseness of those who disagreed.

Remarkable though China's success in remaining a "gardening state" while adapting to the rules of "gamekeeper states" has been, the near-hegemony of the officially endorsed discourse of modern nationhood is tenuous. Leisure travel abroad is creating public and media spaces that are less firmly linked to state-endorsed interpretations. The creation of more self-conscious subjects of a modern Chinese nation-state retains the potentiality of more critical and reflexive positions, which are already being reflected in online discussions.

On the other hand, encounters with Chinese tourists—especially those who are now, in increasing numbers, traveling independently—are likely to confuse and discredit "securitized" discourses of Chinese migration in the West and the various (partly self-contradictory) stereotypical representations of Chinese abroad as precarious illegal laborers, global businessmen who snap up suburban real estate, and industrial spies. These processes have the potential to impact both Chinese and non-Chinese views of the place of Chinese subjects in the modern world.

Notes

Introduction

1   An ambitious recent essay on the persistence of China's "etatist aesthetic" is Zhu Dake's *Liumang de shengyan* (The hooligans' feast, 2006). Zhu makes a complex argument about the oppositional but mutually constitutive relationship between the position of the mobile, subversive "hooligan" and that of etatist stability in Chinese cultural history.

2   In translating contemporary Chinese public discourse, particularly when cultural control is the question at hand, the choice between finding idiomatic equivalents and insisting on literary translation is a particularly important and charged one. Is *laowai* a "whitey" or simply a "foreigner"? Is *zuohao gongzuo* to "gooddo the work" of something or simply to "complete something"? In contrast to earlier translators who tended to exoticize Chinese texts by coining new terms or leaving them untranslated, today's translations tend to be enterprises in cultural brokerage that choose the smoothest colloquial equivalents,

while ignoring the power implications of language. Trying to balance these approaches, I emphasize the "ideologemes" present in contemporary mainland Chinese vernacular in some cases and gloss over them in others. The point is to reflect on the presence and influence of these ideologemes, even as time erodes their erstwhile ideological nature.

3 See Greenblatt, *Cultural Mobility* (Cambridge, UK: Cambridge University Press, 2009).

1 Internal Migration in Reform China

1 Though officially abolished after the collapse of the Soviet Union, this system has been retained in a modified form and continues to be used by the Moscow city government to limit migration to the city.

2 A number of works have been published on the topic in English, including Chan 1996, Solinger 1999, Davin 1999, L. Zhang 2001, and Murphy 2002.

3 See Kojima (1996:378–81) for the various measures adopted to suppress migration under the *hukou* system.

4 On migration in pre-reform China, see Diana Lary (1999) and Yang Yunyan (1994:90–122).

5 State Council, "Guanyu keji renyuan heli liudong ruogan wenti de guiding."

6 Tianjin City People's Government Office, "Notice on reforming our city's population control work" (Guanyu gaige wo shi renkou kongzhi gongzuo de tongzhi), cited in Li Ruojian (2001:54).

7 "Pilot measures for regulating certain questions of the mechanical growth of our city's population" (Guanyu kongzhi ben shi renkou jixie zengzhang ruogan wenti de shixing guiding).

8 State Council, "Memorandum on stopping certain cities' and counties' practice of openly selling township *hukou*" (Guanyu zhizhi yixie shi, xian gongkai chumai chengzhen hukou de tongzhi; 1985) and "Memorandum on strictly controlling the overly rapid growth in 'agricultural-to-non' [-agricultural *hukou*] transfers" (Guanyu yange kongzhi "nong-zhuan-fei" guokuai zengzhang de tongzhi; 1992).

9 Ministry of Public Security, "Opinion on a pilot project to reform household registration in small towns and on perfecting the household registration management system in villages" (Guanyu xiao chengzhen huji gaige de shidian fang'an he guanyu wanshan nongcun huji guanli zhidu de yijian). State Council Document no. 20 (1997).

10 CCP Central Committee and State Council, "Some opinions on promoting the healthy development of small towns" (Guanyu cujin xiao chengzhen jiankang fazhan de ruogan yijian). Central Committee Document no. 11 (2000).

11 Ministry of Public Security, "Opinion on promoting the reform of small towns' household registration management system" (Guanyu tuijin xiao chengzhen

huji guanli zhidu gaige de yijian). State Council Document no. 6 (2001).

12   Ministry of Public Security, "Opinion on resolving some outstanding issues in current *hukou* management work" (Guanyu jiejue dangqian hukou guanli gongzuo zhong ji ge tuchu wenti de yijian), State Council Document no. 24 (1998).

13   For example, regulations issued by Guangdong Province left it up to each county's government "to determine the scale of migration in accordance with the overall absorption capacity and scientific demographic plan" of the area (Xia 2004).

14   Article 2, Beijing wailai lai Jing wugong jingshang renyuan guanli tiaoli, cited in Human Rights in China (2002a:60).

15   They also have to own their place of residence. Based on this rule, a *Peking Youth Daily* article in 2001 estimated that, to qualify for a Peking *hukou* as an entrepreneur, one had to invest 13 million yuan, achieve sales of 17 million yuan, and purchase a house worth 500,000 yuan (Zhang Tao 2001).

16   For example, in Ningbo, Jiangsu, migrants who are "not willing to till the land" must surrender their plots to a village land pool, which is then collectively rented out, and the migrants receive 200 to 300 yuan per year (He Wei 2001).

17   The 1994 Temporary Regulations on the Management of Interprovincial Movement and Employment of Rural Labour (Nongcun laodongli kuasheng liudong jiuye guanli zanxing guiding) and the 1995 Rules of Applying for and Issuing Temporary Residence Permits define the procedure in a general manner. There are variations depending on the province and locality. For example, Peking's Rules for the *Hukou* Management of Outside Personnel specify that landlords may not rent housing to "outside personnel" without a temporary residence permit and that they have to obtain separate permits from the housing, land administration, and public security departments to do so (Beijing shi waidi lai Jing renyuan huji guanli guiding, decree number 11 of the Peking City People's Government, 1995). Under threat of fines, the rules make landlords and employers responsible for ensuring their lodgers or employees register with the authorities and require them to report any illegal activities by them. They also have to sign a "responsibility declaration" to the Public Security Bureau. A separate set of Rules on the Management of Rental Housing for Outside Personnel in Peking (Beijing shi waidi lai Jing renyuan zulin fangwu guanli guiding, decree number 12 of the Peking City People's Government, 1995) requires landlords who wish to rent property to "outside personnel" to obtain a permit first. The permit has to be displayed outside the premises, which, as Human Rights in China (2002a:62) notes, allows everyone to determine which housing is occupied by migrants (for example, in case of a crackdown). The number of permits in each neighborhood is to be kept under a limit so that the share of outsiders within the population does not exceed a certain ratio (not specified in the rules). The rules contain a number of obligations for lodgers, includ-

ing not to use the housing "to engage in activities violating family planning"! Even stricter regulations are in place in Shanghai (see Human Rights in China 2002a:64–70).

18 "Rules of *Hukou* Management of Outside Personnel in Peking" (Beijing wailai renkou hukou guanli tiaoli), 1995.

19 Several authors point out additional aspects of poor health care that distinguish migrants from local residents, such as low ratios of children's vaccination and preventive health checkups (Xiang 2005; H. X. Zhang 2006). H. X. Zhang (2006) cites government statistics showing that migrant workers respectively account for 100, 80, and 70 percent of the workforce in so-called township and village mines, construction, and processing and manufacturing, officially classed as dangerous occupations.

20 The school Woronov (2004) studied went up to sixth form, after which children either went back to their home villages to continue their education or began working. See also Human Rights in China (2002b).

21 For example, eighty-seven workers died in the 1993 fire at the Zhili Toy Factory in Shenzhen (Human Rights in China 2002a:92).

22 On the other hand, marriage with an urban *hukou* holder is highly attractive for those without: Murphy (2002:43) found that an urban *hukou* was a key attribute of a desirable husband for her fifteen-year-old informants in rural Jiangxi Province.

23 Other terms for rural migrants are *mingong*, the "transient population" (*liudong renkou*), "temporary population" (*zanzhu renkou*) and "outside labor" (*wailai laodong*).

24 "Custody and repatriation" of so-called "three withouts people" (without proper documents, without fixed abode, and without a stable income) was one of the central functions of the system until 2003. It was abolished following the highly publicized death in custody of a student who had been detained because he was not carrying the documents proving the lawfulness of his stay in Canton. Under the system, those detained were placed in camps where they had to work to generate the income necessary to pay for their deportation to their place of *hukou* registration.

25 Shenzhen jingji tequ shehui zhian zonghe zhili tiaoli (Shenzhen Special Economic Zone Regulations on the Comprehensive Control of Social Order).

26 Guanyu jiaqiang shehui zhian zonghe zhili de jueding.

27 Beginning in about 1999, practically all newspapers listed in the National Periodicals Database of the Shanghai Library, as well as a range of academic journals published such articles. See Froissart (2005) for a review of influential scholarly publications and reports to the government, including Liu (2003 and 2004) and Huang (2002).

28 State Council Office, Notice on Gooddoing the Management and Service Work of Peasants Entering Cities for Work and Employment (Guanyu zuohao nongmin jincheng wugong jiuye guanli he fuwu gongzuo de tongzhi), 5 January 2003.

29 Since the reform of the urban welfare system, urban residents generally receive no state welfare benefits either, as the system relies on employer and employee contributions; but those within a low income bracket do, on paper, receive free inpatient care and a state allowance for outpatient care (Froissart 2005). Given that migrants are overrepresented in this bracket, their being denied these benefits is significant.

30 "Guanyu queding laodong guanxi" (On defining labor relations), 25 May 2005.

31 "Rules of *Hukou* Management of Outside Personnel in Peking" (Beijing wailai renkou hukou guanli tiaoli), 1995.

32 I spotted this slogan in the Liangmaqiao neighborhood of Peking in 2005.

33 Wu Hong, "China to clear out students, refugees before Olympics." http://news.monstersandcritics.com/asiapacific/features/article_1400345.php/China_to_clear_out_students_refugees_before_Olympics (accessed 25 April 2008).

34 Zhang Juan, personal communication, December 2006.

2 International Migration from China

1 The authors do not provide the size or filter criteria of the sample.

2 "Regulations on Questions Regarding Personnel Studying Overseas" (Guanyu zai wai liuxue renyuan youguan wenti de guiding).

3 "Guanyu chuangjian shehuizhuyi shichang jingji ruogan wenti de jueding."

4 "Zhonghua Renmin Gongheguo chujing rujing guanlifa."

5 "Gongmin yin sishi chuguo huzhao shenqing, shenpi guanli gongzuo guifan" (Working standards for the work of managing passport applications and approvals for citizens going abroad on private business," attachment to Ministry of Public Security Department of Exit and Entry document no. 744 [1996]).

6 "Guanyu geti siying qiye renyuan chuguo (jing) kaocha he zongshi shangwu huodong de zanxing guiding" (Temporary regulations on employees of individual and private enterprises going abroad on inspection trips and for business activities), *Yunnan Ribao*, 7 December 2000, A04.

7 "Gongmin yin sishi chuguo huzhao shenqing, shenpi guanli gongzuo guifan."

8 These include anyone whose departure will, according to "the appropriate supervisory body of the State Council, cause harm to state security or seriously compromise state interests."

9 The section on Eastern Europe is based largely on Nyíri 2003. See references there.

10 Unlike the National People's Congress, the People's Political Consultative Conference has overseas Chinese delegates.

11 "Regulations on the composition and expenses of the Qiaolian" (Guanyu Qiaolian bianzhi he jingfei de guiding), see *Huaqiao Huaren Baike Quanshu* (2000:134).

12 Interview with President Sun Lei in Vientiane, 5 December 2008.

13 Interview in Phnom Penh, 27 August 2008.

14 Interview in Vientiane, 6 December 2008.

15 http://www.hxuc.com (accessed 11 April 2009).

16 This is reported in the summary of the Qiaoban's Overseas Propaganda Work Conference (Qiaoban document no. 58 [1996]). See also Li Minghuan 2002.

17 See, for example, the top story on Tianya, "Lundun, wo suo jiandao de huoju jieli—cong meiyou ba gouge chang de zheme jidongguo" (London, the torch relay I saw: never been so excited to sing the national anthem), 11 April 2008. http://www.cache.tianya.cn/publicforum/content/funinfo/1/1124786.shtml (accessed 14 April 2008).

18 For those who have been cybersocialized in China, the lack of influence of Web sites produced outside the PRC may well stem in large part from the fact that the popularity of foreign sites, even those that are freely accessible, is low among mainland users (Giese 2005).

3 Tourism in Contemporary China

1 "Guomin lüyou jihua," document provided by Wei Xiaoan, then head of the Policy and Regulation Division.

2 In 2007, the government split the three golden weeks into six shorter periods to mitigate the overcrowding of transport systems and tourist destinations.

3 On the role of consumption in spiritual civilization campaigns, see Lewis 2002.

4 Article 27, Sichuan Province Tourism Management Guidelines (Sichuan sheng lüyou guanli tiaoli), revised and reissued by the Sichuan People's Congress, 20 July 2002 (published in *Sichuan Ribao*, 13 August 2002, 8).

5 For example, Article 18, Sichuan Province Tourism Management Guidelines.

6 Data from the official Chinese Internet Information Centre, cited in www. Travel.ru, 7 July 2003.

7 In 2002, their number was further raised to 528.

8 http://www.cambodianculturalvillage.com/index.php (accessed 13 July 2007).

9 Zhongguo gongmin chuguo lüyou banfa (State Council decree no. 354, 27 May 2002).

10 Speech at the Second International Forum on Chinese Outbound Tourism (IFCOT), Peking, 20–21 November 2005, summarized in the China Outbound Project Newsletter, January 2006. http://www.china-outbound.com/Newsletter/2006_01_COP_Newsletter.pdf

11. There is a fascinating parallel between this article and one published seventy years earlier in another Shanghai magazine, *China Traveler*: "I love traveling because I am a modern person. . . . Modern people are mobile." Yet instead of emphasizing national pride, that earlier article focuses on the erasure of national differences in the cosmopolitan experience: "A traveler has no nationality. He has no prejudice—except his *Taste* [original in English]. . . .

Hatred among different nations, discrimination among different races . . . can all be given up by a traveler" (quoted in Dong 2006:195).

4 The Usefulness of Mobility

1   It relies in large part on a systematic analysis of press articles and books published since 1978 on migration, tourism, and spiritual civilization. The analysis covered articles whose titles contained the terms immigration (*churujing*), travel (*lüyou*), and spiritual civilization (*jingshen wenming*). The articles were obtained in three ways: (1) electronically searching China's national social science journals database and the national periodicals database since 1978 using these keywords, (2) electronically searching the entire *People's Daily* and *Economic Daily* databases for the same, and (3) manually searching a one-month sample of four representative mass periodicals every five years between February 1978 and February 2003, for every article dealing with migration, travel abroad, or spiritual civilization. These periodicals are the *People's Daily* (the central newspaper of the Communist Party), the *People's Pictorial* and *Beijing Youth Daily* (popular mass-market papers in the 1980s and 1990s–2000s, respectively), and *Southern Weekend*, the preferred daily of the young, educated urban professionals in the 2000s. This has been supplemented by a review of books for which these keywords were entered in the National Library's catalogue in 2005.

2   Xin Liu (1997) has earlier drawn a parallel between Chinese villagers going to the city to work and students going overseas. He argued that, in both cases, a "spatial hierarchy" was at work that endowed returnees with a higher status by virtue of their having lived in more modern places.

3   State Council Office, Notice on Gooddoing the Management and Service Work of Peasants Entering Cities for Work and Employment (Guanyu zuohao nongmin jincheng wugong jiuye guanli he fuwu gongzuo de tongzhi), 5 January 2003.

4   Andrzej Kwieciński at the 8th European Conference on Agriculture and Rural Development in China, Yiwu, Zhejiang, 1 September 2006.

5   *Pudong xinqu wailai wugong qingnian wenming shouce.*

6   This expression has been applied to migrant women by other Chinese authors; see Gaetano 2004:41.

7   Yan Hairong (2003) contrasts this with the Mao era, when Anhui maids working for high officials in Peking were hidden from the public eye as incompatible with the socialist ideals preached by the Party.

8   Shanghai City People's Congress, Shanghai shi wailai liudong renyuan guanli tiaoli, 1 January 1997.

9   According to various surveys, most migrants' leisure is quite different from what Wang Xiangfen describes. In one study, for example, 52 percent of female

migrant workers said they used their spare time to call their families, 35 percent went window shopping, 28 percent visited with their fellow villagers, and only 27 percent read books or newspapers (Chen Chaobing 2005). The point here, of course, is not what Wang actually does but how she would like to depict herself.

10 www.godpp.gov.cn (accessed April 2005).

11 For example, in April 2006, as part of Peking's campaign to improve residents' "quality" ahead of the 2008 Olympics, the city's Anti-Heresy Committee, Anti-Gambling Committee, and an advertising agency have jointly put up cartoons inside buses displaying examples of civilized behavior that range from rejecting gambling to refusing superstition, opposing heresy, and engaging in healthy activities such as harvest-song festivals. On other buses, passengers were merely requested to contribute to creating a "harmonious vehicle" (*hexie chexiang*) by wearing clean clothes and going to work and returning home happily.

12 These have included the Ministry of Science and Technology's project, "Policy research on developing science popularization work in our country's urban communities and raising the quality of the masses' cultural and spiritual life" (Fazhan wo guo chengshi shequ kepu gongzuo yu tigao gongzhong wenhua jingshen shenghuo zhiliang de duice yanjiu) (2002); the Ministry of Culture's project, "Leisure time: A survey and research on the cultural and spiritual life of our country's masses" (Xianxia shijian: wo guo gongzhong wenhua jingshen shenghuo xianzhuang de diaocha yu yanjiu) (2001); the National Soft Sciences Project, "The social conditions and support system of the leisure industry and development policies" (Guojia Ruan Kexue Yanjiu Xiangmu "Xiuxian chanye yu shehui tiaojian zhichi xitong ji fazhan duice) (2000); and the National Social Sciences Grant project, "The importance of youth leisure time education" (Guojia Shehui Kexue Jijin Xiangmu "Qingshaonian xianxia shijian jiaoyu de zhongyaoxing"). Adding the term culture to make a subject appear more legitimate or high-class has been a rhetorical strategy widely employed by both commercial and official organizations; at the same time, it provides new spaces for disseminating the state's cultural discourse. Thus, tourism developers advertise wine culture, tea culture, and even chieftain culture (*tusi wenhua*), and a Sichuan hotpot restaurant chain, the Taoranju Chongqing Yinshi Wenhua Jituan, calls itself a Culinary Culture Group. See Wang Gan's (2001) analysis of the penetration of Chinese folk songs and dances, promoted by the government, in Shenzhen night clubs.

13 Yet it appeared in 1920s and 1930s Shanghai as well. Madeleine Yue Dong (2006:205) quotes Yu Songhua, a reporter for the German-owned *Shenbao* newspaper, as having written in 1934: "people in our country like to drink and play mahjong to kill time. The German way is so much better. Travel and music are what we should advocate in China as respectable and beneficial forms of entertainment." Although at this point the Nazi *Kraft durch Freude* tourist movement had not yet been set up, German tourism was strongly connected

to the nationalist and socialist movements. A letter to the editor of *China Traveler* published in 1932 directly advocated emulating the Italian Fascist youth tourist movement (ibid.:214). At the time, however, these ideas had very little impact beyond the Shanghai elite.

14 CNTA, "Guanyu jixu fazhan jiari lüyou de yijian" (Opinion on further developing holiday tourism).

15 Thanks to Zhang Juan for pointing out this post.

16 Weiyi Shi (2008:49) reports similar attitudes among Dai and Akha from China to their co-ethnics in Laos.

17 This reflection on cultural conservation was prompted by an Internet campaign to close a Starbucks outlet inside Peking's Forbidden City.

18 A famous quote from Deng Xiaoping.

19 Litzinger (2004) came to similar conclusions in Deqin, a Tibetan-inhabited area in northwestern Yunnan.

20 Reportedly, however, Tibetans in Qinghai Province did protest against turning a traditional festival into a tourist attraction by refusing to sing, dance, or wear fur (explaining that the latter was inconsistent with Buddhism) (*China Rights Forum* 2007).

21 Parts of this section are based on Nyíri 2001, 2002a, 2005a and 2006b and Pieke et al. 2004.

22 *Who's Who of Chinese Origin Worldwide* (Budapest), 4 (2000):31–32.

23 "Cong dagong jilei dao chaoshi qi jia de chuangyezhe; jinchukou maoyi de kaituozhe; Zhonghua minzu wenhua de fuchengzhe" (*Fujian Qiaobao* 2004b).

24 "Zhongguo geti shangren taojin Feizhou: jianku chuangye, gan shang, gan gan" (*People's Daily Online* 2005).

25 Interview with the chairman of the Mingxi branch of the Federation of Returned Overseas Chinese, 23 June 2000; *Fujian Qiaobao* 18 April 2002; *Fujian Ribao*, 17 April 2002. The local authorities in Mingxi County have in fact been so keen on promoting migration to Eastern Europe that they approached the Hungarian embassy in Peking with a proposal to establish a visa office in the prefectural center, Sanming (interviews in Peking on 29 July 1999 with the director of the Sanming City Government Liaison and Trade Office, Peking, and in Fuzhou on 4 August 1999 with the head of the Sister Cities Division, Fujian Province Foreign Affairs Office). On support for migrants from rural Zhejiang Province, see Xu Qing 1999.

26 Interview with the official in charge of European affairs in the Overseas Department of the Fujian Province Overseas Chinese Affairs Bureau, Fuzhou, 5 August 1999.

27 Luova (2007:185) found similar arrangements in Yanbian Prefecture, Jilin, in 2004.

28 Unlike Western narratives of trafficking, Chinese authors tend not to criminalize migration brokers—on whom the majority of students and workers going abroad rely—in a blanket fashion, but rather differentiate between honest and bad intermediaries. In 2001, after issuing a number of documents ban-

ning commercial agencies (other than labor export agencies working on contracts) from providing help in obtaining visas, immigrant status, or university placement abroad, it introduced regulations for the licensing of such agencies (Xiang Biao 2003).

29 Overseas Chinese Affairs Bureau and Ministry of Public Security, "Notice on Taking Forceful Measures to Stop the Illegal Emigration of Our Citizens" (Guanyu caiqu youli cuoshi zhizhi wo guo gongmin feifa yiju guowai de tongzhi), 15 February 1993.

30 Ministry of Foreign Affairs and the Ministry of Public Security, "Notice on Replacing Illegal Emigrants' Passports" (Guanyu wei feifa yimin bu, huan huzhao de tongzhi), 30 October 1992.

31 Personal communication, Heather Peters, consultant to UNESCO's Southeast Asian anti-trafficking project, 2005.

32 The subtitle of the book reads "Two Generations of Chinese Men Go to Harvard from Peking: There, They Demonstrate to You the Wisdom and Strength of the Chinese Male."

33 Haiyan Lee points out a recent shift in plot patterns, in which Chinese women marrying foreigners is no longer cast as a contestation of national power but, on the contrary, as a sign of a more self-confident China fitting into global patterns of romantic love. The condition is that a "foreigner's desire for China must take the form of reverence, longing, and love. He can access a Chinese woman's body only if he makes her his lawful wife, his emotional equal, and his partner in global enterprise" (Lee 2006:525). Kong Shuyu (personal communication) also argues that in the late 2000s, soap operas with transnational plots have shifted from the nationalistic to youth idol drama.

34 *Ouzhou Shibao* (Journal d'Europe) is one of the largest-circulation Europe-based Chinese newspapers. It was one of the first European Chinese papers with a pro-PRC stance and has had strong ties with state media conglomerates in China. See Li Minghuan 2002.

35 Such statements should be read against the background of widespread violence against Chinese traders in Russia. In 2006, a group of Russian students firebombed the Cherkizovo market, aiming to drive out Chinese and other foreign merchants. Shortly afterwards, with the explicit intention, voiced by President Putin, of returning control over markets to the local population, the government issued a decree banning the employment of foreign citizens in retail. The law went into effect in 2007.

36 Several studies have documented the negative attitudes to African students in China. As a student from Benin in Gillespie's (2006) study said, "the Chinese unconsciously think of an African as someone they should set straight." Another interviewee, a counselor at the embassy of an African country, described the way Africans are seen in China in this way: "You come here [because] you need assistance, but you can't give anything. . . . Black stupid, black poor, black strange, black very ugly, AIDS. . . . Black—any negative adjective you can put on it." Gillespie's study is particularly significant as it

was conducted around the time of the China-Africa summit, when Peking was plastered with posters praising Chinese-African friendship and portraying Africa as a land of ancient civilizations and exotic nature, in an effort to show that China does not subscribe to the negative Western discourse of Africa as a failed continent.

During her research in Tanzania, Hsu (2007:116) observed that "it did not take very long before they [Chinese construction workers] started pouring out one story after another about how the locals were stupid, cheating and malingering."

37 "Haiwai laodongzhe shi women shidai de pingmin yingxiong." Reproduced on the website of the Fujian Qiaolian, http://www.fjql.org/fjrzhw/do86.htm, 27 January 2005.

38 The term *jianku fendou* was originally used to describe the hardships the Communists had endured on the way to victory. Later, in a well-known speech, Mao Zedong urged cadres to preserve the spirit of arduous struggle even though they were now in power. As Jacka (2006:53) points out, the terminology of struggle, hardship, and endurance is also applied to rural migrants in Chinese cities. These qualities are seen as "virtues to be retained: . . . In fact, it is precisely the ability to tolerate years of low-paid backbreaking toil, abuse, and exploitation without welfare or security of employment that makes them heroes." In the same way, these qualities can redeem the low quality of overseas entrepreneurial or labor migrants and propel them toward higher social status.

39 In a new soap opera, *Admiral Zheng He*, co-produced by China and several Southeast Asian countries, Zheng He is portrayed explicitly as a bringer of development (Johanes Herlijanto, personal communication).

40 While overseas Chinese had loomed large in China's modernization project at several earlier points in the twentieth century, migration itself was never before seen as an essential part of modernity.

41 As James Cook points out, regional elites in Fujian and Guangdong provinces in the first half of the twentieth century emphasized similar characteristics— "a valorization of wanderlust, or a spirit of adventure, that permitted both a strong sentimental attachment to one's homeland and a desire for exploration and maritime activity; the celebration of a commercial acumen . . . and a historically and experientially formed savvy about . . . modernization"—in arguing that they were better suited for modernizing China than the elites of the old capitals or of Westernized Shanghai (Cook 2006:159–60).

42 Yao (2002:54) asserts that the traders did not turn local villagers "into another version of the lazy natives, the opposite of the Chinese cultural perfection of hard work and endurance," and that this had the effect of undercutting "the Chinese self-perception of racial and economic superiority." This appears to contrast with at least the public narratives of new migrants, buoyed by China's new discourse of national self-confidence.

43 Interview in Udomxay, 11 December 2008.

44 Interview in Vientiane, 5 December 2008.

45 Interview in Phnom Penh, 7 August 2008. Similar comments have been made by other Chinese factory managers and supervisors. For example, an article in the *Phnom Penh Post* (Lo 2006) quotes a merchandiser as saying: "Cambodians cannot work in high positions as we do because they are backward and not educated enough."

46 Sumie Arima, personal communication.

47 Anagnost (1997:117–37) has pointed out the high degree to which ordinary Chinese, even those who personally wished to circumvent the government's one-child policy, internalized the discourse of family planning and population quality.

48 Indeed, *dagong*, a term that means work for a wage or salary and has a connotation of casualness (as opposed to career or vocation), is equally frequently used in narratives of domestic and international migration. But while in the context of domestic migration, *dagong* is unequivocally associated with lower status (Jacka 2006:44), in overseas migration, the stint behind a McDonalds counter or Woolworth till, while humiliating, is portrayed as a necessary educational experience for students. Thus, psychologist Yue Xiaodong (2004:2) writes: "At first, when I got a job, I felt very impatient and regretted the precious time wasted on *dagong*. But later, I realized that dagong was my social university. . . . *Dagong* developed my ability to survive, it was an investment in building my character." (See also Qian Ning 2002:117–23.)

49 Parts of this section are based on Nyíri 2002b.

50 King (2006) points out that the careful avoidance of development aid terminology is designed to differentiate China's policy toward the "Third World," which it asserts is one of mutually beneficial cooperation, from the patronizing discourse of Western donors, in which Africa continually fails to meet targets or measure up to standards.

51 This does not mean that there is no difference between the internal and external civilizing projects. There are indications that internally, China may be paying more attention now to environmental protection (manifested in reforestation projects, grazing bans and so on), and that this may be coming at the expense of exporting polluting development, mining, and soil-extensive farming such as soy bean production to South America and Africa. Similar accusations were leveled against Japan's development strategy in the 1970s.

52 Recent mainland Chinese migrants who live in Europe and other white-majority societies usually call locals "foreigner" (*laowai*), a term perhaps better translated as "whitey" and normally applied only to whites. Chinese in Africa tend to refer to locals as blacks (*heiren*) or niggers (*heigui*), whereas those in Indochina use the local ethnonym (e.g., Lao) to refer to their neighbors.

53 As has been pointed out by many authors (including Harrell and Dikötter), the current Chinese phrase for "Chinese nation," *Zhonghua minzu*, often carries an overtone of biological heredity, as did—in Dikötter's comparison—the term

Anglo-Saxon in the Victorian era or the phrase "das deutsche Volk" in the first half of the twentieth century.

54 But it is important to note that they do not generally perceive their civilizing project as one opposed to that of the Chinese state, but rather as one perfecting it. It is interesting to compare this current Chinese Christian civilizing project and its cooptation of the state's civilizing project to the earlier, Western Christian experience in China; see Harrell 1995. A similar discourse, according to which the Chinese are God's vehicle for spreading the faith and modernizing the world, exists among Chinese Muslims and has been popular among certain Indonesian Chinese Muslim intellectuals (Johanes Herlijanto, personal communication).

5 The Dangers of Mobility

1 Article 9, "Zhong-E bianjing lüyou zanxing guanli banfa" (Temporary procedure for managing Chinese-Russian border tourism), issued jointly by the Inner Mongolia Autonomous Region Foreign Affairs Department, Tourism Office, and Public Security Bureau, 8 April 1992.

2 Ibid., Article 10.

3 Literally, "superior thinking," but Orwell's term captures its meaning better (see note 2 to the Introduction).

4 "Guanyu chuguo liuxue renyuan gongzuo de ruogan guiding" (Regulations on work with students overseas).

5 "Guanyu yingong chuguo renyuan shencha de guiding," approved by the State Council on 15 August 1991.

6 Zhang Juan, personal communication, February 2007.

7 "Gongchandangyuan zai shewai huodong zhong weifan jilü dangji chufen de zanxing guiding," issued by the CCP's Discipine and Investigation Commission (Jilü Jiancha Weiyuanhui) on 23 May 1988.

8 CNTA, "Guanyu zuzhi wo guo gongmin fu Dongnanya san guo lüyou de zanxing guanli banfa" (Temporary management procedures for organizing the travel of our citizens to the three Southeast Asian countries), 5 December 1990.

9 *Action Plan to Raise the Civilizational Quality of Chinese Tourists* (Tisheng Zhongguo gongmin lüyou wenming suzhi xingdong jihua), www.cnta.gov.cn/Upfiles/200681784098.doc, published 8 August 2006, accessed 6 October 2006.

10 "Guide to Chinese tourists' civilized behaviour abroad" (Zhongguo gongmin chujing lüyou wenming xingwei zhinan), http://www.chinanews.com.cn/cj/xftd/news/2006/10-02/799335.shtml, published 2 October 2006, accessed 6 October 2006.

11 "Civilized behaviour convention of Chinese domestic tourists" (Zhongguo gongmin guonei lüyou wenming xingwei gongyue), http://www.chinanews.

com.cn/cj/xftd/news/2006/10-02/799333.shtml, published 2 October 2006, accessed 6 October 2006. The most interesting variation is in Item 7, entitled "Respect the rights of others": this includes, among other things, not forcing foreign guests to take photos with oneself and respecting the work of service personnel.

12   A case described by Zhu Li (2006:150) shows how state authority harnesses commercial consumption to guide the thinking of mobile individuals. The government of Jinhua City invited companies to bid for free film screenings for migrant workers. The films were selected by the city Propaganda Department, but the sponsors got to air their advertisements before the screening.

13   David Bray (2005:184ff) describes the "Shenyang model" of "community building," which served as the basis of the nationally adopted model. "Floor leaders" in each residential building form the bottom of an elaborate hierarchy of "community volunteers." According to a "community compact," every resident makes seven "promises," which include not viewing pornography, refraining from "feudal superstition," avoiding disputes with neighbours and maintaining a harmonious family. The community office keeps a file on each family, and the yearly bonus of its officials depends on there being no protests or petitions in the "community."

14   www.cnta.gov.cn/21-wxzw/2j/zrj-3.asp, accessed 10 December 2004.

15   Xizang Zizhiqu lüyou guanli tiaoli, http://www.cnta.gov.cn/22-zcfg/2j/lydy-2003-3-1.htm, accessed 10 December 2004.

16   These were later published by the Xiamen City Tourism Bureau as *Youbian Xiamen* (Around Xiamen, 1999) and *Xiamen daoyouci* (Xiamen guides' talks, 2001). Information from Lin Xin, then a student of tourism management at Xiamen University and a part-time tour guide.

17   "Chujing lüyou lingdui renyuan guanli banfa" (Procedure for the management of outbound tour group leading personnel), 28 October 2002, CNTA decree no. 18.

18   Interview with Shi Yaling, tour guide in Vienna, December 2005.

19   www.cnta.gov.cn/21-wxzw/2j/zrj-3.asp, accessed 10 December 2004.

6 Conflicting Impulses

1   *Liudong renkou* is often also translated as "floating population." For an analysis of "water terminology" in English-language reporting on refugees and immigrants, see Harris 1995.

2   That the passport was an official (*gongwu*) one, originally intended to be used by individuals traveling on government business though in practice used more widely, rather than an ordinary (*putong*) one, adds to the insult.

3   Zhang Juan, personal communication, December 2006.

4   Interview in Fuzhou, 6 August 1999.

5   Interview with Secretary-General Peng Zhenghua, Vientiane, 6 December 2008.
6   Overseas Chinese Affairs Bureau, Ministry of Foreign Affairs, Ministry of Public Security, Ministry of Trade and Foreign Economic Cooperation, and Ministry of Labour, "Guanyu jin yi bu fangfan he zhizhi wo guo gongmin feifa yiju guowai de yijian," CCP Central Committee document no. 1992, 3.

Conclusion: Mobility and Cultural Control

1   Interview with Zhou Yimin, International Center manager, China Comfort Travel, Chengdu, 10 September 2003.

References

English titles of Chinese texts and periodicals without brackets mean that they are provided in the original. English titles in brackets are my translations.

The Age (Melbourne newspaper)
    2006 "Old Is New for Chinese Tourism." 5 December.
Ai Jun
    2004 "Lüli huji zhidu de bu heli gongneng" (Eliminate inappropriate functions of the *hukou* system). *Xinjingbao*, 14 March, A02.
Alden, Chris
    2007 *China in Africa*. London and Cape Town: Zed Books and David Philip.
Alden, Chris, and Martyn Davies
    2006 "Chinese Multinational Corporations in Africa." Paper presented at the China-Africa Links Workshop, Center for China's Transnational Relations, Hong Kong University of Science and Technology, 11–12 November.
Alneng, Victor
    2002 "The Modern Does Not Cater for Natives." *Tourist Studies* 2, no. 2:119–42.

Anagnost, Ann

1997   *National Past-Times: Narrative, Representation, and Power in Modern China.* Durham, N.C.: Duke University Press.

Anderson, Benedict O'G.

1983   *Imagined Communities.* London: Verso.

Ap, John

2003   "An Assessment of Theme Park Development in China." In *Tourism in China*, ed. Lew et al., 195–214.

Arlt, Wolfgang

2004   "Into a bright future: Chinese Outbound Tourism to Europe is getting more professional, reliable and tailor-made for special interests." Speech at the Second European Travel Fair for the China Incoming Market, Cologne, 3–4 January. Reprinted in *Travel & Trade in Europe*, nos. 1–2:15.

Arnold, Wayne

2005   "Video Sets off Furor between Malaysia and China." *International Herald Tribune*, 9 December.

Association Chinoise Vientiane (Wanxiang Zhonghua Lishihui)

2007   *Qiaoshe ji huaren Huaqiao gaikuang* (The general situation of overseas Chinese organizations and the overseas Chinese people). Vientiane.

Bai Yun and Hong Xiao

1989   "'Chuguochao' zhong de shiluozhe" (The losers in the "emigration fever"). *Fazhi Liaowang*, nos. 3–4:18–20.

Bao Qingde

2002   Presentation at the conference "Leisure and Social Progress." Peking, 27 October.

Barabantseva, Elena

2005   "Shifting Boundaries of the Chinese Nation: Overseas Chinese and Ethnic Minorities in the People's Republic of China's Modernisation Project." Ph.D. diss., School of Social Sciences, University of Manchester.

Barmé, Geremie

1999   *In the Red.* New York: Columbia University Press.

Bauman, Zygmunt

1987   *Legislators and Interpreters.* Cambridge: Polity Press.

Blair, David

2006   "Rioters Attack Chinese after Zambian Poll." *The Telegraph* (London), 3 October 2006. http://www.telegraph.co.uk/news/main.jhtml?xml=/news/2006/10/03/wzambo3.xml

Bray, David

2005   *Social Space and Governance in Urban China.* Stanford: Stanford University Press.

Bredeloup, Sylvie, and Brigitte Bertoncello

2006   "La migration chinoise en Afrique: accélérateur du développment ou 'sanglot de l'homme noir'?" (Chinese migration to Africa: accelerator of development or "the black man's burden"?). *Afrique contemporaine* 218, no. 2:199–224.

Brooke, James
2004 "In the Pacific, Vying for Elusive Prey: China's Rich Tourists." *The New York Times*, 24 May.

Bu Wei
2006 "Looking for 'The Insider's Perspective': Human Trafficking in Sichuan." In *Doing Fieldwork in China*, ed. Maria Heimer and Stig Thøgersen, 209–24. Honolulu: University of Hawai'i Press.

Callahan, William A.
2003 "Beyond Cosmopolitanism and Nationalism: Diasporic Chinese and Neo-Nationalism in China and Thailand." *International Organization* 57:481–517.
2007 "Tianxia, Empire and the World: Soft Power and China's Foreign Policy Discourse in the 21st Century." British Inter-University China Centre Working Paper 1. Manchester.

Campus France
2008 *Les étudiants internationaux: Chiffres clés / International Student Mobility: Key Figures*. Paris.

Cao Feilian
2006 "Rural-Urban Migration in Contemporary China: Discuss with Reference to Shanghai." MPhil diss., Department of Sociology, Chinese University of Hong Kong.

Cao Peiyun and Shuangshuang
2004 "Chuguo dagong re Nongan" (Nongan in overseas labour fever). *Jilin Ribao* (Changchun), 23 April, 5.

Cao Peng
1992 "Zouchu guomen de laowu da jun" (A great labour army leaves the country's gates). *Gongren Ribao*, 7 June, 1.

CCTV (China Central Television)
2007 *Liu Jianjun yu Fezhou "Baodingcun"* (Liu Jianjun and Africa's "Baoding villages"). 25 January. Transcript online: "http://www.all-africa.net/Get?gsfz/14074574.htm" (accessed 2 October 2008).

Chan, Kam Wing
1996 "Post-Mao China: A Two-Class Urban Society in the Making." *International Journal of Urban and Regional Research* 20, no. 1.

Chen Ailing
1997 "Lüyou shengdi geng yao zhongshi jingshen wenming jianshe" (At holy places of tourism, the construction of spiritual civilization is even more important). *Chuangzao* (Kunming), no. 3:25–26.

Chen Chaobing
2005 "Bangzhu nongmingong zouchu wenhua shamo" (Help migrant workers get out of cultural desert). http://www.cnhubei.com/200502/ca689405.htm (accessed 15 October 2005).

Chen Dian and Chen Mei

    1997   *Sheng he* (Sacred river). Peking: Wenhua Yishu Chubanshe.

Chen Feng

    1998   "Shi lun yifa guifan gongmin churujing huodong zhong cunzai de zhongjie jigou" (Legally regulating middleman agencies in citizen's cross-border travel: a tentative discussion). *Gongan Xuekan*, no. 3:89–91.

Chen Guohong

    2006   "Chen Daming huo Agenting zongtong jiejian" (Chen Daming received by Argentine president). *Shijie Rongyin* (Hong Kong), no. 21:30–31.

Chen Linhui

    2005   "Xiuxian wenhua: shehui fazhan de xin jiyu" (Leisure culture: a new opportunity for society's development). *Tansuo yu zhengming*, no. 12:28–31.

Chen Renjie

    2006   "Lin Wenjing faqi chuangban Fuqing Daxue" (Lin Wenjing initiates establishment of Fuqing University). *Shijie Rongyin* (Hong Kong), no. 21:36.

Chen Xiurong

    2004   "Haiwai huaren xin yimin de quanqiuhua yu Zhongguo xibu da kaifa" (The globalisation of new Chinese migrants overseas and China's Great Western Development). Paper presented at the 5th conference of the International Society for the Study of Chinese Overseas, Copenhagen, 10–14 May.

Chen Wei

    2006   "Lüyoudi nongmin wenti yanjiu: Yi Guangdong Danxiashan jingqu wei li / A Study on Peasants Problems in Scenic Area: Case Study of Danxia Mountain in Guangdong Province." Paper presented at the 3rd China Tourism Forum, Hong Kong, 15–16 December.

Cheng Guanglong

    2002   "Huji gaige: shenzhong er xi ren de huati" (*Hukou* reform: a heavy but heartening topic). *Zhongguo laonian bao*, 19 April, 1.

Cheng, Joseph Y. S., and King-lun Ngok

    1998   "Interactions between China's Organs Responsible for Overseas Chinese Affairs and the Overseas Communities: The Cases of Guangdong and Fujian in the Economic Era." Paper presented at the International Convention of Asia Scholars, Noordwijkerhout, The Netherlands, 25 June.

Cheng Xi

    1999   "Liuxuesheng di dailiu yu Zhongguo zhengfu di duice" (Chinese students' remaining abroad and the response of the Chinese government). *Overseas Chinese History Studies*, no. 2:63–76.

    2003   *Dangdai Zhongguo liuxuesheng yanjiu* (China's overseas students today). Hong Kong: Hong Kong Press for Social Sciences.

    2005   *Qiaowu yu waijiao guanxi yanjiu: Zhongguo fangqi "shuangzhong guoji" de huigu yu fansi* (Overseas Chinese work and diplomacy: rethinking China's abolition of dual citizenship). Peking: Zhongguo Huaqiao Chubanshe.

Chin, James K.
    2003   "Reducing Irregular Migration from China." *International Migration* 41, no. 3:49–72.

China Cultural Relics Research Association (Zhongguo Wenwu Xuehui) et al., eds.
    1998   *Zhongguo Zhuming Fengjing Mingsheng Lüyou Daguan* (Tourist Encyclopedia of China's Famous Scenic Areas). Beijing: Zhongguo Ditu Chubanshe.

China News Agency
    2007   "Faguo huashe kaitong boke, jilu kangyi meiti mohei weiquan quan guocheng" (France's Chinese community opens blog, documents full course of rights-protection [movement] against media slander). *Xin Daobao / Új Szemle* (Budapest), 19 December 2007–3 January 2008, F10.

China Rights Forum (Hong Kong)
    2004   "News Update," no. 4:6–11.
    2007   "Tibetan Festival Turns into Silent Protest," no. 4:11.

Chinese Academy of Social Sciences (CASS)
    2006   *Shijie shehuizhuyi huangpishu* (Yellow paper on world socialism). http://www.cass.net.cn/file/2006051559241.html (accessed 18 November 2006).

Chinese Embassy in Mozambique
    2005   "Zhongguo zhu Mosangbike shiguan juxing huaqiao chunjie zhaodaihui" (Chinese Embassy in Mozambique holds Spring Festival reception for overseas Chinese). In *Feizhou Huaqiao huaren shehuishi ziliao xuanji / Social History of Chinese Overseas in Africa: Selected Documents (1800–2005)*, ed. and ann. Li Anshan, 366. Beijing Daxue Huaqiao Huaren Yanjiu Zhongxin Zhongshu (Peking University Overseas Chinese Research Centre Series), no. 28. Hong Kong: Hong Kong Press for Social Sciences.

Chinese Outbound Tourism Blog
    2007   "The Shopping Behaviour of Chinese Travellers—Now available as E-Book." http://www.china-incoming.com, 25 April.

Chiu, Ann Shu-ju
    2005   "Historical Memory, Ethnic Identity and the Internet that Connects the Chinese Transmigrants to their Home." Paper presented at "People on the Move: The Transnational Flow of Chinese Human Capital," conference at the Center on China's Transnational Relations, Hong Kong University of Science and Technology, 21–22 October.

Chiu, Ann Shu-ju, and Chee-Beng Tan
    2004   "Old Chinese Overseas Communities and New Chinese Migrants on the Internet." Paper presented at the 5th Conference of the International Society for the Study of Chinese Overseas, Elsinore, Denmark, 10–14 May.

Clifford, James

    1992   "Traveling Cultures." In *Cultural Studies*, ed. Lawrence Grossberg, Cary Nelson, and Paula Treichler, 96–116. New York: Routledge.

Cong, Cao

    2005   "China's Brain Drain and Brain Gain: Why First-Rate Overseas Chinese Academics Still Hesitate to Return or Be Deeply Involved in China's Education and Scientific Enterprises." Paper presented at the conference "People on the Move: The Transnational Flow of Chinese Human Capital," Center on China's Transnational Relations, Hong Kong University of Science and Technology, 21–22 October.

Cook, James A.

    2006   "Reimagining China: Xiamen, Overseas Chinese, and a Transnational Modernity." In *Everyday Modernity in China*, ed. Madeleine Yue Dong and Joshua Goldstein, 156–94. Seattle: University of Washington Press.

Cresswell, Tim

    2006   *On the Move: Mobility in the Modern Western World*. Abingdon, Oxfordshire: Routledge.

Cui Chuanyi

    2003   "Shiying nongmin jincheng tiaozheng chengxiang guanxi: dui jin Jing nongmingong ji qi zinü jiuye jiuxue he juzhu wenti de diaocha" (Adapting to peasants' influx into cities, adjusting rural-urban relations: a study of employment, schooling and housing problems of peasant workers in Peking). In *Nongmingong: Zhongguo jincheng nongmin de jingji shehui fenxi* (Migrant workers: economic and social analysis of peasants in Chinese cities), ed. Li Peilin, 161–71. Peking: Zhongguo Kexue Wenxian Chubanshe.

Cui Dan

    2002   "Wo shi si xiang fagui quxiao huji xianzhi tiaokuan: Meiyou Shenzhen hukou ye keyi zai Shen sheli kuaijishi, jingji, dichan zixun deng jigou" (*Hukou* requirements struck from four city regulations: now possible to set up accountant offices, brokerages and real estate agencies in Shenzhen without *hukou*). *Shenzhen Shangbao*, 27 April, A02.

D. T.

    2007   "Uyghur Culture Faced with Endless Campaigns," *China Rights Forum*, no. 4:97–107.

Dai Adi and Lin Xiaochun

    2005   "Zhongwen baozhi '*Xifei Tongyi Shangbao*' yansheng ji" (How the Chinese newspaper *Xifei Tongyi Shangbao* was born). In *Feizhou Huaqiao huaren shehuishi ziliao xuanji / Social History of Chinese Overseas in Africa: Selected Documents (1800–2005)*, ed. and ann. Li Anshan, 400. Beijing Daxue Huaqiao Huaren Yanjiu Zhongxin Zhongshu (Peking University Overseas Chinese Research Centre Series), no. 28. Hong Kong: Hong Kong Press for Social Sciences.

Dai Wen

2002 "Chuguo dagong xiaoxin shangdang" (Going overseas to work? Beware of fraud!). *Renmin Ribao*, 25 March, 9.

Dai Wenhai

2001 "Beijing weihe quxiao zhaogong hukou xianzhi" (Why Peking abolished *hukou* restrictions in job recruitment). *Jingji Ribao*, 28 August, 4.

Davies, Martyn

2007 "China's Special Economic Zone model comes to Africa." *The China Monitor* (Stellenbosch), no. 17:4–6 (April).

Davin, Delia

1999 *Internal Migration in Contemporary China*. New York: St. Martin's Press.

Deng Xiaoping

1990 Speech at meeting with Thai businessman Charoen Phokpand, Peking, 7 April.

Diana, Antonella

Forthcoming. "Reconfiguring Belonging in Post-Socialist Xishuangbanna, China." In *Spirits, States and Scooters: Tai Communities on the Move*, ed. Andrew Walker, 163–80. Singapore: NUS Press.

Dikötter, Frank

2005 "Race in China," in *China Inside Out. Contemporary Chinese Nationalism and Transnationalism*, ed. Pál Nyíri and Joana Breidenbach, 177–204. Budapest and New York: CEU Press.

Dobler, Gregor

2008 "Cheapness and Resentment: Chinese Traders and Local Society in Oshikango, Namibia." Paper presented at the Asian Studies Centre seminar, Leiden University, 27 March.

Dong, Madeleine Yue

2006 "Shanghai's *China Traveler*." In *Everyday Modernity in China*, ed. Madeleine Yue Dong and Joshua Goldstein, 195–226.

Dong Shaoping

2003 "Lun wo guo huji guanli zhidu de gaige quxiang" (On the choices of reform in our country's household registration regime). *Xingzheng yu fa*, no. 3:56–58.

Dongfangming

2004 "Zhongguo shangcheng bianbu shijie" (Chinese shopping centres spread across the world). *Qiaoyuan* (Shenyang), no. 6:9.

Dott, Brian R.

2002 "Signifying Mount Tai: Modern Meanings of an Ancient Site." Paper presented at the Association of Asian Studies Annual Meeting, Washington, D.C.

Du Ping

2005 Statement by the Director of the State Department's Western Development Bureau, 21 June. http://news.xinhuanet.com/newscenter/2005-06/21/content_3115051.htm (accessed 3 January 2008).

Duan Ying and Yang Hui

2001 "Quanli bianyuan de Manchunman: Lüyou zuowei xiandaixing yu minzu yishi de gean yanjiu" (Manchunman at the periphery of power: Tourism as a case study in modernity and ethnic consciousness). In *Tourism, Anthropology and China*, ed. Yang Hui, Tan Chee-Beng, and Sydney C. H. Cheung, 94–115. Kunming: Yunnan Daxue Chubanshe.

Edensor, Tim

2001 "Performing Tourism, Staging Tourism." *Tourist Studies* 1, no. 1:59–81.

Edwards, Penny

2002 "Time Travels: Locating *xinyimin* in Sino-Cambodian Histories." In *Globalizing Chinese Migration: Trends in Europe and Asia*, ed. Pál Nyíri and Igor Saveliev, 254–89. Aldershot: Ashgate.

Erdös Ákos and Léderer Pál

1988 *Világútlevél* (World passport). Budapest: Láng.

Fan, C. Cindy

2004 "Out to the City and Back to the Village: The Experiences and Contributions of Rural Women Migrating from Sichuan and Anhui." In *On the Move: Women in Rural-to-Urban Migration in Contemporary China*, ed. Arianne M. Gaetano and Tamara Jacka, 177–206. New York: Columbia University Press.

Fang Lie and Kong Lingquan

2003 "Chuguo dagong leng yu re" (Overseas work: The cold and the hot of it). *Renmin Ribao*, 21 June, 2.

Fang Xinqi

1994 "Huji zhidu gaige, chengshihua de tupokou" (Reform of the *hukou* regime: springboard of urbanization). *Jingji Ribao*, 26 May, 8.

Fang Xiong and Chen Donghu

1991 "Shanghai shi gongmin yinsi churujing huodong gaikuang he weifa fanzui de dongxiang ji qi duice" (Exit-and-entry activities of Shanghai citizens: overall situation, illegal and criminal tendencies, and policy responses). *Xingzheng Yanjiu*, no. 4:19–22.

Fazhan Daobao

2003 "Huji gaige weishenme wu ren hecai" (Why no one benefits from *hukou* reform). 4 April, 1.

Ferry, Megan

2007 "Chinese Travels to Africa: Cultural Representation in the Age of Globalization." Paper presented at the workshop "Class and place: cosmopolitan perspectives on a 'grounded' sensorium," Institute of International Studies, University of Technology, Sydney, 18 June.

Financial Times

2007 "China Is Facing Backlash in Africa." 29 April.

Friedman, Sara L.

2004 "Embodying Civility: Civilizing Processes and Symbolic Citizenship in Southeastern China." *Journal of Asian Studies* 63, no. 3:687–718.

Friman, H. Richard

2002 "Evading the Divine Wind Through the Side Door: The Transformation of Chinese Migration to Japan." In *Globalising Chinese Migration: Trends in Europe and Asia*, ed. Pál Nyíri and Igor R. Saveliev, 9–34. Aldershot, Hampshire: Ashgate.

Froissart, Chloé

2005 "Creating a social insurance system for migrant workers in Chengdu: Which model of social integration?" Paper presented at the first Graduate Student Conference on China, Chinese University of Hong Kong, 11–15 January.

Fu Tengxiao

2003 "Yimin wenhua yu wenhua xiandaihua (bitan)" (Migrant culture and cultural modernization: a comment). *Shenzhen Daxue Xuebao (renwen shehui kexue ban)/Journal of Shenzhen University (Humanities & Social Sciences)* 20, no. 5: 64–65.

Fu Xiaobo

1995 "Kuachu guomen de siying laoban" (Private bosses transcend nation's boundaries). *Wenhuibao* (Shanghai), 2 June, 7.

Fujian Qiaobao (Fuzhou)

2004a "Wo sheng Qiaolian jiceng zuzhi jianshe huo kexi chengji" (Province Overseas Chinese Association ground-level construction achieves heart-warming results). 6 September.

2004b "Xin Nanfei zhu huihuang" (New South Africa moulds glory), 27 September; "Bang zai, lü A minren gan pin hui ying" (Great! Fujianese in Argentina: Willing to toil, able to win). 11 October.

Fuller, Thomas

2008 "In Isolated Hills of Asia, New Roads to Speed Trade." *New York Times*, 31 March.

Fuqing Ribao

2000 "Juanzhu baiwan yuan xingban jiaxiang gongyi shiye" (Donated millions to uplift homeland's projects for common good), 30 October, 1.

Gaetano, Arianne M.

2004 "Filial Daughters, Modern Women: Migrant Domestic Workers in Post-Mao Beijing." In *On the Move*, ed. Gaetano and Jacka, 41–79.

Gaetano, Arianne M., and Tamara Jacka, eds.

2004 *On the Move: Women in Rural-to-Urban Migration in Contemporary China.* New York: Columbia University Press.

Gan Lin and Deng Congyi

1993 "Xinan tielu zai shenyin: Jin chunyun song 'Chuan jun' jishi" (The southwestern railway is groaning: A report on seeing off the 'Sichuan Army' this Spring Festival). *Renmin Ribao*, 25 February, 2.

Gao Chao

1999 "Shi lun fei gongwu huodong chuguo de ruogan wenti" (A preliminary discussion of some questions of going abroad to pursue nonofficial activities). In *Selected Articles on Exit-Entry Management,* ed. Chinese Police Association Exit-Entry Management Committee, 115–23. Peking: Qunzhong Chubanshe.

Gao, Jia

2006 "Radio-activated Business and Power: A Case Study of 3CW Melbourne Chinese Radio." In *Media and the Chinese Diaspora*, ed. Wanning Sun, 150–77. London and New York: Routledge.

Ge Hongbin

1999 "Hukou ningzhi: dailai shehui luohou baoshou" (*Hukou* stagnation creates backward, conservative society). *Tansuo yu zhengming*, no. 3:42.

Gelbras, Vilya G.

2002 "Contemporary Chinese Migration to Russia." In *Globalising Chinese Migration*, ed. Nyíri and Saveliev, 100–107.

Giese, Karsten

2005 "Surfing the Virtual Minefield: Doing Ethnographic Research on the Chinese Internet." *Berliner China-Hefte* 28:20–43.

Gillespie, Sandra

2006 "Voice of African Students in China." Paper presented at the China-Africa Links Workshop, Center for China's Transnational Relations, Hong Kong University of Science and Technology, 11–12 November. http://www.cctr.ust.hk/china-africa/papers/Gillespie,Sandra.pdf

Gray, Denis D.

2008 "Laos Fears China's Footprint." Associated Press, 7 April. http://www.time.com/time/world/article/0,8599,1728340,00.html?xid=rss-topstories (accessed 10 April 2008).

Greenblatt, Stephen, ed.

2009 *Cultural Mobility: A New Manifesto for Cultural Studies*. Cambridge: Cambridge University Press.

Guan Jinping and Jiang Miaoyi

2003 "Chengshi wailai renkou de jiben shenghuo yu jiankang fuwu" (Basic living and health services for outside population in cities). In *Nongmingong: Zhongguo jincheng nongmin de jingji shehui fenxi* (Migrant workers: economic and social analysis of peasants in Chinese cities), ed. Li Peilin, 253–63. Peking: Zhongguo Kexue Wenxian Chubanshe.

Guangdong Shiji (Canton)

2003 "Beijing zai ci fangsong hukou xianzhi" (Peking relaxes *hukou* restrictions again), no. 10:24.

Guangming Ribao

2007 "You Xingbake kan wenwu huanjing de baohu" (Through Starbucks, looking at the protection of cultural monuments' surroundings). Reproduced at http://news.sina.com.cn/0/2007-01-18/060511027554s.shtml, 18 January 2007 (accessed 5 February 2007).

Guo Jing

2001 "Chuguo dagong lu fen liang tou zou" (The way to working abroad has to be paved at both ends). *Xiandai Gongren Bao* (Chonqing), 9 April, A2.

Guo, Yingjie
2004 *Cultural Nationalism in Contemporary China: The Search for National Identity under Reform*. London and New York: RoutledgeCurzon.

Halskov Hansen, Mette
2005 *Frontier People: Han Settlers in Minority Areas of China*. Vancouver and Toronto: UBC Press.

Harajiri Hideki
2008 "Trans-modern Relocation of South-Koreans: From American Dream to Asian and World Dreams." Paper prepared for the International Congress of Ethnologists, Anthropologists and Sociologists, Kunming, 15–21 July.

Harrell, Stevan
1995 *Cultural Encounters on China's Ethnic Frontiers*. Seattle: University of Washington Press.

Harris, Nigel
1995 *The New Untouchables: Immigration and the New World Worker*. London: I. B. Tauris.

He Guangwei
1992 "Bianjing lüyou gongzuo xianzhuang yu fazhan" (The current state and development of border tourism work). Speech at the First Border Tourism Work Conference, 16 August. Reprinted in *Zhongguo Lüyou Nianjian*, 14–15, 1993.
1997 "Baozhang Zhongguo gongmin chuguo lüyou jiankang fazhan" (Ensuring the healthy development of Chinese citizens' tourism abroad). *Zhongguo Lüyoubao*, 1 May, F9.

He Jianming
2000 "Jingti 'xiaomianlang'" (Beware of the "smiling wolf"). *Wenyibao*, 16 September, 2.

He Wei
2001 "Ningbo huji gaige jingqiaoqiao" (Ningbo *hukou* reform proceeds quietly). *Renmin Ribao*, 17 September, 2.

He, Xin Frank
2003 "Regulating Rural-Urban Migrants in Beijing: Institutional Conflict and Ineffective Campaigns." *Stanford Journal of International Law*, 177–205.

He Yifan
2007 "Wang Jiazhu: yongyuan de qiantu" (Wang Jiazhu, the indefatigable globetrotter). *Zhongguo Qiyejia*, reproduced on http://www.sina.com.cn, 19 March 2007 (accessed 2 June 2007).

Hillman, Ben
2003 "Paradise under Construction: Minorities, Myths and Modernity in Northwest Yunnan." *Asian Ethnicity* 4, no. 2:176–88.

Hong Jun

1995 "Jiasu fazhan guonei lüyouye de sikao" (Thoughts on accelerating the development of the domestic tourism industry). *Lüyou Wenhua Bao* (Chengdu), 10 November, 3.

Horizon Research (Lingdian Shichang Yanjiu Gongsi)

2002 *2002 nian chengshi jumin jiari lüyou xiaofei yanjiu baogao* (2002 research report on urban residents' holiday tourism consumption). Peking.

Hsu, Elisabeth

2007 "Zanzibar and Its Chinese Communities," *Population, Space, and Place* 13:113–24.

Hu Jintao

2004 Speech at the second meeting of the Tenth People's Political Consultative Conference, Peking, 7 March.

Hu Ping and Zhang Sheng

1988 "Shijie da chuanlian" (The great worldwide linkup). *Dangdai*, no. 1:4–32.

Hu Shanfeng

1996 "Fazhan guonei lüyou zhi qian jian" (A superficial opinion on developing domestic tourism). *Xueshujie* (Hefei), April, 90–93.

Hu Xuequn

2004 "Xiaogan shi chengzhen huji zhidu gaige de jiben silu (The basic thinking clue to the city and town's household register system reformation in Xiaogan city [sic])." *Jilin gongan gaodeng zhuanke xuexiao xuebao*, no. 3:42–44.

Hu Zhigang

2003 "Wo guo xianxing huji zhidu de baiduan ji qi duice (On malpractice of census register management system and it's countermeasures [sic])." *Journal of Sichuan Police College (Sichuan jingguan gaodeng zhuanke xuexiao xuebao)* 15, no. 5:55–58.

Huang Peizhao, Zhao Gang and Zhou Yisi

2006 "Zhongguoren weihe ai qu Feizhou" (Why Chinese love going to Africa). *Huanqiu Shibao* (Peking), 31 October.

Huang Renzong

2002 "Chengzhenhua yihuo qiancong ziyou" (Urbanization or freedom of movement). *Qiushi*, no. 5:38–41.

Huaqiao Huaren Baike Quanshu bianji weiyuanhui (editorial committee of the Overseas Chinese Encyclopedia), ed.

2000 *Huaqiao Huaren Baike Quanshu* (Overseas Chinese Encyclopedia), *Falü Tiaoli Zhengce juan* (volume of laws, regulations and policies). Peking: Zhongguo Huaqiao Chubanshe.

Huaren Jingji Nianjian bianji weiyuanhui (editorial committee of the Overseas Chinese Economic Yearbook)

1994–2001 *Huaren Jingji Nianjian* (Overseas Chinese economic yearbook). Peking: Chaohua Chubanshe.

Huaxia Shibao (2002) "Ge di fenfen qidong huji gaige" (One city after another starts *hukou* reform), 2 January 2002, 2.

Hubei Province Tourism Bureau and Centre for Tourism Development and Planning Research, Sun Yat-sen University

2003 *Hubei sheng lüyou fazhan zongti guihua / Hubei Province Tourism Development Master Plan*. Peking: Zhongguo Lüyou Chubanshe.

Huber, Toni

2006 "The *Skor lam* and the Long March: Notes on the Transformation of Tibetan Ritual Territory in Southern Amdo in the Context of Chinese Developments." *Journal of the International Association of Tibetan Studies*, no. 2:1–42 (August).

Hugo, Graeme

2005 "Chinese Academic Migration to Australia." Paper presented at the conference "People on the Move: The Transnational Flow of Chinese Human Capital," Hong Kong University of Science and Technology, 20–22 October.

Hulbert, Ann

2007 "Re-education." *The New York Times Magazine*, 1 April.

Human Rights in China

2002a *Institutionalized Exclusion: The Tenuous Legal Status of Internal Migrants in China's Major Cities*. New York and Hong Kong.

2002b *Shutting Out the Poorest: Discrimination against the Most Disadvantaged Migrant Children in City Schools*. New York and Hong Kong.

Hyde, Sandra Theresa

2001 "Sex Tourism Practices on the Periphery: Eroticizing Ethnicity and Pathologizing Sex on the Lancang." In *ChinaUrban. Ethnographies of Contemporary Culture*, ed. Nancy N. Chen, Constance D. Clark, Suzanne N. Gottschang, and Lyn Jeffery, 143–64. Durham, N.C.: Duke University Press.

Ip, David

2007 "From battlers to transnational entrepreneurs? Immigrants from the People's Republic of China in Australia." In *Chinese Ethnic Business: Global and local perspectives*, ed. Eric Fong and Chiu Luk, 120–31. Abingdon, Oxfordshire, and New York: Routledge.

Jacka, Tamara

2006 *Rural Women in Urban China: Gender, Migration, and Social Change*. Armonk, N.Y.: M. E. Sharpe.

Jacobs, Andrew

2008 "Bracing for Games, China Sets Rules That Complicate Life for Foreigners." *New York Times*, 24 April.

Ji Dingjie

2006 "Tuanjie aixiang fazhan, zai tao Yurong huihuang" (Unity, patriotism, development: Resurrecting Fuqing's glory). *Shijie Rongyin* (Hong Kong), no. 21:14.

Ji Fang, ed.

2004 *Green Book of Population and Labor: Demographic Transition and Educational Development*. Zhongguo renkou yu laodong wenti baogao (China Population and Labour Issues Reports), no. 5. Peking: Social Sciences Documentation Publishing House.

Ji Guotao and Xing An

2004 "Guangzhou gaige huji zhidu: 'tiaojian' qudai jihua zhibiao" (Canton reforms *hukou* regime: "conditions" replace quotas). *Xinhua Meiri Dianxun*, 1 April, 1.

Ji Xiaomei and Zhang Chaoji

2002 "Qingnian lüshe zai Zhongguo de xingqi" (The emergence of youth hostels in China). In *2001~2003 nian Zhongguo lüyou fazhan: fenxi yu yuce* (China's tourism development, 2001–2003: Analysis and forecast), ed. Zhang Guangrui, Wei Xiaoan and Liu Deqian, 305–19. Peking: Social Sciences Documentation.

Jiang Yihua

2003 "Huji gaige yu nongye renkou zhuanyi" (*Hukou* reform and migration of the agricultural population). *Xiandai Jingji Tantao / Modern Economic Research*, no. 11:46–48.

Jiang Zemin

1999 Speech at the State Council's Overseas Chinese Work Conference, Peking, 18 January.

Jin Hua

1994 "Cong Wulingyuan kan ziran fengjing kaifaqu de quyu shehui xiaoying" (Looking at the regional social impact of natural scenery development areas from Wulingyuan). *Jingji Dili / Economic Geography* 14, no. 4:89–92 (December).

Jin Huanling

2005 "Dangdai Zhongguo nongmingong shou bu gongping daiyu de shehui lunli fenxi" (An analysis of social norms in the unequal treatment of rural migrant workers in contemporary China). Paper submitted to the first Graduate Student Conference on China, Chinese University of Hong Kong, 11–15 January.

Johnson, Scott

2007 "China's African Misadventures." *Newsweek*, 3 December.

Kahn, Joseph

2006 "China, Shy Giant, Shows Signs of Shedding Its False Modesty." *The New York Times*, 9 December 2006.

Kang, Xiaofei

2005 "Tourism, Two Temples and Three Religions: A Three-Way Contest on the Sino-Tibetan Border." Paper presented at the 2005 Annual Meeting of the Association of Asian Studies, Chicago, 31 March.

King, Kenneth

2006 "Aid within the Wider China-Africa Partnership: A view from the Beijing

Summit." Paper presented at the China-Africa Links Workshop, Center for China's Transnational Relations, Hong Kong University of Science & Technology, 11–12 November.

Kipnis, Andrew

2006 "Suzhi: A Keyword Approach." *The China Quarterly*, no. 186: 295–313.

Kojima Reeitsu

1996 "Breakdown of China's Policy of Restricting Population Movement." *The Developing Economies* 34, no. 4:371–401.

Kolås, Åshild

2006 *Ethnic Tourism in Shangrila: Representations of Place and Tibetan Identity*. Ph.D. diss., University of Oslo.

2007 *Tourism and Tibetan Culture in Transition: A Place Called Shangrila*. Abingdon, Oxfordshire: Routledge.

Ku, Ming-chun

2006 "The Construction of the Self in the Diversified References of Past-ness: Domestic Tourists in China's Heritage Tourism." Paper presented at "Of Asian Origin": Rethinking Tourism in Contemporary Asia, Asia Research Institute, National University of Singapore, 7–9 September.

Lary, Diana

1999 "The 'Static' Decades: Inter-provincial Migration in Pre-reform China." In *Internal and International Migration*, ed. Pieke and Mallee, 29–48.

Le Weizhong, ed. in chief

2000 *Maixiang xin shiji de liudong renkou guanli yanjiu: "Shanghai shi wailai liudong renkou guanli lilun yu shijian yantaohui" youxiu lunwen huibian* (Research on transient population management towards the new century: a collection of outstanding papers from the Transient Outside Population Management in Shanghai: Theory and Practice symposium). Shanghai: Huadong Shifan Daxue Chubanshe.

Lee, Haiyan

2006 "Nannies for Foreigners: The Enchantment of Chinese Womanhood in the Age of Millennial Capitalism." *Public Culture* 18, no. 3:507–29.

Leu Siew Ying

2005 "Guangdong to suspend migrant hiring ban." *South China Morning Post* (Hong Kong), 13 January, A6.

Lew, Alan A., Lawrence Yu, John Ap, and Zhang Guangrui.

Tourism in China. Binghamton, N.Y.: Haworth Hospitality Press.

Lewis, Steven Wayne

2002 "What Can I Do for Shanghai? Selling Spiritual Civilization in China's Cities." In *Made in China: Consumption, Content and Crisis*, ed. Stephanie Hemelryk Donald, Michael Keane, and Yin Hong, 139–51. London and New York: RoutledgeCurzon.

Li Changping

2003 "Huji zhidu de yanbian" (The transformations of the *hukou* regime). *Nanfang Zhoumo* (Canton), 3 April.

Li Chunsheng and Liu Jun

2003 "Changchun chutai shi'er tiao churujing bianmin cuoshi" (Changchun issues twelve people-benefiting articles of exit-entry regulations). *Jilin Ribao* (Changchun), 18 August, 6.

Li Honggu, Jin Yan, and Zhuang Shan

2003 "Weishenme women bu neng zhouyou shijie" (Why we can't tour the globe), *Sanlian Shenghuo Zhoukan*, no. 2 (13 January):22–36.

Li Jinghua

1982 "Zhongguoshi lüyou daolu qianyi" (A shallow opinion on Chinese-style tourism). *Renwen Zazhi*, no. 5:31–36.

Li Maichan

1997 "Lun ba yimin gongzuo naru shehuizhuyi xiandaihua jianshe zhi zhong" (On making migration work part of socialist modernizing construction). *Henan jiaoyu xueyuan xuebao (zhexue shehui kexue ban)*, no. 4:67–70.

Li Minghuan

2002 "Ouzhou zhongwen chuanmei de xingqi, fazhan yu xianzhuang" (The emergence, development and current state of Chinese media in Europe). *Ouzhou*, no. 6:85–92.

2004 "Qunti xiaoying, shehui ziben yu kuaguo wangluo: cong 'Ou Hua Lian-hui' kan quan-Ou-xing huaren shetuan de jianli, yunzuo yu gongneng / Collective Representation, Social Capital and Transnational Links: A Study of the Development and Functions of European-wide Chinese Associations." Paper presented at the 5th conference of the International Society for the Study of Chinese Overseas, Elsinore, Denmark, 10–14 May.

2005 "Transformation of Contingency into Meaning: Emergence of a New *Qiaoxiang* in South China." Paper presented at the conference "People on the Move: The Transnational Flow of Chinese Human Capital," Hong Kong University of Science and Technology, 20–22 October.

Li Minghuan, Jiang Hongzhen and Yu Yunping

2003 "Yi ge lü Ou xin qiaoxiang de xingcheng, yingxiang, wenti yu duice / The emergence of a new qiaoxiang: Its development, influences, problems and countermeasures," *Huaqiao Huaren Lishi Yanjiu / Overseas Chinese History Studies*, no. 4:8–15 (December).

Li Mu

2007 "'Rustification' Revival to Create Jobs, Reverse Brain Drain." *China Development Brief*, 3 March. Online: "http://www.chinadevelopment-brief.com/node/1165" (accessed 2 February 2008).

Li Narangoa

2006 "Nationalism and Globalization on the Inner Mongolia Frontier: The Commercialization of a Tamed Ethnicity." *Japan Focus*, 15 November. "http://www.japanfocus.org/products/topdf/2575" (accessed 27 November 2007).

Li Peilin

2003 "Jubian: Cunluo de zhongjie" (Tremendous change: The end of the village). In *Nongmingong: Zhongguo jincheng nongmin de jingji shehui fenxi* (Migrant workers: Economic and social analysis of peasants in Chinese cities), 55–69. Peking: Zhongguo Kexue Wenxian Chubanshe.

Li Qiang

1996 "'Hualu' yijing zhuanyi la!" (Hualu has moved!). *ZhongOu Shangbao* (Budapest), 19 February, 1–2.

Li Qiang

1998 "Nongmingong yu Zhongguo chengshihua daolu" (Peasant workers and China's path to urbanization). *Renmin Ribao*, 18 February, 11.

2000 "Issues of the Dual Labour Market and the Underclass Elite in Urban China." *Tsinghua Sociological Review*, special issue, 151–67.

Li Yiping

2003 "Development of the Nanshan Cultural Tourism Zone in Hainan, China: Achievements Made and Issues to Be Resolved." *Tourism Geographies* 5, no. 4:436–45.

Lin Sheng'r

2002a "Nü beibao du chuang Yindu" (Female backpacker, alone, hits India). *Travel Times* (Shanghai), 11 July, A3.

2002b "Zhen xiwang lai shi zuo yi zhi niao" (I really hope to be reborn as a bird). *Travel Times* (Shanghai), 11 July, A3.

Lin Zhishen

2006 "Lüju Kenniya Huaqiao huaren qipan 'ziji de jia'" (Chinese sojourners in Kenya hope for "own home"). In *Feizhou Huaqiao huaren shehuishi ziliao xuanji / Social History of Chinese Overseas in Africa: Selected Documents (1800–2005)*, ed. and ann. Li Anshan, 388–89. Beijing Daxue Huaqiao Huaren Yanjiu Zhongxin Zhongshu (Peking University Overseas Chinese Research Centre Series), no. 28. Hong Kong: Hong Kong Press for Social Sciences.

Lingdao juece xinxi

2003a "Weishenme shuo huji gaige neng rang chengshi geng youxiao" (Why household registration reform can make cities more efficient), 12 April, 18.

2003b "Cong 'Beijing lüka' dao 'Zhongguo lüka'" (From a "Peking green card" to a "China green card"), 27 July, 19.

Lintner, Bertil

2002 "Illegal Aliens Smuggling to and through Southeast Asia's Golden Triangle." In *Globalising Chinese Migration,* ed. Nyíri and Saveliev, 108–119.

Litzinger, Ralph

2004 "The Mobilization of 'Nature': Perspectives from Northwest Yunnan." In *China's Campaign to "Open Up the West": National, Provincial and Local Perspectives,* ed. David S. G. Goodman. Special issue of *The China Quarterly* (n.s.), no. 5:174–90.

Liu Bowen

2004 "Wo guo huji zhidu gaige de zongti qushi" (Overall trends in our country's *hukou* reform). *Jingji tizhi gaige / Reform of Economic System*, no. 1:10–14.

Liu Fei

1998 "Wo guo guonei lüyouye fazhan chutan" (Our domestic tourism business: a preliminary investigation). *Beijing Shangxueyuan Xuebao*, no. 2:61–64.

Liu Jing

1999 "Hukou gaige chunchao rongdong" (The spring thaw of *hukou* reform). *Renmin Gongan*, no. 12:12–13.

Liu Juhua

2001 "Huji gaige zenyang tangguo falü zhe tiao he" (How *hukou* reform crosses the river of law). *Beijing Qingnian Bao*, 4 September.

Liu Kaiming

2003 *Bianyuanren* (At the margin). Peking: Xinhua Chubanshe.

2004 *Shenti de jiage* (The price of the body). Peking: Renmin Ribao Chubanshe.

Liu Quan and Luo Jun-chong

2004 "Current status measures of export of labor services in China" (in Chinese). *Overseas Chinese History Studies*, no. 1:22–27.

Liu, Xin

1997 "Space, Mobility, and Flexibility: Chinese Villagers and Scholars Negotiate Power at Home and Abroad." In *Ungrounded Empires: The Cultural Politics of Modern Chinese Transnationalism*, ed. Aihwa Ong and Donald Nonini, 91–114. New York: Routledge.

Liu Weihua and Zhang Xinwu

2000 *Hafo nühai Liu Yiting suzhi peiyang jishi* (Harvard girl Liu Yiting: a record of quality improvement). Peking: Zuojia chubanshe.

Liu Wujun

2001 "Huji zhidu gaige bu yi huanxing" (Household registration system reform hard to postpone). *Beijing Guancha*, no. 3:99–104.

Liu Zhaoping

2001 "Zhongguo jiari lüyou de xianzhuang yu duice" (The current state of China's holiday tourism and policy responses). In *2000 ~ 2002 nian Zhongguo lüyou fazhan: Fenxi yu yuce* (China's tourism development, 2000–2002: Analysis and forecast), ed. Zhang Guangrui, Wei Xiaoan, and Liu Deqian, 174–88. Peking: Social Sciences Documentation.

Liu Zhishan, ed.

2003 *Yimin wenhua yu shichang lunli* (The culture of migration and the ethics of the market). Peking: Zhongguo Funü Chubanshe.

Lo, Norris

2006 "The Chinese/Khmer Divide in Factories." *Phnom Penh Post*, 16–29 June.

Lomanov, Alexander V.

2005 "On the Periphery of the 'Clash of Civilisations': Discourse and Geopolitics in Russian-Chinese Relations." In *China Inside Out. Contemporary Chinese Nationalism and Transnationalism*, ed. Nyíri and Breidenbach, 71–98.

Lu Jing

2002 *Lun qianyi ziyou* (On the freedom of movement). Master's thesis, Central Party School.

Lu Miaogeng

2004 "Nanfei huaren xiqing Aomen huigui jishi" (An account of South African Chinese celebrating the return of Macau). *Renmin Ribao (Haiwaiban)*, 20 December.

Lu Yilong

2001 "Huji geli yu eryuanhua tonghunjuan de xingcheng" (The stratification of household registration and the emergence of a two-tiered endogamous structure). *Kaifang shidai* (Shenzhen), no. 9:97–103.

Luan Jingdong

2000 *Fada diqu nongcun wailai laodongli he yimin guanli yanjiu* (A study of outside labour and migrant management in villages in developed regions). Ph.D. diss., Nanjing Agricultural University.

Luova, Outi

2007 "Ethnic Transnational Capital Transfers and Development: Utilization of Ties with South Korea in the Yanbian Korean Autonomous Prefecture, China." Ph.D. diss., Turku University.

Lute

2003 "Zhongguoren taojin Jianbuzhai" (Chinese gold diggers in Cambodia). *Ouzhou Shibao* (Paris), 24 March.

Lü Zhisheng, Hai Tao and Lu Xiong

2004 "Chuguo dagong: xianbing duo xianjing shao" (Going overseas to work: Few pies, many traps). *Jiancha Ribao*, 11 August.

Ma Huidi

2004a *Zouxiang renwen guanhuai de xiuxian jingji* (Toward a leisure economy with humanistic concerns). Peking: Zhongguo Jingji Chubanshe.

2004b *Xiuxian: Renlei meili de jingshen jiayuan* (Leisure: The making of a beautiful home for the human spirit). Peking: Zhongguo Jingji Chubanshe.

Ma Huidi and Zhang Jing'an, eds.

2004 *Zhongguo gongzhong xiuxian zhuangkuang diaocha* (Survey studies of the state of leisure life among the Chinese public*)*. Peking: Zhongguo Jingji Chubanshe.

Ma Ping

2001 "Xibu da kaifa dui dangdi minzu guanxi de yingxiang ji duice" (The impact of the Great Western Development project on local ethnic relations and ways of dealing with it). *Minzu Wenti Yanjiu*, no. 5:37–42.

Ma Zhendong

    2002   "Tansuo shihe Shanghai tedian de churujing guanli jigou moshi (A probe into the exit-entry sdministrative body model suited to Shanghai character)." *Journal of Shanghai Public Security Academy (Shanghai gongan gaodeng zhuanke xuexiao xuebao)* 12, no. 5:13–16.

Ma Zhonggui

    2000   "Gaizao 'cheng zhong cun' shi jianshe xiandaihua chengshi de xuyao" (Reforming "urban villages" is a requirement of constructing a modernized city). *Guangdong Jingshen Wenming Tongxun*, 87–88.

MacCannell, Dean

    1976   *The Tourist: A New Theory of the Leisure Class.* New York: Schocken.

Mao Rongjun and Zhou Dan

    2007   "Fang Xifei Zhongguo Heping Tongyi Cujinhui mishuzhang Hu Jieguo" (An interview with Hu Jieguo, secretary-general of the West African Association for the Peaceful Reunification of China). In *Feizhou Huaqiao huaren shehuishi ziliao xuanji / Social History of Chinese Overseas in Africa: Selected Documents (1800–2005)*, ed. and ann. Li Anshan, 470–74. Beijing Daxue Huaqiao Huaren Yanjiu Zhongxin Zhongshu (Peking University Overseas Chinese Research Centre Series), no. 28. Hong Kong: Hong Kong Press for Social Sciences.

Mao Xiaomei

    2003   "Laodong he shehui baozhang bu fabu si diqu mingong xuqiu xinxi" (Ministry of Labour and Social Security publishes information on four regions' migrant labour demand). *Renmin Ribao*, 9 February, 2.

Matisoff, Adina

    2004   "News Update: Mid-May to Early August, 2004." *China Rights Forum*, no. 3:7–13.

McGreal, Chris

    2007   "Thanks China, Now Go Home: Buy-up of Zambia Revives Old Colonial Fears." *The Guardian*, 5 February.

Mengin, Françoise

    2007   *La présence chinoise au Cambodge: Contribution à une économie politique violente, rentière et inégalitaire.* Paris: CERI (Les Études du CERI, No. 133.)

Mian Xiaohong

    2004   "Burdened Youth." In *On the Move*, ed. Gaetano and Jacka, 289–93.

MIT (équipe)

    2002   *Tourismes 1: Lieux communs* (Common places). Paris: Belin.

Mu Yunkai

    2001   "Hen Budapeisi dao yongyuan" (Budapest, I hate you forever). *OuYa Xinwenbao* (Budapest), 1–8 February.

Murphy, Rachel

    2002   *How Migrant Labour Is Changing Rural China.* Cambridge: Cambridge University Press.

2004   "Turning Peasants into Modern Chinese Citizens: 'Population Quality' Discourse, Demographic Transition and Primary Education." *The China Quarterly*, no. 177:1–20.

Nader, Laura

1997   "Controlling Processes: Tracing the Dynamic Components of Power." *Current Anthropology* 38, no. 5:711–37.

Nanfang Dushibao (Canton)

2004   "Guangzhou hukou you he yongchu" (What are the uses of a Canton *hukou*?), 14 March.

Nanfang Ribao (Canton)

2002   "Wang Jianxu: Wo xiang gaojie xiang lai Feizhou zuo shengyi de Zhongguoren" (I would like to warn Chinese people who want to come to Africa), 6 December.

National Tourism Administration

2001   *The Tenth Five-Year Plan of China's Tourism Development and the Main Long-Term Targets for 2015 and 2020.* Peking.

2005   *Zhongguo Lüyou Nianjian* (China Tourism Yearbook). Peking.

Népszabadság (Budapest)

2002   "Cipöt a cipöboltból" (Shoes from the shoe shop), 18 April, 32.

Northern Laos Industrial Economic Development and Cooperation Planning Preparation Group

2008   2008 ~ 2020: *Planning for Industrial Economic Development and Cooperation in Northern Part of Lao People's Democratic Republic.* Kunming.

Notar, Beth

2006   *Displacing Desire: Travel and Popular Culture in China.* Honolulu: University of Hawai'i Press.

Nyíri, Pál

1999   *New Chinese Migrants in Europe.* Aldershot: Ashgate.

2001   "Expatriating Is Patriotic? The Discourse on 'New Migrants' in the People's Republic of China and Identity Construction among Recent Migrants from the PRC." *Journal of Ethnic and Migration Studies* 27, no. 4: 635–53.

2002a   "Mobility, Entrepreneurship, and Sex: How Narratives of Modernity Help Chinese Women in Hungary Evade Gender Constraints." In *Globalising Chinese Migration*, ed. Nyíri and Saveliev, 208–41.

2002b   "Moving Targets: Chinese Christian Proselytism among Transnational Migrants from the PRC." *European Journal of East Asian Studies* 2, no. 2:263–302.

2003   "Chinese Migration to Eastern Europe." *International Migration* 41, no. 3:239–66.

2005a   "The 'New Migrant': State and Market Constructions of Modernity and Patriotism." In *China Inside Out*, ed. Nyíri and Breidenbach, 141–76.

2005b   "Global Modernizers or Local Subalterns? Parallel Perceptions of

Chinese Transnationals in Hungary." *Journal of Ethnic and Migration Studies* 31, no. 4:659–74.

2006a *Scenic Spots: Chinese Tourism, Cultural Authority, and the State*. Seattle and London: University of Washington Press.

2006b "The Yellow Man's Burden: Chinese Migrants on a Civilizing Mission." *The China Journal* 56:83–106 (July 2006).

2006c "Transnationalism and the Middleman Minority Model: Chinese Entrepreneurs in Hungary." In *Global Conjectures: China in Transnational Perspective* (*Chinese History and Society / Berliner China-Hefte* 30), ed. William C. Kirby, Mechthild Leutner, and Klaus Mühlhahn, 73–91. Münster: Lit.

2007 *Chinese in Russia and Eastern Europe: A Middleman Minority in a Transnational Era*. Abingdon, Oxfordshire: Routledge.

Nyíri, Pál, and Feischmidt Margit, eds.

2006 *Nem kívánt gyerekek? Migránsok a magyar közoktatásban* (Unwanted children? Migrants in Hungary's public education system). Budapest: Centre for International Migration and Refugee Studies, Institute for Political Sciences, Hungarian Academy of Sciences.

Nyíri, Pál, and Igor R. Saveliev, eds.

2002 *Globalising Chinese Migration*. Aldershot, Hampshire: Ashgate.

Oakes, Tim

1998 *Tourism and Modernity in China*. London and New York: Routledge.

2007 "Welcome to Paradise! A Sino-American Joint Venture Project." In *China's Transformations: The Stories Beyond the Headlines*, ed. Lionel Jensen and Timothy Weston, 240–64. Lanham, Md.: Rowman and Littlefield.

Ong, Aihwa

1999 *Flexible Citizenship: The Cultural Logic of Transnationality*. Durham, N.C.: Duke University Press.

2002 *Buddha Is Hiding: Refugees, Citizenship, the New America*. Berkeley: University of California Press.

2006 "Labor Arbitrage: Displacements and Betrayals in Silicon Valley." In *Neoliberalism as Exception: Mutations in Citizenship and Sovereignty*, 157–75. Durham, N.C.: Duke University Press.

Open Net Initiative

2005 *Internet Filtering in China in 2004–2005: A Country Study*. http://opennet.net/studies/china

Østbø Haugen, Heidi, and Jørgen Carling

2005 "On the Edge of the Chinese Diaspora: The Surge of Baihuo Business in an African City." *Ethnic and Racial Studies* 28, no. 4:639–62.

Ouzhou Shibao (Paris)

2004 "Zhongguo yimin zai Eluosi: ku gan cheng yi wan fuweng gu shangxiao zuo baobiao" (Chinese migrants in Russia: Billionaires through hard toil, they hire majors as bodyguards), 11–13 September.

Pan Yiyong

1993 "Zouchu xiaonong wenming yao gaige huji zhidu" (Leaving small-peasant civilisation behind needs *hukou* reform). *Gaige yu zhanlüe*, no. 2:46–49, 58.

Peng Decheng

2003 *Zhongguo lüyou jingqu zhili moshi / The Governance of Tourist Attractions in China*. Peking: Zhongguo Lüyou Chubanshe.

Peng Xizhe and Yao Yu

2006 "Social Protection for Migrant Workers in the Informal Economy – Issues and Options." In *Labour Mobility in Urban China: An Integrated Labour Market in the Making?* ed. Michaela Baur, Bettina Gransow, Yihong Jin, and Guoqing Shi, 195–204. Münster: LIT (Berliner China-Studien, no. 46).

People's Daily Online

2003 "Chinese tourists' unsocial behavior sparks concern at home," 22 September. "http://English.peopledaily.com.cn" (accessed 6 September 2006).

2005 "Zhongguo geti shangren taojin Feizhou: jianku chuangye, gan shang, gan gan" (Private Chinese businessmen on Africa gold rush: struggling to set up business, daring to think, daring to act), 17 August. "http://chinese.people.com.cn/GB/42316/3622666.html" (accessed 26 May 2007).

Petersen, Ying Yang

1995 "The Chinese Landscape as a Tourist Attraction: Image and Reality." In *Tourism in China*, ed. Lew et al., 141–54.

Picard, Michel

1993 "Cultural Tourism in Bali: National Integration and Regional Differentiation." In *Tourism in South-East Asia*, ed. M. Hitchcock, V. King, and M. Parnwell, 71–98. London: Routledge.

Pieke, Frank N., and Hein Mallee, ed.

Internal and International Migration: Chinese Perspectives, Richmond, Surrey: Curzon.

Pieke, Frank N., Pál Nyíri, Mette Thunø, and Antonella Ceccagno

2004 *Transnational Chinese: Fujianese Migrants in Europe*. Stanford: Stanford University Press.

Pieke, Frank N., and Xiang Biao

2007 "Legality and Labour: Chinese Migration, Neoliberalism and the State in the UK and China." British Inter-University China Centre working paper no. 5. Oxford.

Piore, Michael

1970 "The Dual Labor Market: Theory and Implications." In *The State and the Poor*, ed. Samuel H. Beer and Richard E. Barringer, 55–59. Cambridge, Mass.: Winthrop.

Polian, Pavel

2003 *Against Their Will*. Budapest: Central European University Press.

Pun Ngai

1999   "Becoming *Dagongmei* (Working Girls): The Politics of Identity and Difference in Reform China." *The China Journal* 42:1–16.

2005a   *Made in China: Women Factory Workers in a Global Workplace*. Durham, N.C.: Duke University Press.

2005b   "Putting Transnational Labour Process in its Place: Dormitory Labour Regime in Post-Socialist China." Paper presented at the conference "People on the Move: The Transnational Flow of Chinese Human Capital," Hong Kong University of Science and Technology, 20–22 October.

Qian Ning

2002   *Chinese Students Encounter America*. Seattle: University of Washington Press.

Qiao Yu

2001   "Construction of 'big museum': a new thought about the future development of Badaling Great Wall scenic spot." *Tourism Tribune* (Peking), no. 3:41–43.

Qiaoqing (internal publication of the State Council's Overseas Chinese Affairs Bureau)

2002   "Xila, Maerta, Jieke qiaoqing jinkuang" (The recent situation of overseas Chinese in Greece, Malta and the Czech Republic), no. 25:1–6.

Qin Lingnan

2006   "Dui 'chujing lüyou yajin' de falü fenxi ji xianzhuang fansi / A Study on Outbound Tourist's Deposits: A Legal Perspective." Paper presented at the Third China Tourism Forum, Hong Kong, 15–16 December.

Renmin Ribao

1978   "Bixu zhongshi qiaowu gongzuo" (Overseas Chinese work must be taken seriously). 4 January.

1981   "Guowuyuan zuochu jiaqiang lüyou gongzuo de jueding" (State Council issues decision on strengthening tourism work), 19 October, 1.

1983   "He zhi Anxiang xian!" (Who will stop Anxiang County!), "'Xiao guo zhi jun' he qi duo" (Why so many kingpins), and "Jue bu neng rang tamen menghun guoguan" (Don't let them get away with this!), 23 February, 8.

1985   "Beijing shi waidi lai Jing renyuan huji guanli guiding" (Peking City's Regulations on *hukou* management of outside personnel in Peking), 5 July, 7.

1986   "Liuxue renyuan an xu paiqian shuliang bu jian" (Planned number of personnel to study abroad not to decrease), 8 July, 3.

1990   "Wo guo gongmin yinsi chuguo renshu suinian zengjia" (Number of our citizens going abroad for private purposes increases year by year), 12 May, 1.

2001   "Guomin jingji he shehui fazhan di-shi ge wu nian jihua gangyao" (Essentials of the tenth five-year Plan of National Economic and Social Development), 18 March.

Rose, Nikolas
    1999   *Powers of Freedom: Reframing Political Thought*. Cambridge: Cambridge
           University Press.

Sachs, Susan
    2002   "Immigrants See Path to Riches in Phone Cards." *New York Times*, 11
           August.

Schein, Louisa
    2005   "Mediated Transnationalism and Other Elusive Objects: Anthropology,
           Cultural Studies and Questions of Method." In *China Inside Out*, ed.
           Nyíri and Breidenbach, 99–140.

Schramma, Fritz
    2004   Speech by the Head Mayor of Cologne at the Second Annual Chinese
           Travel Fair in Europe. *Travel & Trade in Europe* (Cologne), no. 1–2:1.

Schwandner, Gerd, and Gu Huimin
    2005   "Beer, Romance, and Chinese Airlines. Mindsets and Travel Expecta-
           tions of Chinese Tourism Students." In *New Tourism for Asia-Pacific,*
           Conference Proceedings, ed. Suh Seung-Jin and Hwang Yeong-Hyeon,
           110–18. Seoul: Asia Pacific Tourism Association.

Shaanxi Shifan Daxue Chubanshe
    2003   *Zhongguo tubu chuanyue (Traversing China on foot;* English title: *A Guide*
           for Chinese Hikers). Taiyuan.

Shandong Youyi Shushi
    1988   *Lüyou xiaobaike* (Pocket Tourism Encyclopedia). Jinan.

Shanghai New Migrants Research Project Team
    1997   "Shanghai shi xin yimin yanjiu" (A study of Shanghai's new migrants).
           Zhongguo renkou kexue, no. 3:36–41, 52.

Shanghai Transient Outside Population Management Leading Group
    1995   *Ru Hu zhinan: zhi lai Shanghai wugong de dixiong jiemei* (A guide to
           entering Shanghai: For brothers and sisters who come to Shanghai to
           work). Shanghai: Sanlian Shudian.

Shen Hongfei
    2003   "Zhongguoshi yidong" (Mobility Chinese style), *Sanlian shenghuo zhou-*
           kan, no. 8:70 (24 February).

Shen Ying
    2004   "Mingong zidi shangxue zaoyu 'geli zhengce'?" (Do migrant children
           face apartheid at school?). *Nanfang Zhoumo*, 3 June, 6.

Shi Fayong
    2004   *Social Capital and Collective Resistance in Urban China Neighbourhoods*.
           Singapore.

Shi Hanrong
    2004   *Tanjie Zhongguo qiaowu* (Understanding China's overseas Chinese
           affairs). Hong Kong: China Review Academic Publishers.

Shi, Lijing
    2006   "The Successors to Confucianism or a New Generation? A Questionnaire

Study on Chinese Students' Culture of Learning English." *Language, Culture and Curriculum* 19:122–47.

Shi, Weiyi

2008 *Rubber Boom in Luang Namtha: A Transnational Perspective*. Vientiane: Lao-German Development Cooperation.

Shi Xiangjiu and Ye Huancong

1989 "Gaige chengshi hukou guanli de tansuo" (A discussion on urban *hukou* reform). *Renmin Gongan*, no. 10:40–42.

Shi Yaoxin

2000 "'Huji' zhe dao men he ri neng shangkai" (When can the door of *hukuo* open?). *Shenghuo Shibao*, 24 March.

Shi Yulong

2002 "Huji zhidu gaige tuijin Zhongguo chengshihua" (Household registration system reform advances China's urbanization). *Zhonghua Ernü (Overseas Edition)*, no. 7:29–32.

Shichang (Budapest)

2003 "Huaren nüqiyejia Lai Hua" (Lai Hua, Chinese businesswoman), 12 August, 11. (Originally broadcast on Tilos Rádió, Budapest, 6 August 2003, 9–10 pm.)

Shijie Rongyin (Hong Kong)

2000a "Cheng qian bi hou, jiwang kailai" (Learning from the past, preparing for the future; building on the past, marching ahead), no. 2:2.

2000b "Shu gao qian chi ye wangbuliao gen" (May a tree be a thousand feet tall, still it cannot forget its root!), no. 2:3.

2001 "Zheng Changhou tan Aozhou Rong-qing" (Zheng Changhou about Fuqing fellowship in Australia), June, 17.

2006 "162 wei qiaoxian huo shi fu biaozhang" (City government honours 106 overseas worthies), no. 21:17.

Shu Boyang and Yuan Jirong

2003 "Zhengfu zhudao yu lüyou mudidi xingxiang tuiguang yanjiu (Study on Government Domination and Tourist Destination Image Promotion). *Guilin Lüyou Gaodeng Zhuanke Xuexiao Xuebao / Journal of Guilin Institute of Tourism* 14, no. 5:51–53, 67.

Siemons, Mark

2006 "Der alte Preusse, das ist der Mann" (The old Prussian, that's the guy). *Frankfurter Allgemeine Zeitung*, 14 December, 35.

Sik, Endre

1999 "The Spatial Distribution of Informal Marketplaces and Informal Foreign Traders in Contemporary Hungary." In *Underground Economies in Transition*, ed. Edgar F. Feige and Katarina Ott, 275–306. Aldershot: Ashgate.

Siu, Helen F.

2005 "The Cultural Landscape of Luxury Housing." In *Locating China. Space,*

Place, and Popular Culture, ed. Jing Wang, 72–93. Abingdon, Oxfordshire: Routledge.

Skeldon, Ronald, and Graeme Hugo
1999 "Of Exceptionalisms and Generalities." In *Internal and International Migration*, ed. Pieke and Mallee, 333–45.

Smart, Alan, and George C. S. Lin
2007 "Local Capitalisms, Local Citizenship and Translocality: Rescaling from Below in the Pearl River Delta Region, China." *International Journal of Urban and Regional Research* 31, no. 2:280–302.

Smith, Paul J
1994 "The Strategic Implications of Chinese Emigration." *Survival* 36, Summer, 60–77.

Sofield, Trevor H. B., and Fung Mei Sarah Li
1998 "Tourism Development and Cultural Policies in China." *Annals of Tourism Research* 25, no. 2:362–92.

Solinger, Dorothy J.
1991 "China's Transients and the State: A Form of Civil Society?" SC Seminar Series no. 1. Hong Kong: Chinese University of Hong Kong Press.
1999 *Contesting Citizenship in Urban China: Peasant Migrants, the State, and the Logic of the Market*. Berkeley: University of California Press.

Song, Xianlin and Gary Sigley
2000 "Middle Kingdom Mentalities: Chinese Visions of National Characteristics in the 1990s." *Communal/Plural* 8(1):47–64.

Song Zhida
2004 *Di-shi dai: Yi ge pingmin jiating song zi chuguo liuxue de zuji* (The tenth generation: An ordinary family's path to sending their child to study abroad). N.p.: Xuelin Chubanshe.

Spiegel
2007 "Die gelben Spione" (The yellow spies), no. 35 (27 August).

Stanley, Nick
1998 *Being Ourselves for You: The Global Display of Cultures*. London: Middlesex University Press.

State Statistics Bureau International Statistics and Information Centre (Guojia Tongjiju Guoji Tongji Xinxi Zhongxin)
2002 *Chuguo renyuan guoji xinxi gailan / Brief Introduction of International Information for the Personnel Going Abroad*. Peking: China Statistics Press, 4th ed.

Steinberger, Karin
2007 "Die Eilkunst der Chinesen" (The Chinese art of haste). *Süddeutsche Zeitung* (Munich), 26–28 May, 3.

Sun Hong and Lei Zhenglang
1999 "'Xiuxian wenhua yu dangdai shenghuo xueshu yantaohui' zongshu" (Report on the "Scholarly Conference on Leisure Culture and Contemporary Life" [organized by the Jiangxi Research Institute for Develop-

ment Strategy and Aixi Lake Holiday Village, Aixi Lake Holiday Village, Jiangxi, 8 June 1999]). *Jiangxi Shehui Kexue*, no. 7:123–24.

Sun Hongling

2000 "Qian lun zhuanxing shiqi liudong renkou zinü de jiaoyu gongping wenti" (The question of education equality of the children of the mobile population in the transitional period: a shallow discussion). Paper presented at the annual meeting of the professional committee of middle-age and young theoretical workers of the Chinese Association for Education Research.

Sun Jing and Yang Yuhong

2001 "Chuguo laowu, lu zai he fang?" (Going abroad to work: Where does the road lead?). *Xinhua Ribao* (Nanjing), 15 January, A02.

Sun, Wanning

2002 *Leaving China: Media, Migration, and the Transnational Imagination.* New York and Oxford: Rowman and Littlefield.

2004 "Indoctrination, Fetishization, and Compassion: Media Constructions of the Migrant Woman." In *On the Move*, ed. Arianne M. Gaetano and Tamara Jacka, 109–28.

2006 *Media and the Chinese Diaspora: Community, Communications and Commerce.* London and New York: Routledge.

Sun Xiaoli

2004 "Xiuxian yu xin de shenghuo fangshi" (Leisure and the new lifestyle). Talk at the seminar "2004–Zhongguo: Xiuxian yu shehui jinbu" (2004–China: Leisure and social progress). Peking, 2–6 June.

Sun Yinglan

1996 "Xiuxian lüyouye: yi men fang xing wei ai de chanye" (The leisure travel industry: a business in the making). *Liaowang*, no. 33.

Tan Chee-Beng, Sydney C. H. Cheung and Yang Hui, eds.

2001 *Tourism, Anthropology and China.* Bangkok: White Lotus Press.

Tan Ke, Arthur

2003 *"The Influence and Significance of Household Reform on Floating Population Based on the Survey in Shijiazhuang / Huji zhidu gaige dui chengshi liudong renkou de yingxiang ji qi yiyi – yi Shijiazhuang huji zhengce gaige wei li."* Master's thesis, People's University of China.

Tan Shen

2002 *Funü yu laogong* (Women and labor). Manuscript.

2006 "Labour Services for China's Migrant Workers: New Ideas and Practises" (sic). In *Labour Mobility in Urban China: An Integrated Labour Market in the Making?* ed. Michaela Baur, Bettina Gransow, Yihong Jin, and Guoqing Shi, 100–112. Münster: LIT (Berliner China-Studien, no. 46).

Tan Tianxing

1997 "Jin nian lai wo guo gongmin yiju haiwai qingkuang zhi guan jian" (The official view on PRC citizens' settling overseas in the past years). *Overseas Chinese History of Bagui*, no. 1:1–6.

Tang Diao

2002 "Gaige huji: chengxiang yiti bu zai yaoyuan" (*Hukou* reform: unification of country and town no longer far away). *Beijing Qingnianbao*, 10 January, 32.

Tian Dezheng

2003 "Huji zhidu gaige bu neng ge zi wei zheng" (*Hukou* reforms should not differ from place to place). *Shenzhen Shangbao*, 3 September, A06.

Tong Dahuan

2004 "Huji zhengce yao zunzhong shichang xuanze" (*Hukou* policy must respect market's choices). *Xinjingbao*, 26 March.

Traub, James

2006 "China's African Adventure." *New York Times Magazine*, 19 November.

Urry, John

2000 "Mobile Sociology." *British Journal of Sociology* 51, no. 1:185–203.

Travel & Trade in Europe (*Ouzhou shang-lü bao*, Cologne)

2004 "Ouzhou huaren lüyou nianhui wanmei luomu" (Annual Chinese travel fair in Europe a resounding success), no. 1–2:1.

Walsh, Eileen R., and Margaret Byrne Swain

2004 "Creating Modernity by Touring Paradise: Domestic Ethnic Tourism in Yunnan, China," *Tourism and Recreation Research* 29, no. 2:59–68.

Wan Xingya

2004 "Gonganbu youguan renshi biaoshi: Wo guo hugai qushi reng shi fangsong hukou qianyi xianzhi" (PSB officials in charge say liberalizing *hukou* migration remains the trend in our country's *hukou* reform). *Zhongguo Qingnianbao*, 20 September.

Wang, Fei-Ling

2004 "Reformed Migration Control and New Targeted People: China's *Hukou* System in the 2000s." *The China Quarterly*, no. 177: 115–32.

Wang Fuming, Sun Liping, and Zhu Liming

1998 "Shanghai shi jiaqiang wailai liudong renkou guanli: Tigao chengshi xiandaihua guanli shuiping" (Shanghai strengthens management of transient outside population: Raise the management standards of city modernization). *Chang'an*, no. 10:56–57.

Wang Gan

2001 "A Field of Cultural Contestation: Nightclubs in Shenzhen." *Tsinghua Sociological Review* 1:1–16.

Wang Guixiao and Liu Xinghua

2003 "Gucheng nongmin chuguo zheng 'yangqian'" (Peasants from ancient towns go abroad to make "overseas money"). *Hebei Jingji Ribao* (Shijiazhuang), 13 February, A01.

Wang Guixin

2001 "21 shiji renkou qianyi jiang tuidong Zhongguo xiandaihua jiasu fazhan" (Population movement will speed up China's modernization in the 21st century). *Renkou Xuekan*, no. 5:31–33.

Wang Gungwu

1998 "Upgrading the Migrant: Neither *Huaqiao* nor *Huaren*." In *The Last Century of Chinese Overseas*, ed. Elizabeth Sinn, 15–34. Hong Kong: Hong Kong University Press.

Wang Haiguang

2003 "Dangdai Zhongguo huji zhidu xingcheng yu yange de hongguan fenxi" (A macro-level analysis of the emergence and reform of the household registration system in contemporary China). *Xinhua Wengao*, no. 10.

Wang Huan

2004 "Chuguo wugong: Jiaobu weihe zheme zhong?" (Going abroad to work: Why are the steps so heavy?). *Sichuan Ribao*, 3 July.

Wang, Jing

2001 "The State Question in Chinese Popular Cultural Studies." *Inter-Asia Cultural Studies* 2, no. 1:35–52.

Wang Jun

2003 "Yonggan zouchuqu" (Go out bravely!). *Renmin Ribao*, 21 June, 2.

Wang Minghao

2003 "Wei nongmin jincheng wugong 'chengqi yi pian lan tian'" (Propping up a piece of blue sky for peasants coming to work in the city). *Renmin Ribao*, 17 February, 5.

Wang Qun

1993 "Quanguo lüyou wenyu gongzuo" (National tourism culture and entertainment work). In *Zhongguo Lüyou Nianjian*, 102–4. Peking: Zhongguo Lüyou Chubanshe.

Wang Shizhong

2000 "Fayu Wandongnan lüyouye gouxiang" (A vision to develop Southeast Anhui's tourism). *Anhui Ribao*, 8 July, A03.

Wang Shucheng and Li Renhu

1996 "Wuwei: Baomu xiaoying" (Wuwei: The nanny effect). *Banyuetan*, no. 8:23–25.

Wang Wenlu

2003 "Renkou chengzhenhua beijing xia de huji zhidu bianqian / Changes in the Household Registering System Against the Urbanization Background: Shijiazhuang City as a Case." *Renkou Yanjiu (Population Research)* 27, no. 6:8–13.

Wang Xiangfen

2004 "Looking Back, I Am Proud." In *On the Move*, ed. Arianne M. Gaetano and Tamara Jacka, 295–97.

Wang Ying

2001 "Qiancong ziyou yu huzheng guanli feizhianhua / Moving on Freely and Census Management Without Police" (Freedom of movement and the delinking of *hukou* management from public safety). *Xiandai Faxue (Modern Law Science)* 23, no. 6 (no page numbers).

Wang Yutian

2003 "Huji zhankai renwen guanhuai de lian" (Household registration reveals humanitarian face). *Renmin Gongan*, no. 16:15–17.

Wang Zhengjun

2004 *Hafo zhi Lian* (Love at Harvard). Peking: Zhongguo Huaqiao Chubanshe.

Wanshui Yifang

2006 "Yuenan ji xing" (Notes on my trip to Vietnam), 11 November 2006. "http://www.tianya.cn/New/PublicForum/Content.asp?flag=1&idWriter =0&idArticle=99550&strItem=travel" (accessed 22 March 2007).

Watts, Jonathan

2007 "China Fears Brain Drain as Its Overseas Students Stay Put." *Guardian*, 2 June.

Weber, Eugene

1976 *Peasants into Frenchmen: The Modernisation of Rural France 1870–1914.* Palo Alto: Stanford University Press.

Wei Jun

2001 "Feichu hukou!!!" (Get rid of the *hukou*!!!). *Zhongguo Shehui Daokan*, no. 4:21–24.

Wei Xiaoan

2001 *Muji Zhongguo lüyou* (Witnessing China's tourism). Shijiazhuang: Hebei Jiaoyu Chubanshe.

2003a "Zhongguo lüyou guihua fazhan de xianzhuang yu qushi" (The present state and trends of China's tourism planning development). Paper presented to the tourism planning class held by the Peking City Tourism Bureau, 13 March.

2003b *Lüyou qiangguo zhi lu: Zhongguo lüyou chanye zhengce tixi yanjiu / Path to Great Tourism Country: Research on China Tourism Industry Policy System.* Peking: Zhongguo Lüyou Chubanshe.

2004 "Xiuxian dujia de tedian ji fazhan qushi" (The characteristics of leisure holidaymaking and trends in its development). Manuscript courtesy of the author.

n.d. "Zhongguo gongmin chujing lüyou shichang de guifan yu fazhan" (The regularization and development of Chinese citizens' outbound travel). Manuscript courtesy of the author.

Wei Xiaoan, Liu Zhaoping, and Zhang Shumin

1999 *Zhongguo lüyouye xin shiji fazhan da qushi* (Trends in China's Tourism Development in the New Century). Canton: Guangdong Lüyou Chubanshe.

Williams, Raymond

1961 *The Long Revolution.* London: Chatto and Windus.

Wines, Michael

2007 "China's Influence in Africa Arouses Some Resistance." *New York Times*, 10 February.

Woeser

    2007   "Decline of Potala Palace." *China Rights Forum,* no. 4:44–51.

Woronov, T. E.

    2004   "In the Eye of the Chicken: Hierarchy and Marginality among Beijing's Migrant Schoolchildren." *Ethnography* 5, no. 3:289–313.

Wu Hung

    2005   *Remaking Beijing: Tiananmen Square and the Creation of a Political Space.* Chicago and London: University of Chicago Press and Reaction Books.

Wu Jincai and Ge Xueqin

    2000   "Mingxi 'xin yimin' xianxiang pouxi" (An analysis of the "new migrant" phenomenon in Mingxi). *Fujian Gongan Gaodeng Zhuanke Xuexiao xuebao: Shehui gonggong anquan yanjiu* (Fuzhou) 14, no. 3:69–71 (May).

Wu Liang and Xiang Kailai

    2004   "Chuguo dagong: dixia zhongjie anliu xiongyong" (Underground intermediaries for overseas jobs: turbulent waters of the dark stream). *Renmin Ribao,* Overseas Edition, 28 July.

Xia Xueqin

    2004   "Zhengzhou 'huji xin zheng' de san ge cuowu" (Three errors of Zhengzhou's "new *hukou* policy"). *Xinjingbao,* 23 September.

Xiang Biao

    1999   "Zhejiang Village in Beijing: Creating a visible non-state space through migration and marketized networks." In *Internal and International Migration,* ed. Pieke and Mallee, 215–50.

    2003   "Emigration from China: A Sending Country Perspective." *International Migration* 41, no. 3 (special issue 1):21–48.

    2005a "An Institutional Approach towards Migration and Health in China." In *Migration and Health in Asia,* ed. Santosh Jatrana, Mika Toyota, and Brenda S. A. Yeoh, 161–76. London and New York: Routledge.

    2005b *Transcending Boundaries.* Leiden: Brill.

    2007   "The Making of Mobile Subjects: How Migration and Institutional Reform Intersect in Northeast China." *Development* 50, no. 4:69–74.

Xiangnan

    1994   "Duonao xiasi" (Summer thoughts on the Danube). *Ouzhou Daobao* (Budapest), 13 July, 3.

Xiao Shuchen and Zhang Kedan

    2004   "Huji menkan weihe 'chao jiang xi cheng'" (Why did the *hukou* threshold 'go down at morn and up at eve'?). *Gongren Ribao,* 18 September.

Xing Heping

    2008   *Hong Sen Shidai (The Era of Hun Sen).* Phnom Penh: Lucky Star.

Xing Jiang

    2001   "Ulumuqi fangsong hukou qianyi xianzhi" (Urumqi loosens *hukou* transfer limits). *Jingji Ribao,* 29 August, 11.

Xu Changle, Yuan Wen, Luo Zuyi, Hua Wei, and Le Weizhong

2000   "Shanghai shi liudong renkou guanli gongzuo san nian guihua yanjiu"
        (Research on the three-year plan of Shanghai's transient population
        management work). In Le Weizhong, ed. in chief, *Maixiang xin shiji de
        liudong renkou guanli yanjiu: "Shanghai shi wailai liudong renkou guanli
        lilun yu shijian yantaohui" youxiu lunwen huibian* (Research on transient
        population management towards the new century: a collection of out-
        standing papers from the Transient Outside Population Management in
        Shanghai: Theory and Practice symposium), 1–18. Shanghai: Huadong
        Shifan Daxue Chubanshe.

Xu Deming, ed.-in-chief
2003   *Shanghai shequ wailai renkou sixiang gongzuo yanjiu* (Research on com-
        munity thought work among Shanghai's outside population). Shanghai:
        Shanghai Renmin Chubanshe.

Xu Qing
1999   "Qian tan gongmin yinsi chuguo guocheng zhong de zhuyao maodun
        yu xuanjie fangfa" (A superficial discussion of the main contradictions
        in the process of citizens' going abroad for private purposes and of ways
        of alleviating them). In *Selected Articles on Exit-Entry Management*, ed.
        Chinese Police Association Exit-Entry Management Committee, 143–54.
        Peking: Qunzhong Chubanshe.

Yan Hairong
2003   "Neoliberal Governmentality and Neohumanism: Organizing Suzhi/
        Value Flow through Labor Recruitment Networks." *Cultural Anthropol-
        ogy* 18, no. 4:493–523.
2006   "Self-Development of Migrant Women and the Production of *Suzhi*
        (Quality) as Surplus Value." In *Everyday Modernity in China*, ed. Mad-
        eleine Yue Dong and Joshua Goldstein, 227–59.

Yan Shanping
1998   *Zhongguo jiushi niandai diqujian renkou zhuanyi de shitai ji qi jizhi* (The
        current state and structure of interregional migration in 1990s China).
        Shehuixue yanjiu, no. 2.

Yan Taorui
2005   "Wo renshi de Nanfei," *Shijie Rongyin* (Hong Kong), no. 19:56.

Yang, Mayfair Mei-hui
1997   "Mass Media and Transnational Subjectivity in Shanghai: Notes on (Re)
        Cosmopolitanism in a Chinese Metropolis." In *Ungrounded Empires*, ed.
        Aihwa Ong and Donald M. Nonini, 287–322. London: Routledge.

Yang Yijia and Wang Zhenyu
1998   *Ouzhou huaqiao huaren funü yanjiu baogao* (Chinese women in Europe:
        a research report). Presented to the 6th congress of the European Federa-
        tion of Chinese Organisations, Budapest.

Yang Yunyan
1994   *Zhongguo renkou zhuanyi yu fazhan di changqi zhanlüe* (Migration and
        long-term development strategy in China). Wuhan: Wuhan Chubanshe.

Yangge

    1997   *Chuguo weishenme?* (Why did we go abroad?). Peking: Zuojia Chubanshe.

Yao, Souchou

    2002   *Confucian Capitalism: Discourse, Practice and the Myth of Chinese Enterprise.* Abingdon, Oxfordshire: RoutledgeCurzon.

Yao Wen

    2003   "Mingnian 1 yue 1 ri qi shishi de Guangzhou changzhu renkou tiaokong guanli zhidu you duo xiang da gaige: Guangzhouren hukou ke ziyou qianru qianchu" (Several major changes in Canton's resident population control and management regime effective 1 January next year: Canton residents can freely move *hukou* in and out). *Yangcheng Wanbao* (Canton), 22 December.

Ye Nanke

    1995   "Nongyeguo zhong de xin yimin: Lun yi-gong-yi-nong jieceng de xiandaihua zhuanxing" (New migrants in an agrarian country: On the modern transformation of the worker-cum-peasant stratum). *Shehuixue yu shehui diaocha*, no. 1:8–13, 52.

Yeo, Kwang-Kyoon

    2008   "A Transnational Community and Its Impact on the Local Power Relations in Urban China." Paper prepared for the International Congress of Ethnologists, Anthropologists and Sociologists, Kunming, 15–21 July 2008.

Yizhi

    2002   *Zang di niupi shu* (Tibetan lands: A cowhide-bound book). N.p.: Zhongguo Qingnian Chubanshe.

Yong Xiaoru, ed.-in-chief

    1999   *Zhongguo mingsheng gailan* (An almanac of China's famous sites). Peking: Zhongguo Renshi Chubanshe.

Young, Nick, and June Shih

    2004   *The Chinese Diaspora and Philanthropy.* Global Equity Initiative, Harvard University. http://www.fas.harvard.edu/~acgei/PDFs/ Philanthropy PDFs/Phil_Chinese_Diaspora.pdf

Yu Dapeng

    1994   "Chengxiang guanxi zhong de 'cheng che xiaoying'" (The "riding the train effect" in urban-rural relations). *Shehui*, no. 3:37–39.

Yu Hai

    2003   "Linyu jinqi yi xie jingneiwai feifa zhongjie he geren youpian laowu renyuan chuguo, Shangwubu jiu chuguo laowu zuochu tebie tishi" (Faced with some illegal intermediaries and individuals enticing labour personnel to go abroad recently, Ministry of Trade issues special warning regarding work abroad). *Xinhua Meiri Dianxun*, 21 September, 2.

Yu Jun

    1994   "Bai nian da ji zaiyu tigao ren de suyang" (The great project of a hundred years lies in improving the quality of the people), *Huikan* (bulletin of the Hungarian Chinese Association, Budapest), no. 25:6 (30 April).

Yuan Ning and You Haohuan

2002 "Wo guo xianxing huji zhidu de baiduan ji duice sikao / On the Drawbacks of China's Household Register System and Countermeasures," *Guangdong Xingzheng Xueyuan Xuebao / Journal of Guangdong Institute of Public Administration* 14, no. 4:38–41.

Yuan Yue, Victor, and Xin Wang

2000 "Leaders among the Migrants in Beijing." In *Inequality Mobility and Urbanisation: China and India*, ed. Amitabh Kundu. Delhi: Manak and Indian Council of Social Science Research.

Yuan Zhipei

1997 "Gaohao zanzhu renkou de dengji, zhuxiao gongzuo; tigao dui renkou de kongzhi nengli" (Gooddo the registration and cancellation work of temporary population, raise the capacity to control temporary population). *Henan Gongan Xuebao*, no. 6:3–8.

Yue Xiaodong

2004 *Yu zhenli wei you / Let Your Friend Be Truth: My Harvard Experience.* Shanghai: Shanghai People's Publishing House.

Zeng Shan

1995 "Nongmin chuangru lüyou dachao mian mian guan" (Peasants gallop into the great wave of tourism: a many-sided view). *Lüyou*, no. 2:7–9.

Zha Jinxiang and Zeng Lingxiang

2000 "Wo guo xianxing huji zhidu de gongneng quexian he jiaozheng silu" (Dysfunctions in our country's current household registration system and a plan to correct them). *Xiao Chengzhen Jianshe*, no. 3:42–43.

Zhang Ansheng and Zhang Xiaoming

2002 "New Ideas on Immigration." *Journal of Yunnan Public Security College*, no. 3:89–92 (in Chinese).

Zhang Ensheng and Guo Jie

2002 *Zui xin chuguo renyuan bi du* (The latest must-read for personnel going abroad). Peking: Jincheng Chubanshe.

Zhang Fa

2006 "Wangfujing buxingjie: Zhongguo zhuanxing shidai de wenhua tuxiang" (The Wangfujing pedestrian street: a cultural icon of China's era of transition). In *Chengshi wenhua pinglun* (Essays on urban culture), 108–14. Shanghai: Shanghai Sanlian Shudian.

Zhang Gu

2000 "Gengxin wu da guannian, jiakuai fazhan Sichuan lüyou chanye" (Refresh five big concepts, accelerate the development of Sichuan's tourism industry). *Lilun yu Gaige*, no. 5:120–22.

Zhang Guangrui

1992 "Dui fazhan guonei lüyouye de ji dian renshi" (Some observations on the development of the domestic tourism industry). *Caimao Jingji* (Peking), no. 3:57–60.

2003a "China's Tourism since 1978: Policies, Experiences, and Lessons Learned." In *Tourism in China*, ed. Lew et al., 13–34.

2003b "2002~2004 nian Zhongguo chujing lüyou de zhuangkuang fenxi yu qushi yuce" (The situation of China's outbound tourism in 2002–2004: Analysis and trend forecast). In *2002~2004 nian Zhongguo lüyou fazhan: Fenxi yu yuce* (China's tourism development, 2002–2004: Analysis and forecast), ed. Zhang Guangrui, Wei Xiaoan, and Liu Deqian, 77–95. Peking: Social Sciences Documentation.

Zhang Guangrui, Wei Xiaoan, and Liu Deqian

2001 *2000 ~ 2002 nian Zhongguo lüyou fazhan: Fenxi yu yuce* (China's tourism development, 2000–2002: Analysis and forecast). Peking: Social Sciences Documentation.

2002 *2001~2003 nian Zhongguo lüyou fazhan: Fenxi yu yuce* (China's tourism development, 2001–2003: Analysis and forecast). Peking: Social Sciences Documentation.

2003 *2002~2004 nian Zhongguo lüyou fazhan: Fenxi yu yuce* (China's tourism development, 2002–2004: Analysis and forecast). Peking: Social Sciences Documentation.

Zhang Guofang

1998 "Lun churujing zhongjie huodong de guifan guanli" (On regulating and managing the activities of middleman agencies in the international movement of people). *Gongan Xuekan,* no. 6:48–51.

Zhang Guoyu

1993 *Zhongguo laowu shuchu shouce* (Handbook of China's labour export). Peking: Zhongguo Jianzhu Gongye Chubanshe.

Zhang, Heather Xiaoquan

2006 "Citizenship and Livelihood Sustainability: A Study of Migration and Health in China." Paper presented at the 8th European Conference on Agriculture and Rural Development in China, Yiwu, Zhejiang, 1 September.

Zhang Huzheng

1995 "Dushi damen banyanzhe" (City gate opens a crack). *Zhongguo Gongqingtuan,* no. 1:46–48.

Zhang Lala

2003 "Wailaigong zinü paihui zai chengshi jiaoyu bianyuan" (Children of immigrant workers marginalised in urban education). *Kaifangchao,* no. 4.

Zhang, Li

2001 *Strangers in the City.* Stanford: Stanford University Press.

Zhang Liuhao

2006 "City Faces Challenge in Rising Tide of Migrants." *ShanghaiDaily.com,* 30 October 2006. "http://202.101.38.80/art/2006/10/30/295621/City_

faces_challenge_in_rising_tide_of_migrants.htm" (accessed 30 October 2006).

Zhang Lu
2005 "Hegemonic Regime? Globalization, Market Reform and Changing Labor Politics in China's Automobile Industry." Paper presented at the first Graduate Student Conference on China, Chinese University of Hong Kong, 11–15 January.

Zhang Mingshan and Du Juanying
2001 *Wo jia Benben shang Jianqiao* (Our Dummy Goes to Cambridge). Peking: Zhongguo Shehui Chubanshe.

Zhang, Ning
2006 "Fieldworker, Donkey Friend and Cyberspace." Paper presented at the Questions of Methodology: Researching Tourism in Asia Graduate Workshop, Asia Research Institute, National University of Singapore, 5–6 September.

Zhang Qunsheng
2006 "Zhengque bawo kexue fazhanguan de lilun yiyi yu shijian yaoqiu" (Correctly grasp the theoretical meaning of the scientific view of development and the requirements for its practical implementation). *Renmin Ribao*, 31 March, 5.

Zhang Shengchun
1995 "Bianxiang xiandaihua guoji da dushi jincheng zhong de Guangzhou liudong renkou guanli" (Towards a transient population management in setting up a modern international metropolis in Canton), *Zhengfa Xuebao*, no. 2:9–13.

Zhang Tao
2001 "Beijing hukou: menkan jiujing you duo gao" (Peking *hukou*: how high is the threshold?). *Beijing Qingnian Bao*, 15 October.

Zhang Xiaodong
2003 "Chengdu quxiao hukou rucheng zhibiao xianzhi" (Chengdu abolishes *hukou* quota limits for moving into city). *Fazhi Ribao*, 2 June.

Zhang Xiaoli
1998 "Chuguo zhao shihui" (Going abroad for bargains). *Sanlian Shenghuo Zhoukan*, no. 3:46–47.

Zhang Zhiye
1990 "'Chuguore' jiemi" (Exposing the secrets of "going-abroad fever"). *Falü Zixun*, no. 5:6–12.

Zhang Zhongbin
1997 "Mingxi lü Ou xin yimin chengwei jiaxiang jianshe di xin sheng liliang" (New Mingxi migrants in Europe become a newborn force in the home county's construction). *Fujian Qiaobao*, 21 December.

Zhao Guoqing and Geng Lian
2004 "Dagongzhe, bu gai pian zheng chuguo chujing" (Workers should not go abroad with fraudulent documents). *Xinhua Ribao*, 9 February.

Zhao Jin

2003 "Jiangsu huji gaige lengqing kaichang" (Jiangsu *hukou* reform proceeds coolly). *Zhongguo Jingji Shibao*, 19 May.

Zhao Limei

1999 "Shi lun shangwu chuguo renyuan huzhao shenban zhidu de wanshan" (An attempt to discuss the improvement of the passport application and approval process for business travellers). *Yunnan Gongan Gaodeng Zhuanke Xuexiao Xuebao / Journal of Yunnan Public Security College*, no. 2:42–44.

Zhao Ling

1998 "Yunnan lüyou wenhua jianshe de zhanlüe gouxiang" (A strategic plan to construct tourism culture in Yunnan). *Chuangzao*, no. 5:33–35.

Zhao Shengyu

2003 "Chuguo laowuye zengyu san dao nanti" (Three difficulties of the labour export business). *Xinhua Ribao* (Nanjing), 17 September.

Zhao Weixiong

2000 "Wailai liudong renkou fanzui chengyin de xinli tanxi he duice yanjiu" (A psychological analysis of the factors of outside transient population criminality and policy responses). In *Maixiang xin shiji de liudong renkou guanli yanjiu: "Shanghai shi wailai liudong renkou guanli lilun yu shijian yantaohui" youxiu lunwen huibian* (Research on transient population management towards the new century: A collection of outstanding papers from the Transient Outside Population Management in Shanghai: Theory and Practice symposium), ed. Le Weizhong, 74–81. Shanghai: Huadong Shifan Daxue Chubanshe.

Zheng Deyi

1994 "Gaige chengshi hukou guanli zhidu" (Reforming cities' *hukou* management regime). *Jingji Ribao*, 18 February, 8.

Zheng, Tiantian

2004 "From Peasant Women to Bar Hostesses: Gender and Modernity in Post-Mao Dalian." In *On the Move*, ed. Arianne M. Gaetano and Tamara Jacka, 80–108.

Zhong Chengxiang

2003 "Xin de minzu qingdian, mei de wenhua da can" (A new folk celebration, a beautiful cultural feast). *Renmin Ribao*, 11 February, 14.

Zhou Bingrong and Sheng Keming

1989 "Liuru renkou dui shehui zhian de yingxiang ji duice" (The public safety impact of population inflow and policy responses). In *Shanghai liudong renkou* (Transient population in Shanghai), 77–84. Peking: Zhongguo Tongji Chubanshe.

Zhou Daming

2003 "Waichu wugong yu shuchudi zhengzhi jigou de bianqian: yi Jiangxi sheng wei li" (Labour migration and change in political structures of sending areas: the example of Jiangxi). In *Nongmingong: Zhongguo jincheng nongmin de jingji shehui fenxi* (Migrant workers: Economic and social analysis of peasants in Chinese cities), ed. Li Peilin, 185–195. Peking: Zhongguo Kexue Wenxian Chubanshe.

Zhou Xiaoyang and Yang Guocai

2006 "Tuanjie xiangqin liange xiangqing ningju qiaoxin fuwu qiaomin: Agenting Rongji huaqiao shetuan you wei you wei" (Uniting fellow countrymen, linking feelings of homeland, bringing together overseas hearts, serving overseas Chinese: Fuqing overseas Chinese associations in Argentina have both function and status). *Shijie Rongyin* (Hong Kong), no. 21:32.

Zhu Dake

2006 *Liumang de shengyan* (The hooligans' feast). Peking: New Star Press.

Zhu Guangxi, Zhu Lixia, and Wu Guangyun

2004 "The Value Analysis of Tour Golden Week Policy." *Yunnan Geographic Environment Research* 16, no. 3:70–72 (in Chinese).

Zhu Huiling

1995 "Dangdai Zhongguo liu Ri xueren ji qi zuoyong" (Chinese students and scholars in Japan and their role today). *Overseas Chinese History Studies*, no. 2:22–31.

Zhu Li

2006 "Cultural Life of Rural Migrants and Urban Integration." In *Labour Mobility in Urban China: An Integrated Labour Market in the Making?* ed. Michaela Baur, Bettina Gransow, Yihong Jin and Guoqing Shi, 140–52. Münster: LIT (Berliner China-Studien, no. 46).

Zhu Qing, Li Heping, and Fan Zihan

1989 "Qian tan wailai renkou dui Shanghai de yingxiang ji duice" (Shallow observations on the impact of outside population on Shanghai and policy responses). In *Shanghai liudong renkou* (Transient population in Shanghai), 70–76. Peking: Zhongguo Tongji Chubanshe.

Zhuang Guotu

2000 "Policies of the Chinese Government Toward Overseas Chinese Since 1978." In *Ajia Taiheiyō Sekai to Chūgoku: Kaihatsu no naka no ningen* (The Asia-Pacific world and China: Human development), 45–52. Shirizu Chūgoku Ryōiki kenkyū (China Area Studies Series), no. 10. Tokyo: Ministry of Education, Science, Sports, and Culture, Scientific Research in Priority Areas, no. 113: Structural Change in Contemporary China.

n.d. "Er zhan yilai Jianpuzhai huaren shehui diwei de bianhua" (Changes in the social status of Cambodian Chinese since WWII." Manuscript courtesy of author.

Zweig, David, and Chung Siu Fung

2004 "Redefining the Brain Drain: China's 'Diaspora Option.'" Working Paper no. 1, Center on China's Transnational Relations, Hong Kong University of Science and Technology.

Index

and use of migrant labor in China, 13, 21, 28–29
entrepreneurship. *See* enterprises
environmentalism, 78, 84, 92, 95, 180n51
Ethiopia, 43
ethnicity, 10, 33, 44, 59, 128, 161, 164–65; and minorities in China, xv, 16, 64–68, 73, 85, 93–96, 138, 141, 163–65
eugenics, 78, 84, 89
European Federation of Chinese Organizations (EFCO), 54

Falun Gong, 54–58
family planning, 19, 25, 30, 84, 149, 172n17, 180n47
Ferry, Megan, 125
Finland, 102, 114
Ford, Henry, 116
Forever Africa (Yongyuan de Feizhou), 126
"four modernizations," 77
freedom of movement, 86, 148, 153
Fujian, Fujianese, 15, 32, 41, 48, 59–60, 98, 102–3, 158–60, 179n41; overseas, 51, 53, 58, 102, 115, 121, 161–65
Fuqing, 32, 54, 98–99, 103, 113–15, 133, 160, 163
Fuzhou, 158, 162–63

"gamekeeper state," xi–xii, 167
"gardening state," xi–xii, 8, 167
gender, 87–88, 117–20
Genghis Khan, 68
Germany, 36, 70, 127, 154–55, 176n13
Golden Venture, 104
golden weeks, 62, 91, 174n2
Great Britain, 36, 70, 128, 158–59
Great Leap, 12
Great Western Development, 16, 84
Guangdong, 15, 32–33, 36, 171n13, 179n41; overseas migration from, 50, 58–59, 87; tourism in, 96

Guangzhou. *See* Canton
guidebooks, 74–75
Guide to Entering Shanghai (Ru Hu zhinan), 25, 83–84
Guizhou, 64
Gypsies, 109, 152

Hainan, 73
Halskov Hansen, Mette, 85
Hangzhou, 65, 93
Hanoi, 93
Harrell, Stevan, 126, 180n53, 181n54
Hefei, 93
Hekou, 34, 157
Henan, 26, 116
Hillman, Ben, 97
Hohhot, 68
Hongcun, 96
Hong Kong, xiii, 13, 25, 32–33, 57, 59, 67, 71, 101, 153, 161; Chinese migrants in, 54; Chinese tourism to, 69–70, 73–74; media, 56, 113; migrants from, 55, 79, 113, 116
household registration: in China (see *hukou*); in the Soviet Union, 10–11
Huaihua, 80
Hubei, 95, 141
Huber, Toni, 96
Hugo, Graeme, 12
Hu Jintao, xiii, 139, 141
Hukou, xiv–xv, 11–30, 47, 80, 84, 148, 152–53, 170–72
human trafficking, 155–56, 159, 177n28
Hunan, 40, 80
Hungary, 134; Chinese in, 42–46, 70, 100, 102, 104, 109–14, 117–23, 128–29, 154, 165, 177n25
hygiene, 81, 83, 94, 126, 155, 176n11

India, Indians, 43, 65; Chinese tourists in, 70, 76; overseas, 43, 111; Tibetans in, 141
Indonesia, 32, 60, 71, 99, 181n54
Inner Mongolia, 12, 68

51, 104–6, 113, 125, 133, 159–66; in
  Russia, 8, 10–11, 170n1
Milošević, Slobodan, 108
Mingxi, 60, 102–4, 110, 158, 177n25
modernity, modernization, xii–xv, 8–9,
  23, 35, 53, 56, 59, 76–129, 149, 153–57,
  163–67, 179n40–41, 181n54; and tour-
  ism, 62–68, 131, 137–38, 145, 174n11
Mongols, 64, 68–69
Morgan, Lewis Henry, 126
Mount Changbai, 73
Mount Meili (Khabad Karpo), 73
Mount Putuo, 73
Mount Tai, 63
Mount Wutai, 141
Murphy, Rachel, 31, 79–81, 130
Myanmar. *See* Burma

Nader, Laura, xii
Namibia, 43–44, 156, 159
nationalism, 59, 63, 76, 178n33, 108;
  and migrants overseas, 57, 107, 128,
  154, 161; and tourism, 124, 176n13,
  143–45
National Tourism Administration
  (CNTA), 64, 67, 72, 90, 135–36, 140–43
native-place associations (*tongxianghui*), 31, 51, 55
neoliberalism, 8, 28, 79; migrants as
  ideal subjects of, 87, 89, 110
Nepal, 65, 70, 73, 141
newspapers, Chinese, overseas, 52,
  56–58, 109, 116–18, 121, 164, 178n34
New York, 51, 101–2, 104–5, 107, 122,
  154, 162–65
New Zealand, 41, 70, 132
Niger, 43
Nigeria, 52, 55
Ningbo, 22, 81, 171n16

Oakes, Tim, 64, 85, 94–95, 142
Olympics, 34, 58, 68, 114, 166, 176n11
Ong, Aihwa, 79, 123, 127, 156
overseas Chinese, 47–58, 97–101,

112–13; China's policies toward,
  47–55, 97, 124, 158, 173n10, 179n40
Overseas Chinese Affairs Bureau (Qiaoban), 47–50, 54–58, 100

patriotic education, 89, 138, 143
Peking (Beijing), 62, 70, 176n11;
  migrants in, 13–36, 46, 81, 87, 104,
  119, 171n15–17, 175n7; tourism, 65,
  73–74
*Pekingers in New York (Beijingren zai
  Niu Yue)*, 105–7
Performance or performativity, 57,
  163–65; in tourism, 64–65, 71, 74, 92,
  97, 124, 139–45
Philippines, 42, 125
Picard, Michel, 64
Pieke, Frank, 158
Pocket Tourism Encyclopedia, 65–66,
  137
population quality. See *suzhi*
Portugal, 127
"post-tourists," 142, 165
Pun Ngai, 23, 88

Qian Ning, 105
Qian Qichen, 54, 105
Qiaoban. *See* Overseas Chinese Affairs
  Bureau
Qiaolian (National Association of
  Returned Overseas Chinese), 47–49,
  58
Qiaoxiang (migrant sending areas),
  30–32, 47–48, 58–60, 82, 98–99,
  102–4, 112, 122, 160–63, 177n25
Qingtian, 58, 122

remittances, 30–31, 112, 158
resettlement, 13, 84
Romania, 42
Rose, Nikolas, 28
Russia, 8, 102, 131, 170n1; Chinese in,
  42, 108, 111, 178n35; and the Far East,
  42–43. *See also* Soviet Union

LIBRARY OF CONGRESS CATALOGING-IN-PUBLICATION DATA

Nyíri, Pál.
Mobility and cultural authority in contemporary China /
Pál Nyíri. — 1st ed.
p. cm.
Includes bibliographical references and index.
ISBN 978-0-295-99015-6 (hardback : alk. paper)
ISBN 978-0-295-99016-3 (pbk.: alk. paper)
1. Migration, Internal—China.
2. Migration, Internal—Government policy—China.
3. China—Cultural policy. I. Title.
HB2114.A3N95 2010   307.20951—dc22   2009049097

www.ingramcontent.com/pod-product-compliance
Lightning Source LLC
Chambersburg PA
CBHW030648270326
41929CB00007B/257